Dedication

This work is dedicated to Our L
gin **Pura** and to Jesus Christ – King (
of Their Two Hearts descend soon i
mankind upon all the earth. Today
dedication as director of "The Father's House of v....
the Holy Family" apostolate in Santa Maria, California. At the
Blessed Mother's direction, this apostolate was founded to form
the beginning of many prayer communities to receive and to teach
the many who will come to take refuge in her serene valley of
Santa Maria, under the "Cross of Peace," which she has asked to be
built there. On September 23, 1997, the Blessed Mother promised:
*"The blessings upon all who participate and who in any way help
bring this about will come through a special grace of protection
for the coming days; and let all who would participate do so for
the greater Glory of God!"* For further information contact:

The Father's House of Victory through the Holy Family,
401 Garnet Way, Santa Maria, CA 93454, 805/928-3994.

© 1998 Signs of the Times Apostolate, Inc.

Published by: **St. Dominic's Media**
P.O. Box 345
Herndon, VA 20172-0345

Phone 703-327-2277
FAX 703-327-2888
ISBN 1-892165-01-5

Declaration

Since the abolition of **Cannons 1399 and 2318** of the former Code of Canon Law, publications about new appearances, revelations, prophecies, miracles, etc., may be distributed and read by the faithful without the express permission of the Church, providing they contain nothing which contravenes faith and morals. This means no *imprimatur* is necessary when distributing information on new apparitions not yet judged by the Church.

In *Lumen Gentium*, Vatican II, Chapter 12, the Council Fathers instructed the faithful:

> "That discernment in matters of faith is aroused and sustained by the Spirit of truth. It is exercised under the guidance of the sacred teaching authority, in faithful and respectful obedience to which the people of God accepts that which is not just the word of men but truly the word of God. (Cf. 1 Thess. 2:13) Through it, the people of God adheres unwaveringly to the faith given once and for all to the saints, (Cf. Jud. 3) penetrates it more deeply with right thinking, and applies it more fully in its life.

> It is not only through the sacraments and the ministries of the Church that the Holy Spirit sanctifies and leads the people of God and enriches it with virtues, but, 'allotting his gifts to everyone according as He wills.' (1 Cor. 12:11) He distributes special graces among the faithful of every rank. By these gifts He makes them fit and ready to undertake the various tasks and offices which contribute toward the renewal and building up of the Church, according to the words of the Apostle: 'The manifestation of the Spirit is given to everyone for profit.' (1 Cor. 12:7) These charisms, whether they be the more outstanding or the more simple and widely diffused, are to be received with thanksgiving and consolation for they are perfectly suited to and useful for the needs of the Church. Extraor-

dinary gifts are not to be sought after, nor are the fruits of apostolic labor to be presumptuously expected from their use; but judgment as to their genuinity and proper use belongs to those who are appointed leaders in the Church, to whose special competence it belongs, not indeed to extinguish the Spirit, but to test all things and hold fast to that which is good." (Cf. 1 Thess. 5:12, 19-21)

All of the messages contained in this volume have been reviewed by three Catholic priests: Fr. John Wishard, Fr. John B. Wang, Ph.D., J.U.D., and Fr. James W. Anderson, M.S.A., J.D., Ph.D., who find nothing in them to be contrary to faith or morals. Nevertheless, both Sadie Jaramillo and the publishers of this Second Edition of her messages unconditionally submit them to the final and official judgment of the Magisterium of the Church.

Declaration of Private Revelation

The messages in this book must be understood not as words spoken directly by God Our Father, Our Lord Jesus, The Holy Spirit, Our Blessed Mother, or the Holy Angels. Rather they were received as interior locutions from Heaven in the heart of Sadie Jaramillo.

St. Paul advises that we: "[N]ever try to suppress the Spirit or treat the gift of prophesy with contempt..." 1 Thess. 5:19-21. St. John advises that not every spirit can be trusted, and instructs us to "test them, to see if they come from God; there are many false prophets, now, in the world. You can tell the spirits that come from God by this: every spirit which acknowledges that Jesus the Christ has come in the flesh is from God; but any spirit which will not say this of Jesus is not from God, but is the spirit of Antichrist, whose coming you were warned about." 1 Jn. 4:1-3.

Before she accepts any message, Sadie tests the voice with one of several challenges: "I rebuke you in the Name of Jesus

Christ." "I command you to go if you are not of God." "Who speaks to me?" "In whose name do you come?"

The heavenly persons whom God sends to her always identify themselves, and regularly reply in the words St. John urges, above. Typically, Sadie tested after hearing Our Lady's voice at 3:20 P.M. on November 3, 1992. Sadie: "In whose name do you come?" Mary: "I am the Queen of Heaven and the Mother of Jesus, come in the flesh, died, resurrected and ascended to The Eternal Father." On February 28, 1994 at 9:30 A.M. Sadie heard Jesus' voice and tested. Jesus replied: "Be still and know I AM your God, your Savior and your Lord. I AM Jesus, I bow and worship My Father. I AM the Alpha and Omega—I AM!"

Sadie has been under obedience to spiritual direction since 1992, when her locutions began.

Acknowledgments

We wish to acknowledge and thank those who have helped prepare this book for publication. Many thanks to Fr. John Wishard, Fr. John Wang and Fr. Jim Anderson for critically reviewing all of the messages prior to this publication, and to Marge Volpe for proofreading this second edition. Charlie and Carol Nole deserve special thanks for meticulously recording each message since 1992. We remain grateful to Joni, to Helen and to Paul for their support and prayers in getting the first edition published. Most especially, we give all the credit to God Our Loving Father for sending His Son, the Holy Spirit, their Holy Angels, Saints and Our Blessed Mother to speak to our hearts.

Preface

When Joshua complained to Moses that the elders Moses had chosen to help him govern the people were prophesying in the camp, Moses prayed that not only he and the elders, but that all of God's people would receive his Spirit and become prophets. Numbers 11:29. God spoke the following words to Israel through the prophet Joel four centuries before Christ, in answer to Moses' prayer:

"After this I will pour out my spirit on all mankind. Your sons and daughters shall prophesy, your old men shall dream dreams, and your young men see visions. Even on the slaves, men and women, will I pour our my spirit in those days. I will display portents in heaven and on earth, blood and fire and columns of smoke.
The sun will be turned into darkness, and the moon into blood, before the day of Yahweh dawns, that great and terrible day. All who call on the name of Yahweh will be saved, for on Mount Zion there will be some who have escaped, as Yahweh has said, and in Jerusalem some survivors whom Yahweh will call." Joel 3: 1-5.

Peter believed the first 2 verses of this prophesy by Joel were fulfilled on the day of Pentecost. Luke reports in Acts that the Apostles with Mary and some women of their company, who had been praying continuously with one heart since Jesus' ascension, were filled with the Holy Spirit and began to speak different languages so as to be understood by pilgrims and visitors to Jerusalem from many lands. Acts 1:12-14, 2:1-13. Peter quotes Joel 3:1-2 to begin his own address to the assembled crowd. Acts 2:14-21. All were then emboldened by the work of the Spirit within them to preach and teach with power and conviction about the love God wanted to shower upon each in Jesus Christ.

The Spirit has always used prophets to bring his people first to personal renewal, and then to accomplish mighty, even impossible deeds. In Ezekiel 37: 1-14 the Spirit brought the dry bones of long defeated armies back to life from their sandy graveyard, covering them with flesh and muscle and comparing the Israel of the prophet's time to those dry bones. In Judges 7:1-22 he moved a fearful Gideon to lead an army of 32,000 warriors against Israel's enemies, and then maintained Gideon's faith and courage as he reduced Gideon's army to 300 to show clearly to his people in every age that he will lead even little persons like you and me to victory if they will believe, obey and remain steadfast. Perhaps, most miraculously of all, God chose the future great King of Israel by overlooking Jesse's mature, warrior sons and sending the prophet Samuel to anoint his ruddy youngest son, the shepherd boy David, and the Spirit never left him. 1 Samuel 16: 1-13. On the day of Pentecost the Spirit launched the Apostles on a truly heroic missionary effort which would bring much of the ancient world to Christ and a martyr's crown to each of them. In Jerusalem 3,000 were added to their number that first day. They worked signs and wonders for all to see and totally changed their own lives, living in Eucharistic prayer communities and sharing what they had. Acts 2:37-47.

That first fulfillment of Joel 3 preceded a first fulfillment of Our Blessed Lord's eschatological prophesy in Matthew 24, Mark 13 and Luke 21. Within a generation the former age of the old covenant had passed away with the destruction of Jerusalem and its temple in 70 A.D. by the Roman army under General Titus. The Christians had followed Christ's warning and on seeing Jerusalem being surrounded by armies had fled to safety in the town of Pella in the Jordon Valley, halfway to the Sea of Galilee. But that first fulfillment had not included Christ's coming as ruler and judge: his *"parousia."* Since then Christians have anticipated and prayed constantly for a second coming of Christ with power and authority. Many believe that a second Pentecost or outpouring of the Holy Spirit as prophesied by Joel will immediately precede it.

I am convinced that we are now in the final moments of that second Pentecost, and that the messages of the Most Blessed Trinity and of the Blessed Mother of Jesus to Sadie Jaramillo are an important part of its fruits. I pray that these messages will be read immediately because of their great urgency. When I hear committed Christians, and especially brother priests, say that they have no need of such contemporary prophesy because their faith is firmly rooted in Jesus and in the Holy Scriptures, I am puzzled. It is just those who are believers to whom contemporary prophets are being sent. Because they are strong in the faith, they should want to hear the prophetic message God sends. It is just to such believers that God is likely to send a prophet to exhort His people to holiness or to warn them of specific dangers to their spiritual well-being. What concerns the well-being of the flock he has entrusted to our care as his shepherds, we priests should hear. The question is not what do I think I need, but what is the Spirit saying to the churches through the prophets. And if Jesus were to send his mother in the role of prophet and Queen, we ought to hear her. Is Jesus standing at the gate, ready to come again? Many contemporary prophets, including Sadie Jaramillo, believe they have been told that now is, indeed the time. Among the many signs of our times, consider that Jesus' first coming was accompanied by the massacre of the Holy Innocents. Matthew 2:16-18. Might not his second coming be the same?

Sadie has sought and followed spiritual direction by experienced priests. She remains completely obedient and docile to the holy scriptures, the doctrine and magisterium of the Church, and to the guidance of her spiritual director. She is very much in love with God, filled with hope and love for God's Church and his children, and totally focused on the mission heaven has given her. Yet she remains warm and outgoing, caring for and home-schooling her children, answering questions and praying for all who call on her, and speaking of heaven's messages to all individuals and

Contents

Editor's Note:

In an effort to protect the privacy of individuals, names have been changed to initials only.

Private and personal revelations have been excluded from this publication. Only those relevant to all persons have been included.

Introduction

The messages contained in this book have been given since 1992, in the form of interior locutions, or "inner conversations" from God Our Father, Our Lord Jesus Christ, the Holy Spirit, the Blessed Virgin Mary and St. Michael the Archangel to the "Little Sorrowful Rose".

The little sorrowful rose is Sadie Jaramillo, a single mother living in Southern California. Her conversion began in 1980 at a private Catholic charismatic prayer and healing service, which she regularly attended for six years. In 1980, while singing of her love for Our Lord she suddenly heard a voice say "I love you too." She was shocked and asked "Lord, is that you?". He replied "Yes, daughter."

Over the next twelve years she received messages (inner locutions) from Our Lord Jesus only. In 1992, she began to hear the voices of Our Father, Our Blessed Mother and the Holy Spirit, warning of world events and chastisements, most of which have been averted in large part, due to the intercession of Our Blessed Mother.

She has carefully recorded and published these messages, because now is the final time for repentance before the Justice of God.

January 31, 1997

Jesus: "Do not let yourselves be deluded into thinking nothing will happen. It should have happened long ago, but I have desired to show mercy and, through the great intercession of the Queen of Heaven, great acts of God's justice have been averted. But we are in the final hours and for this you have been prepared and risen with many others, that God's instructions should be heeded. . .

"Be as the brides with oil in their lamps, for you know not the hour in which the groom will arrive and you will have to flee. The graces for conversion are being showered upon humanity. They are bought by your prayers, fasts, sacrifices and for some, by the shedding of their blood."

"This Lent will be as no other. The sickle is put to the harvest. And if you have seen mighty things, mightier than these will you see, for I speak it! My will be done."

Chapter One

The Mother of All Humanity Warns Her Children

**Messages From August 1, 1992
To December 29, 1992**

Sadie's Introduction

August 1, 1992

Many events have happened in my life which I cannot explain. But with the grace of the Holy Spirit, I will try.

I came home from the cenacle last night feeling not comforted, but very disturbed. I don't know if I did or didn't hear correctly the message from Our Lord that David* had for me, but I was very upset. I felt that what the Lord was saying to me, was scolding me for not having faith, for He asked, "Why are you sad?"

D. - Message For Sadie

Jesus: It is done.
It is finished
Out of the ashes rises the Phoenix.
Unless gold go through the fire, (crucible)
it will not shine.

It is over My child. See the crown you have won for yourself. Feel My arms enfold you.

Rejoice! Just as I lay in the tomb for three days after enduring immeasurable suffering, so will you, only to emerge triumphantly into My Glory! Sound the trumpet of salvation, the day of The Lord is here! Behold, I give you real food to eat and real drink to refresh your soul. I embrace you in My arms.

Just as I lay in the tomb for three days, you have also been awarded the end of your suffering, a period of rest. How pleased I am at your offerings. Prepare your banquet, prepare your feast.

I give you a short period to rejoice and after the reuniting of your family there will come again the need for My work to continue. Are you prepared?

2

(S.J. Whatever Your will is for me, my Lord and my God, I will do as you ask.)

Jesus: Rest My child, I love you.

S.J.: This morning, I woke up and could feel The Lord asking me, "Where is the mercy I have shown you?" So I went up to the house, and this part of the experience Our Mother said I could keep private.

I came home to the apartment to cook some food for the boys. Then I took a shower. While in the shower I started to cry and let go of the anger I had been feeling. I made my peace with The Lord. Then I went to go buy some salt and oil to have blessed at the Family Renewal Home.

As I was leaving the store, a young Mexican man came up to me looking very embarrassed and asked if I could speak Spanish. We talked and he told me he and his uncle were going north to work in the fields near Salinas, but they had no money to complete the trip. I checked in my purse and car, but only had $4.00. So I told him to wait and I would go to the bank.

On the way I asked The Lord, 'Lord I'm always getting taken by people like this. Should I do this?' He replied "Yes". So I withdrew $20 and returned to the store. As I got out of the car I saw my Virgen de Gaudalupe Rosary. I took it in my hand and walked over to the young man and his uncle.

I told them both that I wanted them not to use the money for beer but only for what they needed to get to Salinas. I also asked them to promise they would go to the church in Salinas and thank the Virgen for their safe trip, because She is the one who told me to give this money to you. The uncle shook my hand and looked me in the eyes and said "Oh Senorita, thank you. May God bless you. I wish you could have given me a rosary."

3

As I drove off I was thinking about my rosary and suddenly I heard a beautiful woman's voice say "Don't worry My daughter, you will have many more of my rosaries to give away." I felt the swelling of my heart and I couldn't believe it, for I had never heard Our Mother's voice.

Then I said out loud, "Oh no, this is just me now." Our Lady replied "No My daughter, it is I, your Mother. Your time of visitation is now. That was My Son you gave that money to." I kept saying in my heart over and over, "Oh My Mother, my beautiful Mother."

Then she said I would never have to worry, the adversary could never touch me again. I had three angels who had been instructed to my care. I was never to judge what another was doing, because each of us has something different to do. That there would be more people coming to the cenacle and I would have to share Jesus' love with them. She is pleased with the name I've chosen for the cenacle, which is the Cenacle of the Sorrowful and Immaculate Heart of Mary.

Then I heard Our Lady start to cry. She said, "See My Son and I have felt every tear you have shed, they have fallen like roses of gold on Our laps. But I am also crying because time is so short and there is so much to do!" She then gave me a personal message about my estranged husband. After She said: "Your heart, that is what We have seen and your gift of money was a test. Now you are in a period of rest and restoration, then the work will begin again."

That morning, and since the beginning of the week, my eyes started to tear up uncontrollably. They are now very swollen and I explained to my husband that I couldn't help it. Our Lady said I was right to tell him that I can't help it, because they are not my tears, they are Hers. She asked: "Will you share My sorrow, will you cry My tears?" I hesitated and She gave me another private message, then I said yes.

4

Later, while driving back from Santa Paula, I asked, "If this is really you Blessed Lady, let me smell roses." I smelled roses four different times. When I got to my apartment I was ecstatic and ran to my Pilgrim Virgin statue and fell on my knees. Then I noticed Her face and I could see the tracks of Her tears!

The Time of Visitation

August 2, 1992

(S.J. This morning I heard a voice and tested saying, "I rebuke you in the name of Jesus. Go if you are not of God." Our Lord replied:)

Jesus: Woe, Woe to them who will not recognize the time of their visitation!

Daughter, be sure to tell My people you heard *My* voice, not My Mother's.

August 3, 1992 - In Mass

(S.J. I heard a women's voice and tested. Our Lady replied:)

Mary: Rejoice, daughter, rejoice.

(S.J. Then I heard choirs of angels singing the 'Alleluljah' and an angel said:)

"Behold the Mother of God goes down to leave another sign for God's people!"

Sound the Trumpet

August 14, 1992 - A.M.

(After receiving Communion I saw a vision and tested, and Our Lord told me to come home and write down what I saw.)

First, this morning, Our Lady told me to rejoice and praise the Name of Her Son. For, did I think that in Her asking me to share Her sorrow, or cry Her tears meant only that? Did I not know that it also meant I would share in Her joys? And, Her joys are when the Father grants to Her children their requests.

I didn't know what that meant, but then in Mass I saw Our Lady standing on the head of the serpent. Then, Jesus stood up from His throne and held me in His bosom. He then helped me up the stairs, lifted me up and placed me in the arms of **the Father** and He said to me, **"Yes, I am your Abba,"** and I felt myself cry tears that I haven't been able to cry.

Then He said to me, "Your Saint Joseph awaits you."

Then I saw myriads of angels ready for battle and **Saint Michael** at the head of them and Jesus on a white horse rearing up, and He was dressed all in white with a gold sash across His chest. He had a sword raised above His head, and He said, **"Sound the trumpet, the 'Day of The Lord' has come."**

He then instructed me to come home and write down what I had seen.

(S.J. Later that same day.)

I was eating lunch, for Our Lady said that I should fortify myself and I was thinking about the message My Mother gave to me for 'A.'s' cenacle which is called *The Triumphant Reign of The Immaculate Heart, through the assistance of Saint Michael the Archangel.*

Then I heard a man's voice, not Our Lord, say "Hello, Sadie". I got up and walked around saying: "Oh no, now I'm really going crazy." But he said "No, no you are not."

"It is I, St. Michael, allow me to hold your hand; you will feel the heat." So, I extended my hand and at first didn't feel anything. But as he spoke, I felt heat in my hand. He then said: "Remember the little book you bought about me?" And I replied 'Yes,' for I bought a book about the Prayer to St. Michael and I remember thinking the Church would not be in the state it is in, if they had not stopped saying that prayer.

He said, "From now on you will walk with my valor, my courage and my special protection. Thank you for allowing Our Lady to use you, and this cenacle with His name is going to be specially protected by me and my legions of angels. For by invoking His name and aid, we are opening the doors of victory over Satan."

Many Warnings Given

September 14, 1992

Message to be read at the Sorrowful & Immaculate Heart of Mary Cenacle of the Marian Movement of Priests.

(S.J. I heard a voice and tested. Our Lady answered.)

Mary: Daughter, prepare My message.

Many of you will wonder at the many natural disasters happening around the world. My children, listen to the many warnings being given around the world. Those of you who doubt and refuse to believe continue to cause me great suffering and tears.

Why am I called Our Lady of Sorrows? Not only because of the intense suffering I endured watching My Son, the Son of God, endure for His great love for you, but because in these end times the place of honor bestowed upon Me has been all but diminished. And I cry as a mother cries whose heart is breaking at the agony of her children's cries.

Do you not know I am beside you all, through all life's burdens, trying to lead you to the only answer possible for your peace? That answer is My Beloved Son Jesus, He Who suffered to the point of death, loved you all so that, indeed, He would die for each one of you again!

7

Do not harden your hearts! Sin continues to run rampant in the lives of many of My children. There is a hell, my children! There is a punishment awaiting all who would refuse My call. Consecrate yourselves to My Sorrowful and Immaculate Heart. In that lies your peace of heart and mind. Give Me your burdens and sufferings. I can use them all to convert many more souls to My Son.

He will refuse Me nothing! His first miracle was at My request, as will His last one be!

I will not rest, for the time quickly approaches. There is no more time left to live in complete refusal to convert, completely and totally!

Many are called, few are chosen - Why?

Because of the sin of pride! Do not justify your sins! Confess them and throw them into My Son's ocean of mercy. Only He can change the hearts of My children, but we come together and always, always, implore and ask permission to enter.

Thank you all for coming together, as I request, to pray. Many blessings and answers to prayers are here tonight.

Peace to all who remain in Our hearts!

What I Desire is Obedience

September 15, 1992 - 2:30 A.M.

(S.J. During the night I am awakened and tested. Our Lord answered with these words:)

Jesus: That you may know that I abide in you and you abide in ME. I desire that you pray My Mother's Most Holy Rosary.

(S.J. So, I prayed the Rosary. Then, as it was 3:00 o'clock, I went on to pray the Mercy of God Chaplet. As usual, when I am done, I feel a peace that allows me to go back to sleep.

In the morning I awake and stand in front of the Mercy of God picture and I say, "Good morning, my Jesus;" for through His inspiration I know now that I trust, when I don't even mention my needs for the day, or my worries.

I tell Him, today I offer all my thoughts, deeds and sufferings and I ask that You unite them to Your Most Perfect Sacrifice, that they may become pleasing to you. Then I hear a voice and test and My Lord says to me:)

Jesus: Write these things down.

That you may know that I abide in you and you abide in Me, I tell you now that you are being prepared. For you have submitted your will and all else to Me. It is not because you are great, for even in your prayers, you acknowledge that you are the most despised of sinners. But, you acknowledge My mercy in your life, and for this reason and this reason alone, I can use you. I would use all if they would but submit!

(S.J. Then I heard in my heart a sound like a trumpet or a horn, and His voice is deep and serious.)

Jesus: So behold, My people, to the words you will hear. The time has come for all to submit. If you would do My will and the will of My Father, then I tell you to stop trying to guess or figure out what Our next move will be. Release your fears, for they block what I am trying to do.

Trust in Me! Trust in Me! Trust in Me! What I desire most is obedience. Be still and know that I am your God! Be still and hear my voice. Those that would respond do not do so totally. I ask you to remain in my peace.

You are My children; would I allow anything to harm you? Have I not told you that I have counted even the hairs on your head?

When you gather, pray and pray fervently, fervently! There is so little time left and I would use you all if you would submit. What I desire is obedience! Trust Me. Allow My Mother to lead you

9

where there is need. Be still and know that I am your God, who cares for and loves you. But there is so little time. Release all your needs. See, I know them even before you think them.

Do only what I ask; in this way you will be trusting Me. I love you. Peace to all.

Vision of Disasters

September 22, 1992

(I have been receiving this vision since last week, not understanding and I think not wanting to understand. But, I heard Our Lady say I must come home and write down what I was shown.)

Vision: I see in this vision three parts: In the upper right-hand I see devastation over a large portion of land, with a huge crack running from top to bottom of this part of the vision. I understand this is to be a mighty earthquake.

In the bottom of the vision I see a huge ocean wave and can feel the force with which it is rushing towards the land. I am told this is another tidal wave.

Then, I can see a volcano, which I know is Mt. Pinatubo in the Philippines, because Our Lady has been telling me to pray since last week for Her children in the Philippines.

The Lord told me today in Mass that the tidal wave is headed for Southern California. The earthquake will be where there has never been an earthquake. The volcano will be in the Philippines.

He also told me that He is the Lord God, and God will not be poured into a mold that man makes for Him! He in His Justice will show man, who tries to understand with his own intelligence, that **God is Creator** and no one can understand the ways of His Wisdom or His Justice!

He is angry because of all the signs that have been given, men still continue to try to explain them all as acts of 'mother nature'. They are not! They are warnings of what will be and will continue to be if man does not repent. The Father is already giving the commands to the angel of destruction.

Please, please, pray. Offer sacrifices of atonement to lessen the punishments. For that is all we can do, lessen the punishments to come.

Many Will Be the Conversions

October 2, 1992

(In front of the Pilgrim Virgin of Fatima, as I was praying, I heard a voice and tested. Our Lady answered in Spanish :)

Hoy te doy este mansaje en espanol por con el poder del Espiritu Santo te va ayudar con tu idioma paraque proclamaras todos los mensajes a mi gente pobre con mucha fe, que hoy adelante todos van a saber que tu eres consagrada a mi de un modo especial; y que todos los mensajes son verdaderamente de Mi y mi Hijo Jesus. Todo pa traer todo Gloria y Honor a Dios Padre Celestial y a mi Hijo Jesucristo y al Espiritu Santo.

(Our Lady continued in English.)

Tell My children:

Do not worry, I have prepared in the hearts of all My children who love Me, the desire to supply every need that would arise for My walk. Many will be the conversions. Many will come, and I will manifest My presence in a special way.

My peace and blessings to all My children.

11

There Is No More Time to Waste

October 3, 1992 - 9:00 P.M.

(My dialog with Jesus before the message.)

Jesus, how profoundly I adore you. When will I understand the immensity of Your love for me? I praise and love my Eternal Father for calling me to You. Someday I'll know whose prayers broke the bondage of the evil.

The agony in my heart! I want to cry out and scream at seeing the woman who cared for me when I was a little girl, lying in such a state. But, I suffer in silence, as you My Beloved Mother have asked, to use my suffering to bring more glory to your Beloved Son, by converting more souls, precious souls who will live eternally with Him! What have I to give? Only my heart. That is all.

(The following message was given after my dialog. But, before I start, I realize my blessed candle has gone out, so, I light another candle. I test, then Our Lady speaks:)

Mary: Yes, My children, keep your lamps burning, keep them ever burning and a supply well on hand.

Do not be caught in darkness nor when the darkness comes. These are two different requests, but each lead to the same end, light everlasting. Yes, Jesus is the light that will reflect over His entire Kingdom at the fulfillment of His reign and life everlasting.

Soon your whole valley and indeed the whole world will know of My Presence here. Many will come from near and far. What in the end will stand? Only those living in the light and grace of My Son.

(As I hear and wonder at another voice and test, He says:)

Jesus: Yes, daughter it is I your Lord.

The Eternal Father can withstand no more! End the sins in your life. That is not what keeps you from me, it is the rigidity of

12

your heart. Why do you chose death instead of life? Why? Throw off what you feel is justified! It is not. Your world would tell you differently.

You parents, do you not know the treasure you have been entrusted with in your children? They are not yours. They are My Father's! But He loved you enough to entrust you with the care of your, HIS, children. Each one of you is called in a different way. Stop the killing, the abuse!

I only knew love, total love from My Beloved Mother and Step-Father Joseph.

Your world has falsely said you must abandon the care of your children so you can provide! Provide for what? All that can be given comes from the Eternal Father. Put your priorities in order!

God must be first! He it is who sees to your daily needs.

I tell you, you must turn from your sins while there is still time. I still wait with arms outstretched to receive you and be invited into your hearts.

Soon the warnings will stop and the fulfillment of them will begin! I love you one and all My children. Turn to your God Who loves you. Peace, Peace . . .

Yes, daughter, tonight the Lord gives you a message also. He sees with what tireless actions on My part you try to turn the world to Him. Please My daughter, give My messages, go forth and proclaim them.

Sin is no longer called sin in this world. But it is real and you must turn from it. [Yes, you feel the beatings of the Holy Spirit, allow Him to work in you.]

(S.J. At this time I feel an intense pounding in my heart that seems to literally move my whole body.)

Jesus: You must continue to strengthen all your cenacles by means of prayer and sacrifice to make reparation for the many sacrilegious acts committed against The Father and Your Lord. Only then will My children know peace.

Today everyone here will see a sign of My Presence. It will be a sign that will confirm all that has been said. All will come to pass. Then all will believe. Not all will accept, but they will believe. And there lies all the Sorrow of the Mother and the Son. They will see, believe and not accept.

We bless you in the name of The Father and The Son and The Holy Spirit.

(S.J. I hear another voice and test. Our Lady answers.)

Mary: Tell My daughter to remember I was a young woman when I was also taken as a wife. There is no higher calling than **wife and mother**. There are many who cause me to cry for their failure to live in the sanctity of their calling. She must remain close to Me and I will protect and bless her husband and their children. This is My gift to her, as I Am present with My Son. Peace to all who remain close to Our Hearts.

AMEN!

(S.J. After receiving Communion, I hear a voice and test. Our Lady answers.)

Mary: You must tell Fr. 'N.' [the following message]:

If he would allow himself consecration totally and completely to Me, I will shower him with all the graces needed to achieve the total desire of the Father; that is to allow Me the place of homage He desires for Me. Then this parish will shine ever so brilliantly in this world of complete darkness.

There will be true conversions and he will receive all that he needs to truly prepare his flock for what is to come.

14

There is no more time to waste! The souls of so many are being lost because of the complete refusal to boldly and loudly Proclaim the Good News of My Son.

I desire also that the devotion to **Jesus King of All Nations** be promoted. My Son promises great graces to His consecrated sons who promote this and I am the **Mediatrix of All Graces** and I distribute them freely to whomsoever would call on Me.

The success of My Church is not in the amount of money taken in, but rather the number of souls being saved and converted.

This is a priority for My ministers of My flocks.

Do this first, all else will follow.

Adieu et seru.

Hearts Are Being Prepared

October 5, 1992 - 4:30 A.M.

(S.J. I hear a voice and test. Our Lady speaks.)

Mary: Daughter you must prepare My message:

The hearts of many are being prepared, as they would listen and hear the voice of their Heavenly Mother, they will also know of their mission and call.

Come with wonder and expectation to My pilgrim walk. Offer to Me and My Son all of the burdens you carry. Lay them at the foot of My Son's Most Holy Cross and take My hand. Then you will feel the peace and comfort of My heavenly arms. They will soothe and bind up your wounded hearts, just as they comforted the Wounded Body and Heart of Jesus, My only begotten Son.

From His Cross He would feel the rejection of all humanity to the end of this age and time.

15

Many of you will question and doubt. Many of you will want to see signs. But do you want to experience a change of heart? Do you want to put an end to your own agony and torture?

How many of My children experience nights of no peace? How many look to other means (substitutes) for the genuine peace that comes from Jesus?

How many of you fear the love, comfort and peace Jesus **died to bring you**? It is because you allow Satan, My enemy to blind you and hold you captive!

Once you feel the gentle call of love, for God is **love**, go forward. Hold onto the hand of the loved one who is praying desperately for you to see in light and know it is I, your Heavenly Mother, in reality who is arranging for your arrival at the foot of My Son's cross.

I and all of you are winning the battle as foretold against the evil one. All who have consecrated themselves to Me will experience that gift.

On the 75th anniversary date of the **Miracle of the Sun**, there will also be a **Miracle of the SON**! Who with Me and through ME comes to all who call on Us.

Please my little children, put down your fears. Come forward to experience the genuine peace and love We bring.

Many will believe. For the work of silence and hiddeness is over. Now it is being proclaimed to bring all Glory to God, of His Great Love for the Mother of God.

Blessings and peace for you, My children of light.

Run to My Divine Son's Mercy

October 10, 1992 - 5:00 A.M.

(S.J. I tested and Our Lady answered.)

Mary: Many of you, My dear children, have come to pay Me honor and respond from a love that has long been in your hearts for the Mother of God. Others have come in response to a new love for Me.

But today I announce to you, **you are part of the fulfillment of the Fatima messages**, the Triumph of the Immaculate Heart!

Yes, devotion to the Mother of God is spreading as never before through the **Marian Movement of Priests**. My cenacles are burning with love for Me and I am making My presence felt in an extraordinary way. The fragrance of the Mother permeates every home of My cenacle movement.

God proclaimed from the beginning of all ages that all generations would call Me blessed. Many have fought and denied the place God has given to Me. Many feel this is a 'new age' where love and time spent praying the rosary are old fashioned.

I tell you, My children, there is no other way to fight My adversary, other than by My most holy rosary. Therein lies the very power of heaven!

You have come each and every one with a burden, an illness, a lost loved one, a pain that has drawn you to the Mother of God. Do not despair My children! Have faith! Pray as you have never prayed before, pray constantly and from your hearts. I want to speak to all of My children.

Consecrate yourselves and your whole families to Me. Only then can I begin to move in your lives and families.

Give up the pleasures and treasure hunts of this world; for this world, as we know it today, is passing away.

With your offerings of sufferings and offerings of prayer you are causing many souls that would otherwise be lost to be saved.

17

And that is the whole story of redemption from death: To claim as many souls as possible for The Kingdom of God. To accept freely and completely the free gift from God. Salvation from all of your sins, through the most precious sacrifice My Son suffered on Calvary and on the Cross.

You are allowing yourselves to rot in your own sins by not accepting My Son's gift of Mercy. And in the end your condemnation will not come from your sins. It will come from your refusal to say yes!

Do not allow your hardened hearts to keep you in darkness any longer. Draw close to Me and My love and I will take you to the very bosom of My Beloved Son.

All of you here are needed by My Son to continue His proclamation of the gospel, to share His love.

To all, to all children, God does not love anyone less than another. He is equal and fair in His love for His children. Do not separate from His love by your sins you continue to justify. Nothing is worth giving up your salvation for your dislike and hatred for another child of God.

So, run to My Divine Son's mercy! There is still time.

Cleanse yourselves through the sacrament of confession. Strengthen yourselves through the sacrament of communion and consecrate yourselves and family to My Immaculate Heart.

There is no fear for what is to come for My children of light, living in grace.

Many answers to prayer and blessings are here today. My presence, My place of honor will no longer be denied.

Peace and blessing to all, in the name of the Father, Jesus, the Son, and the Holy Spirit.

Love One Another

October 12, 1992 - 8:40 A.M.

(S.J. I tested and Our Lord answered.)

Jesus: Tell your leaders and sources the message I give you:

(S.J. This message was given in response to a request to move the cenacle to the church.)

Mary: Yes My child, I know the love those two beautiful sources, 'J.' and 'L.' have for Me and the desire they have to venerate Me. However, everything is being prepared solely by Me for the continuous growth of all the cenacles.

Father 'N.' must be made aware of all My cenacles. Prepare a list and take it to him. Tell him how My children are being drawn in great numbers. In particular the Tuesday evening cenacle with you, My child. And you My daughter, call him and invite him to come tonight and tell him the words I give to you.

Continue in prayer, support one another; this is most pleasing to Me. You are touching the very throne of God with your prayers.

Much love to you and all the leaders on My cenacles and to My sources who have served Me so well and been the instruments of spreading the messages. This message is solely for you and the leaders.

We love you.

(S.J. This message was given at 2:10 A.M. the next morning, after I was feeling overwhelmed at the confusion and misinterpretation of the previous message by the leaders of the cenacle.)

Mary: Come to Me, daughter.

There must be no dissension among My children. My enemy sees the fruits of My cenacles and is prowling about to bring division. Each one of you has been called to serve in a different way.

I, Myself, am leading all of you; and not all of you will move in the same way. The exhorter must exhort, the teacher teach, the server serve. Seek the scripture.

There can only and must only be love among you.

I come to warn you to be ever vigilant. Do not let your prayer defenses down. Remain always in the spirit of prayer to discern My call. Many fruits have been seen; but this is only the beginning, with much to do, so very much.

Love one another as your Mother and Lord love you.

Persevere, go forward in Our peace.

Hear the Voice of Your God

October 27, 1992 - 4:00 P.M.

(S.J. Who speaks to me? In whose name do you come?)

Jesus: Thus says the Lord your God:

My children how My Heart anguishes at the refusal of so many to heed the call of My Mother and Myself.

I tell you your fate is even at the doors! The warnings of My Prophets will not go unfulfilled!

Do you not understand the reason My Mother is making Her presence known, felt, seen and heard in so many places as never before in the history of My Church?

Read the prophets of old and know the Spirit which I pour on mankind is to fulfill those prophets' words.

And now as I raise new prophets, they go scoffed at and looked at as an oddity! But My people, hear the voice of your God! They will not be laughed and scoffed at when the time of all times arrives!

You cannot see what awaits you, so you choose to believe you have more time.

(S.J. At this point, Our Lord directed me to read Matthew, Chapter 10.)

Jesus: Enough! Return to your merciful Lord and Savior!

The time arrives, will the Son of God find any faith?

Have faith in your God!

Trust in your God!

There is no other way to salvation.

Love one another, indeed as I have loved you. Allow the flame of love from the hearts of My Mother and Myself to lead you, guide you, teach you and cleanse you.

We await with loving arms and hearts to enfold you.

Peace and blessing to My children.

The Holy Spirit Will Confirm

October 30, 1992

(S.J. Who speaks to me? In whose name do you come?)

Mary: My beloved daughter:

Yes, there comes the end of this test for you. You are about to embark on a new journey.

Do not despair!

21

Continue to pray. All is being prepared by Me. Those who have come against My messengers and sources will soon know that they (these I speak of) are truly sent forth by God, the Eternal Father and that they walk in the power of the Holy Spirit.

They (those who speak against) will be given a chance to have a change of heart for the untruths spoken. Do not worry about what you are to say, for the time comes and indeed is here when you are speaking what you hear from Me and the Holy Spirit will confirm all that is being said.

The time arrives for the marvels of the Holy Mother to appear. Continue to invoke Michael the Archangel for His protection and to remove the antichrists that are indeed in My Holy Church.

Continue to gather in cenacle with leaders and sources; Yes, it is the will of My Son to study His Holy Word as a group. Much teaching and grace will be spread as a result of this.

Love and blessings to all My children of light.

Warn the Priests

November 2, 1992 - 6:30 A.M.

(S.J. Who speaks to me? In whose name do you come?)

Mary: I am the Mother of your Lord and Savior who came in the flesh, died and resurrected to the Eternal Father. I am the Immaculate Conception.

Behold My daughter:

Thus says Your Lord: I come to tell you that indeed you will be expelled from your church and they who come will claim to be serving God. But, My Son will not leave His people unprepared. Thus you are raised to go forth and proclaim the messages given. Do not fear, I will go with you and prepare all that will happen and all that you are to say.

Again read Chapter 10 of the Book of Matthew.

My priest sons refuse to acknowledge that the Mother of God is indeed coming to warn, to ask and to pray with God's people. Cry out and pray, pray, pray, My daughter. They refuse to acknowledge that God chooses those who stand pure of heart. What is there for you to gain? Rejection? Persecution? Rejoice, they did the same to My Beloved Son!

Already you feel the alienation, the distance they put between them and you. But you Must go on. You are directed by the Queen of Heaven and Her Son. It has been predestined by the Eternal Father. But never despair, I am with you and will remain with you until the time of all times arrives, and I, Myself, will warn you interiorly and you will in turn warn those that I tell you. **You will warn the priests and they will stand before God and give accounting of how they lead their flocks!**

Go, My child, tend to your children. I will speak to you when you are able to take the dictation I give you.

(S.J. I take my children to school and then gather with my friends after morning mass to continue to pray for the cenacles and the leaders. Just recently, the Lord directed that this meeting be opened to all His children.

As I leave to pick up my children from school I begin to sing in the Spirit, rejoicing, for in the sharing of prayer, I find that Our Lady is indeed working Her Marvels.)

(S.J. Then The Lord speaks to me as I'm driving so I reach for some scraps of paper and this is what He has to say:)

Jesus: Behold My priests, I the Lord your God say:

You brood of vipers, who do not recognize the time of your visitation! Behold the time arrives and is ever near when you will stand before me with the blood of the souls I placed before you to minister and save for My kingdom!

Their loss will be held accountable to you. Do you preach sin as sin; [do you preach about] heaven and hell? Do you acknowledge My Mother in your ministry? On the contrary; My Mother is forgotten! You ridicule those who are sent to you as being not of God! Look at the fruits! If this was not My Mother's work it would not bear the fruit it has!

Do not remain in your obstinacy! Your place is in the confessional to receive many who are converting through hearing the messages of those I have chosen.

My people will not be left without a Shepherd and unprepared! There is a chastisement coming to purify this world of the filth that has infected the very core of it. Search the words of Scripture and My holy prophets and the words of saints before! Since the very beginning of time, I have spoken of what is to come. Continue in your disbelief and you will be judged on your refusal to hear the voice of Your God!

My patience ends! Do you not know that I see **all** that is happening in the lives of My children? And that My consecrated sons are not living their consecration! The Father is indeed ready to let His arm down to bring this punishment, that will be nothing that mankind has seen since the beginning of all times! But My children are responding. It is the simple of heart who are hearing the good news and responding.

Your world's intelligence? As far as the east is from the west, so are my ways from yours! The abominations have entered into the very sanctity of the Church.

Divinations, teachings of the "new age" are another name for the teachings of the antichrists. Their ears desire to hear only those things that make them feel good.

When My **Word** is spoken it will bring those in sin under conviction. There is no one to tell My children to look only to their God for their needs. Neither parents nor priests are tending to the very center of mankind's need. They are the people who have forgotten their God!

The very acts of Satan are in those places and being taught by persons who claim they are serving their God.

Away from Me you evil doers!! Your father is Satan the father of all lies! Go back to the simplicity of the Gospel. Do you not expect yourselves to undergo the very same persecutions that were meted out to Me? Go back to My Holy Word and listen to what I would have you see and know.

I love all and would receive all that would repent. But those being chosen are arising at My command and you will know the Day of the Lord, the truth and all that shall condemn you!

Now My daughter, give this message to your spiritual director and he will know this indeed is the message from Your Lord and Mother. He will be used as foretold by My Mother to minister to his fellow priests. I Myself will go before him and surround him with My anointing.

I Will Warn Interiorly

November 3, 1992 - 3:20 P.M.

(S.J. In whose name do you come?)

Mary: I am the Queen of Heaven and the Mother of Jesus, come in the flesh, died, resurrected and ascended to the Eternal Father.

My beloved daughter:

Tell My children how pleased I am at their response for prayer and sacrifice offered to Me their Queen and consolation.

The Queen of Heaven is walking among Her children. More and more the triumph of My Immaculate Heart becomes total and complete.

What does this mean for you My children?

25

It means that I your Mother manifest My presence and love in a way that no one can deny. I begin to grant the graces needed for your total consecration to Me. You are then formed and molded according to the plan of The Heavenly Father for your life.

Pray children, with total abandonment to Me. There are those who arise to throw accusations and ridicule at those chosen to go forth and proclaim My messages. My messages which tell over and over again the love the Son has, His forgiveness and My desire to return one and all to the graces of the sacraments.

Do not justify your sins! Don't make excuses any longer Don't wait! How I plead! How can My messages change?

My enemy foolishly believes he has won. Oh no My children, My victory is ever nearer. Those who worry, need not. The Father has willed not to leave His children unprepared.

I will warn interiorly all those who are chosen. I am marking My children with the Sign of the Cross, that all will know they are mine. My Son Jesus has willed it so. Allow Me to lead and console you. Do not continue to sin My children. Pray as you have been, love one another and continue to offer Me your sufferings.

I am leading each and every one of you to that total and complete consecration to Me and My Son. Behold children the days of extreme trial are arriving, as are the terrible chastisements and purification for this sinful world.

Beginning with the house of God to the least of My children, judgement will fall! Now is the time of mercy and forgiveness from My Son. Read God's word, pray My rosary, fast for all those souls still far away from the Truth that will bring peace, forgiveness and love for their fellow brothers and sisters.

We love and bless all here tonight and thank you for praying with Me for this world.

(S.J. Our Lady then asked me to read messages 449 & 450 in Fr. Gobbi's Book.)

My Sons Must Prepare their People for the Punishment

November 5, 1992 - 8:30 A.M. In Mass.

Mary: Complete the message to My priest-son,

(S.J., Who speaks to me?)

Mary: I am the Mother of Jesus, your Lord and Savior of the World, Who lived among men, died, resurrected and ascended back to the Eternal Father.

Thank you My daughter for testing as you are to do. The enemy is ever near as you found out on Tuesday. Continue to do the same, for we will be coming to you more and more, this you know as We have spoken of before.

Tell My beloved son:

I have wanted you to hear the words of your Lord in regards to the many consecrated sons who are in disobedience to their purpose for God's people.

Just as My messengers are sent with a purpose, so also will you be used for the glory of My Son. **Do not expect it to be an easy time**. You will continue to be persecuted, but I will protect and shelter you with My mantle.

You must go forth and reach the many priests of My Son who are no longer taking care of their people. The doors are opening and will continue to do so, because the unlearned are hearing and accepting the messages and doing as I ask. They are in constant prayer for Me and My intentions, which are bringing about the ever nearer triumph of My Immaculate Heart.

My sons must prepare their people for the coming punishment!

This **will** come and for that reason I have come down from Heaven to walk amongst My children and prepare, pray and lead them!

27

But, **woe** to them that refuse My request! The Father and the Son have spoken many times in regard to this. Do not drink of the same cup as Judas!

Listen to those We send to you. My children are simple and pure of heart. What do they have to gain? The same persecutions that have gone on since the beginning of My Son's ministry. Those who are doing the will of God, you will know by the fruits. And the fruits of My Movement are many!

Know this My son. Their are many of My children desiring to return to the sacraments and convert totally back to My Son and acknowledge the place the Mother plays in the redemption plan. Help My children who come to you and reach your brother priests. The time and the means will come, but you must be prepared.

My Movement will not be stopped, precisely for it is My Movement and there are no leaders other than Me! We love and bless you and will continue to send messages to you through the messenger. You will be led by the Spirit and Myself when the time comes.

Peace and blessing to you My little son.

I Am the Mother of All Humanity, Mediatrix of All Graces

November 6, 1992 - 5:51 P.M.

(**S.J.**, Who speaks to me?)

Mary: *I am the Mother of All Humanity, Mediatrix of All Graces, Servant of My Lord.*

Reflect on My words, daughter of mine. I have given you a glimpse of what is to come. From now on you must pray as you never have before.

You have been under tremendous attack of the enemy, this you know. But, you are marked and consecrated for the use of the Lord and he could never touch you. I have already shown you this.

But, Oh My little daughter, you must plead before God and My Son for His poor lost people. How it makes My heart be pierced over and over again as I see many run headlong to their fate. What continues to soothe My pierced heart, is the response of so many of My children in many sorrowing communities.

Unite ever stronger! United prayer among all My cenacles is moving God's Spirit among His children. There is indeed a time of preparation and teaching among My consecrated children under this movement of mine. You are the least of My children, but you are repentant and pure of heart when you love and comfort My Son.

Trust in His forgiveness by running to the confessional every time you fall and each time you come back and say "Here I am Lord, if you can use even me, here I am."

I have indeed shown you in the vision, the disasters on the way to your country. Previously, you were not told specifically where they are to occur. All these disasters are for your country - soon! I was also placing in your heart My beloved Philippine children, by requesting that you pray for them.

Do not despair at your family situation. Very soon, the tide will turn and your family state will be complete. Then you will go forward with your call from your God. I will continue to lead you to all material and messages vital to you.

Stay close to Me daughter of mine. I cover you with My mantle.

Love and blessings to you.

Now is Your Time of Salvation

November 9, 1992 - 2:55 P.M.

(S.J., I tested and Our Lady answered and told me to read messages 398 & 400 in Fr. Gobbi's book.)

Mary: Greetings to all My beloved children:

I your Heavenly Mother come here tonight to pray with you for Peace. Peace in the world and peace in your families.

How it pleases Me to hear you all pray My most Holy Rosary with such love and fervor. Much time I have spent calling My children to respond to My request.

As I pray with all of you I am painfully aware of your needs. Some are physical. Others are spiritual. In the physical sense, it can be a need for the healing of your body, heart or mind. In the spiritual, it can only be to call you from darkness into the light.

There are some who don't need to be told exactly what they are doing wrong. They know, and so does God!

Others are blinded by My foolish adversary into thinking they are not bad people. They perform all duties required of them. These are the ones I especially cry for. They deny their very need for adoring God in His Most Holy Trinity. To know My Son Jesus is to know the Father and to know the Son and the Father is to know the Holy Spirit. These people are the living dead, since they can provide most of their needs, they feel there is no other need.

But how wrong they are!

The poor must live on **faith** day to day.

The persons set free from the bondage of extreme sins know their freedom and therefore cannot help but acknowledge Gods Providence in their lives.

But, My **materialistic** spoiled children!

When will they know their need? For that reason I am walking amongst My children. Listen children. Do not doubt. You will feel and sense My Presence long after you leave this cenacle.

Make that first step by calling out as a small child when it has lost its mother. "Mother! Help me!" And I will enfold you in My arms and cover you with My mantle. I will kiss away all your pain and lead you to perfect union with My Son , Who awaits you with open arms.

Now is your time of salvation.

Do not wait until the disasters that await you are here. This is not to punish or scare, but to give time to prepare. If you are in a state of grace, you have no need to fear.

Do not be foolish in your sins any longer.

I walk among all of you and bless you with My Graces. Peace and love and mercy await you in the flames of Our Hearts!

November 14, 1992 - 11:20 A.M.

Mary: Prepare My message daughter.

(S.J., Who comes to speak to me?)

Mary: I come as your Mother of Consolation and I am the Mother of your Lord Jesus Christ, Who lived, died and ascended to the Eternal Father and Who, very soon will come again!

Yes, My little daughter, I am most pleased about these plans. You must see that when I open the doors for My children, there is no closing. Do not fear, all the plans have been made in advance and you My little ones must continue in prayer, that My desires may become your desires.

This will be the opening for the fulfillment of what has already been spoken. Do not doubt, with all the attacks that have come your way, do you not know that this is the way it is for all My chosen?

31

I am your Mother of Consolation and I am leading all of My Children of light. You must know this and prepare yourselves with prayer. Many will come and once again the marvels of your Heavenly Mother will be seen and felt.

Many will be touched.

Continue to gather in prayer whenever the opportunity is given to you, do not waste it, but pray.

We love and bless all of you in the light of the Son and He pours His peace and blessings on your wounds, and I, your Mother, hold each of you dear to Me in My arms.

Unconditional Love

November 17, 1992

(S.J., I test the voice and Our Lady speaks to the cenacle.)

Mary: Tell My children:

My message to you tonight, My children, is one of encouragement. I am most pleased at the efforts of My children to "live My messages."

What are My messages all around the world? One and all are the same, **love**! Unconditional **love**. The kind of love that God offers to you today and always.

If you love only those whom you choose, are you responding to God's love?

If you are not, My children, I urge you, as your Mother, to put aside your fears and hurts and rejections; for none of it is worth placing yourself outside of God's blessing and protection, due to pride.

Children, help one another learn the messages. Encourage one another. Pray for each other. Persevere in My Son's Divine Mercy.

Pray always to know the will of the Father.

32

Invite us, I your beloved Mother and Jesus, My Beloved Son to walk with you on a daily basis. Do not let your hearts be troubled. I have come to set my small remnant on the right path, rejected by many, but on the right path nonetheless.

We love you and are here with you tonight with blessings of peace and love.

I Am Showing the Signs and Wonders

November 18, 1992

(S.J., I hear a voice and I test.)

Jesus: Who among you is blameless? Who among you has never sinned? I, your Lord, ask this question of you, My children, of light.

When you hold another person before you and criticize who they are, what they are doing or what they have done, do you not understand, My children, that when you stand before the Father, no one else will be with you? Do you think you will be able to justify your shortcomings by pointing to that person who caused you to sit in judgment of them?

No, My children. You will stand before your God who loves you so, and for every reason you try to show Him, He will make you understand, before you are lost forever, that nothing was to have kept you from looking only at yourself!

If My children would keep their eyes only on Me, I would come and help them remove the plank from their eyes. Instead of pointing their fingers and slaying others with their tongue, they would be beating their breasts and crying out for repentance and reparation for their own sins.

This causes Me so much pain; My children, at odds with each other. Look at your brother and sister with love. When you've

33

said all you can say, say no more, but pray, pray for them and yourselves. This is pleasing to My Father.

The truth is being spoken where I am showing the signs and wonders and My children are experiencing true conversion! Woe to them who do not recognize the time of their visitation!

(S.J., Lord, why do you speak to Me?)

Jesus: Because I Am, you exist. Because I Am, I choose who I will and no one will be able to say to Me, I was wrong! I see all. I feel all. I know all.

Your heart is what I have seen and been pleased with. Your total submission, finally, to My will is what I have seen. Do not worry about those who do not believe you. They all didn't believe Me either.

I love you child, I bless you child, rejoice with Me!

Your Loving Lord.

Listen to the Stillness in Your Heats

November 20, 1992 - 8:40 A.M. During Mass

(S.J., I test and Our Lord speaks.)

Jesus: Behold My children, the Lord your God speaks!

It pleases Me greatly to see all who come in faith to pay honor, love and homage to My dearly Beloved Mother!

This is as it has been declared in Heaven. Her presence is the very will of My Father. Her plan of fulfillment is at hand. I come to say, as She has many times before; "Give up your sins and run to Me!"

Fall into the limitless ocean of mercy still at your disposal. It is not possible that all come. For the enemy, Satan, has blinded the hearts of many. That causes Me and My Mother such anguish. Blindness of the heart in reality is coldness of God's love. It is living today in your sins because you only want to think of the moment of pleasure. To break the bondage of the enemy you must **act**!

First, invite My Mother into your heart, life and home. Then, as She brings you to Me, I also await to be invited. **I do not overrule your free will!** Many will feel fear or anger at hearing these words, but that is only the enemy feebly trying to keep his hold on you.

When you invite Us in, then We can act!

And the enemy loses his power, for you are commanding him to go. Then the graces fall from Our Hearts and We lead you to do what you must to gain your peace.

That peace is not able to be understood by the world. And yet they desire it when they look to other means to satisfy.

Do not remain in your sins. Convert and let God's love flood your heart then your life. Your desires are no longer yours, they are Ours.

Listen to the stillness in your hearts. There it is where We speak, where We reign!

Behold My children, the hour draws near, as already the preparations in Heaven are being made and completed.

Do not dwell on your failures, but lift your hearts and your heads and advance forward.

Live the messages in your hearts, then the power of God's love will move in your lives.

Our peace and blessing to Our children of light. We invite all to become the same.

Jesus, your King of All Nations, and Mary, Mediatrix of all Graces!

As in the Days of Noah

December 1, 1992

(**S.J.**, Who speaks to me? In whose name do you come?)

Jesus: I Am - Jesus, King of All Nations, Who is praised and glorified in heaven and Who desires **all** would praise Me on earth.

Write these words my child:

The hour of darkness arrives!

I come to tell you, My daughter, that events will begin to unfold as foretold through many of My chosen.

My children will know the signs!

They, (My children) are simple of heart and, like a child, embrace and accept the truth when they hear it.

But again I say woe! Woe to them who do not recognize their time of visitation!

Do not My Words **strike** the hearts of man?

No! Because of their coldness and hard hearts, they refuse to repent and turn from their evil ways!

How many must I send to go forth and proclaim My Words before they are believed?

I am about to grant My Mother's requests at this time so that Her Immaculate Heart's Triumph will be complete and absolute!

You are on the last one of a year that as been critical for your country - 1993 will bring about even greater turmoil, division and cataclysmic events! But, even greater will be the wonders performed by the manifestation and outpouring of My Holy Spirit.

My Mother's presence, messages and visionaries will become so numerous as not to be able to count!

36

She will draw all men, women and children unto Me. She will cover them with Her mantle to protect Her and My children from the onslaught of evil that is even at the door!

In the end, those who refuse to believe will not be able to stand before Me and say they never heard the warnings. Yes, as in the days of Noah, mankind danced and played and ate and drank, up to the day the deluge began and the doors to the ark shut!

My Mother is the New Ark! All allow themselves to be carried in the safety of Her pierced heart.

As She has suffered silently in the background since I walked the earth; Now, the Father and I have granted Her this time and age so that Her triumph will, over and above, surpass Her suffering. Wait with expectations at the marvels and wonders you will see.

For those who believe they **will** be signs of hope. For those who do not believe, it will be for them their downfall.

Continue in love and prayer and unity. This has been most soothing to Our hearts.

We love and bless all here tonight who have come in faith.

Persevere in Prayer, Love and Unity

December 8, 1992 - 1:45 P.M.

(S.J., Who speaks to me? In whose name do you come?)

Mary: I am your Mother. I am the Immaculate Conception!

I am your Mother of Consolation, who wishes to offer words of encouragement to Her children. It has pleased Me greatly to see the response of My children, living My messages.

The prayers of all My children united in cenacles is indeed moving mountains and behold the wonders which I will manifest

37

tonight. I am leading, teaching, inspiring my children to follow Me and therefore commit entirely to Me their desires and take upon themselves My desires. I will move among My children tonight and God's power will fall. Many will be touched. Many will soothe the bleeding wounds of the Son.

It is My desire that you place My image in the church, where My image will move the hearts of the children of the Mother. The coldness of many hearts will melt by the flame of My love and I will then place this heart in the Sacred Heart of Jesus, where they will enter into the perfect union intended by God for man.

Many will be the occasions when I will pour out the many graces for My children. Draw ever nearer to Me, so as not to lose sight of the Father's will.

Soon, I will reveal the location of all that is being planned on a smaller scale by your brother messenger. Many will come and your priests will be forced to acknowledge God's Divine Providence and manifestation in His chosen instruments.

Persevere in prayer, love and unity. Keep close in cenacles. Your own situation will be resolved quickly. Then you will go forth as a family, united and testifying to God's mighty hand, wondrous and working!

Call on the angels and saints you are being led to. They are resolved in helping you achieve your mission and call. The validity of My words will be proven by God's Divine Will and Providence as He grants all My requests as we enter a crucial time.

Do not despair! See the signs and praise God, for all has been foretold and you will know in your spirits that which the Holy Spirit will quicken. The peace and love of Christ reign in the hearts of all!

I bless all in the name of the Father, Son and Holy Spirit!

Please tell My daughter 'J.' I desire the name: Cenacle of the Flower of Carmel!

Offer Up Fasts

December 13, 1992 - 2:30 A.M.

(S.J., I test and Our Lady answers.)

Mary: Daughter, I come to give you great news of consolation. You have been predestined to suffer much for the glory of God and His kingdom, and your 'J.' is battling inwardly with his enemy, My adversary. Continue in prayer but know that at My intercession along with My beloved son, Padre Pio, and Our Little Flower, your cause has been answered. Soon, very soon, there will be a turnaround of his heart and completion of Father's words on this sorrow.

Then, daughter, the next step in your journey, My image as the Woman Clothed in The Sun must be marched in procession on the church grounds of all three parishes. But in Piru, it (the procession) will bring many revelations to light. There are new people to come in and unite in My love. Sister Guadalupe is one, guide her gently to My movement. Others, with finances, will be brought in to help with the cova grotto.

Many of My children will come from near and far and I will truly manifest My presence in a miraculous way. As in all of My plans, I have provided and will once again place in the hearts of all My little children the desire to supply every need. Do not let yourselves get caught up in worry. All are being led and inspired to My desires for this great night.

Fast and offer up fasts for this night, for My cenacles for all My children responding to My will. I will be present and manifest My leading you tomorrow.

Peace and blessing to all.

A House Divided Cannot Stand

December 15, 1992 - 1:50 P.M.

(S.J., I test and Our Lady answers.)

Mary: Daughter, I require you to take My message.

Today I come to you as the Woman Clothed with the Sun, Your Virgin De Guadalupe, servant of your Lord and My beloved Son:

A house divided cannot stand, this is most important My children. Understand this. When division enters, so enters strife and jealousies of all sorts. Humility is the virtue that keeps division from conquering.

Always be humble, even when it means taking the responsibility unto yourself for something committed by another. Love is always the virtue that renders the enemy powerless.

What if your Lord had responded to His Father in any other way than humility unto obedience? Whatever act, no matter how little or insignificant, is seen and honored by the Father.

Is there division in your heart? Then there will be division in your home. If the truth is light and love, then that is what others must see. Jesus must be seen in everyone you come in contact with.

Does His Word not say:

> You clothed Me
> You fed Me
> You visited Me
> You nursed Me

when you did this to the **least** of your brothers and sisters!

As the time of My Son's birth arrives it is My prayer, for I always pray with you, that His Love will truly be borne into each and every heart. That his peace will reign in every heart and home.

Look around and see who can be Jesus for you to minister to. This world is full of the abandoned and hopeless, lost and sinners. Reach out and minister to Him, My Son and allow the joy of Christ to flood your hearts.

I am much pleased with the offerings of love by prayer and sacrifice. Live united in prayer, and love and Christ's peace, and God's Will, will triumph, as always through My intercession.

Many graces fall unto My children tonight.

A Great Sign of Hope

December 17, 1992 - Before & After Mass.

(S.J., I test and Our Lady speaks.)

Mary: My days of silence and hiddenness are over. Today I will walk with you and pray with you together because of your humility, love and obedience. We will at every attempt of the enemy, thwart his plan and in its place will be My triumph!

Continue to plead, pray and offer Me yourselves, little as you are, as the only way I can accomplish My triumph.

I bless you all and will be with you.

(S.J. I then heard another voice and tested. Our Lord replied.)

Jesus: Today, My daughter, I will leave a great sign of hope at My Cross. You have been brought together by My Mother, who is dressed in Her splendor of battle!

(S.J. Our Lord refers to the site for a cross to be built on a mountain above Piru.)

She is commanding, leading and inspiring Her group. Offer your walk for the unity of My church, peace in your world and invoke

41

My Spirit to cover all My children, it is My gift to you during this season remembering My birth.

Oh, do not doubt! Go forward one step at a time and We will be with you.

We love and bless all Our children of light.

(S.J. After Mass, we climbed up the mountain of the cross. Seeing the miracle of the sun, Our Lord spoke again.)

Jesus: You see My children why I choose a mountain top? For only then can people become aware of God's vast and immense love for all His children. The gold spots, (globes of light we saw) were the 12 angels assigned to protect and begin My holy work, for you are standing on holy ground.

Events Will Unfold Quickly

December 20, 1992 - 6:00 A.M.

(S.J., Who speaks to me? In whose name do you come?)

Mary: Get up, My daughter, I have need of you to take My message. I know you are tired, but would you not respond to Me?

Yo soy la Virgin De Guadalupe. Reina del Cielo. Madre del Salvador!

Today I come to tell you that all events will unfold very quickly. That which is in my plan you cannot fathom. My steps are not yours, so allow yourself to be led by Me. You have been seeing the events that transpired over and over again, marveling at God's wonder - His love, and the love of My Son and me for all Our children.

It gave Us great joy to see and hear My daughter's exclamations of joy. But, that is only the beginning. You must write an account of all that has happened also.

The opportunity to speak to Mr. 'VT' will come later through 'T.' You must tell him all that has happened and what My plans are.

42

Then tell him, "Our Lady has great need of your help. She said you would know how to help us. She also says that She loves you very much and Her Son does too. She wants you to go back to confession and back to Mass."

Now then, all My daughters and brother messenger 'D.' go up the hill. Again sing praises to Me and pray My Rosary. Again We will be with you and manifest our presence to you. Do this soon.

Continue to pray from the depths of your heart and love and support one another's weaknesses.

Continue to Pray in Unity

December 27, 1992

(S.J., I test and Our Lady answers.)

Mary: Behold, My daughter, the Miracle of the Son!

It is necessary for you to convey all events to Msgr. 'B.' The image on this mountain is only the beginning. Behold your St. Joseph awaits you and there will be a miraculous turn for 'J.', this is My gift to you.

All events will happen quickly to usher in a year of triumphant events, all in My plan. Rejoice and sing praise for your obedience and perseverance. The Father has willed to grant you your prayer to reunite your family.

Do not be surprised that you have been called, and yes, I am speaking to daughter 'L.' For the moment she must remain hidden, but only for the moment. When events have unfolded, many will be called. Until then reveal the location of My Image only to certain sources and family. Continue to pray in unity, come together in cenacle.

The Lady of All Nations

December 28, 1992 - 4:00 P.M.

(S.J. I heard a voice and tested.)

Mary: *I am The Lady of All Nations, your Mother Mary, full of graces to bestow on Her children.*

My daughter, you must pray, for the one who devours is ever near. Your prayer of today was most efficacious and significant, for indeed there is a seed of doubt being planted by the spirits of the evil one. Pray these away as you did today.

It is most important all My children remain obedient above all else. No one is above this call to obedience. If my children would look into their hearts they would see if any disobedience remains. All that I request and inspire is a call for My Son's body to be **one**!

If one is in disobedience, the rest of the body must pray that the scales of iniquity would fall from their eyes and ears. We are, for I am leading, on the threshold of the fulfillment of many prayers.

Unity of the body, conversion of many sinners, atoning to My Son [are necessary], for He is so tired and, but for Me, would have let the hand of the Father fall long ago. Do not despair. Continue in prayer. My night of visitation will bring many revelations to light.

You will see the wonders of My works and marvels at My presence. More are being called and purified. Help and counsel one another. This area will indeed be a mark and sign of My presence and miraculous works.

Praise your God and Lord for the answer to prayers you will see quickly.

Peace and love remain in your hearts.

The Defeat of the Enemy Will Come

December 29, 1992 - 6:45 P.M.

(S.J. I heard a voice and tested. Our Lady answered.)

Mary: I ask My children that you abandon yourselves completely and totally to Me. Put all your worries at the foot of My Son's Cross, for He has carried the burden of all your sins, cares and worries, and won for you the victory over all!

Is it not victory when you are going through your own purification, through trial and heartaches, or sickness and you can feel within you the peace that surpasses this world's understanding?

You are on the brink of seeing the marvels of your heavenly Mother! The defeat of the enemy will come ever so swiftly. So I ask as you embark upon a new year, do not be overcome by the burdens, worries, illnesses, or heartaches. Abandon yourselves completely and totally to prayer. Offer all of your actions to the Hearts of My Son and Myself.

It is only through this most simple plan, that you can you help usher in the victory of the Triumph of Mary's Immaculate Heart!

Faith is believing in what you cannot see, or understand with your own intellect. So, continue as My little Children, abandon yourselves to Me and I will lead you as My small children and together we will accomplish this final ascent up the mountain and the world will know of My victory!

And then you will be as pure as the children, to meet again your Beloved Lord and Savior; and He will wipe away every tear and there will be such rejoicing.

Until then, pray, pray, pray! Do not let your prayer defenses down. For the enemy is ever vigilant, and waiting for the opportunity to divide, confuse and destroy. But this is not to be; but Only the

Triumph of My Immaculate Heart, which I have entrusted to My remnant of faithful who believe the messages of Your Mother.

Continue your cenacles of prayer and love, and We bless you all in the name of the Father, Son and Holy Spirit.

Chapter Two

My Mantle Will
Be Your Shield

**Messages From January 5, 1993
To June 29, 1993**

Have Faith and Perseverance

January 2, 1993 - 10:30 P.M.

(S.J. - Beloved Mother: I sit in silence to see if there are any words you would have me know. I call upon the whole celestial court to help me - strengthen me by the graces you pour upon those who ask.

How can I serve thee better? How can I know you better? My time is so limited when I have my - your two angels 'J.' and 'C.'.)

Mary: My little daughter, I bid you a good New Year in My service and that of Jesus Christ your Lord and Savior and My Beloved Son.

How My heart grieves at your sorrow. Have faith! Your words of consolation are such as to set the whole of heaven rejoicing, as has been spoken before. That which has been spoken must come to be by your faith and perseverance. It is good to be in prayer and to fast. Soon, very soon, all will come to pass.

Distract yourself from your thoughts through prayer. Your mind is your worst enemy, for it is where the enemy throws seeds of doubt on the truth you know is upon your heart.

This new year brings about many events in my plan of triumph. Many of those events will coincide with one another. Many, as of now, are being called. To what degree they will be used depends on their willingness to submit.

(S.J., I heard another voice and tested. Our Lord answered.)

Jesus: I speak, My daughter, your Lord and Savior, Jesus Christ.

There is a spirit of spiritual jealousy rearing its ugly head! Step on it through prayer and remain united in love and humility and above all, obedience! I cannot use anyone who chooses to disregard obedience.

You will begin to suffer signs of what has been revealed to you. You will have your day of rejoicing and a lifetime of sorrow! Do you still accept?

(S.J., Oh, yes, My Lord!)

Jesus: The message to 'Dr. V'G.' will be given after the revealing of My Mothers' plan, which even now is happening. The day to ascend the mountain will come soon.

Many Will Be the Signs of My Presence

January 5, 1993 - 9:10 A.M.

Mary: Today, My daughter, I will leave a permanent sign, it will be for the world to see.

The faithfulness of My children has brought this special intercession of graces on My behalf from the Father. He refuses Me nothing. The simplicity of My children, their willingness to believe, this is most pleasing to Our hearts.

As spoken before, all events will happen quickly. Be prepared by remaining in constant prayer. When you pray at My cenacles, unite yourselves to all of My cenacles, thereby bringing many graces to each cenacle.

Tell My daughter 'L." to be of heart and stand firm. It matters not the numbers, [at the cenacle] only the faithfulness. Offer your walk up the mountain for the many who will come, for all those being brought in to unite in My plan.

I will be with you, praying with you all.

Many will come and experience the miracle of conversion as at Medjugorje. Many will be the signs of My presence. Those who will see Me will be revealed later.

Love and blessing to all.

To Deny Me Is To Deny My Son

January 6, 1993 - 8:00 P.M.

(S.J., I tested and Our Lady answered.)

Mary: I am the Mother of your Lord and Savior, Maria, Virgin Pura. My daughter, I want you to write My message:

Today many will see the beginning of God's fury unleashed on mankind. These storms will bring much destruction and devastation. Pray daughter of mine, pray fervently for My children that will be lost, for living without Christ is to exist without source of consolation. There is no organization or government that can console one who exists without Christ.

To deny Me is to deny My Son, for unbeknown to My little ones, I work tirelessly for them; calling them, guiding them, to no avail. Many times these are souls who have no one to pray for them. That is why I am so in need of My little prayer warriors, who faithfully, without fail, pick up the little beads of heaven's most powerful prayer.

I sit and cry with pain, inconsolable pain for My children who deny Me.

I know the black night of your soul, and during this time of total abandonment, you have nowhere else to look for your comfort. When you come in total blind faith, feeling that nothing is coming of your prayers; that faith is most precious in the Father's sight.

You must fight doubts ! Pray ever more fervently, implore the celestial aid of My angels and saints and We will come to send the enemy scurrying away. Do not allow those doubts to take hold on fertile ground. Doubts can grow. It leads to total confusion. Those who do not seek the source of truth first and foremost, My Son's presence in the Eucharist, allow themselves to come under attack.

50

In this time of cold weather and often raining times, the sacrifice of going out to pray in unity is powerful. This small action brings about so much in the spiritual battles being fought.

All the weapons have been given to My children. Continue to read all that I lead you to. Pray and fast. Continue in unity. Your obedience and humility is most pleasing. We do not see your weakness, because you acknowledge them.

Never justify, or try to find excuses for your failings. The Father and Son see all, know all, and My children would only be fooling themselves. You still have a most loving and Merciful Savior.

My children would never begin to understand My Son's love. So capable of melting all in His heart of love.

(S.J., I hear another voice and I test. Our Lord answers.)

Heed My Call

January 10, 1993

(S.J., I test and Our Lord answers.)

Jesus : Go to your Bible daughter, read from the prophet Ezekiel in Chapter 11, verses 19, 20 and 21 and Psalm 92 and write down the words of both.

Ezekiel 11: 19-21

I will give them one heart and I will put a new spirit within you; and I will take the stony heart out of their flesh, and give them a heart of flesh: That they may walk in my statutes and keep mine ordinances and do them: and they shall be my people, and I will be their God.

But as for them whose heart walketh after the heart of their detestable things and their abominations, I will bring down their way upon their own heads, saith the Lord God.

51

Psalm 92: 1-15

A Psalm for the Sabbath Day

It is a good thing to give thanks unto the Lord, and to sing praises unto thy name, O Most High: 2 To shew forth thy loving kindness in the morning, and thy faithfulness every night. 3 Upon an instrument of ten strings, and upon the psaltery; upon the harp with a solemn sound. 4 For thou Lord hast made me glad through thy works: I will triumph in the works of thy hands. 5 O Lord, how great are they works! *and* thy thoughts are very deep. 6 A brutish man knoweth not; neither does a fool understand this.

7 When the wicked spring as the grass, and when all the workers of iniquity do flourish; *it is* that they shall be destroyed forever: 8 But thou Lord *art most* high for evermore. 9 For, lo, thine enemies O Lord, for, lo, thine enemies shall perish; all workers of iniquity shall be scattered. 10 But my horn shalt thou exalt like *the horn of* a unicorn: I shall be anointed with fresh oil. 11 Mine eye also shall see *my desire* on mine enemies, *and* mine ears shall hear *my desire* of the wicked that rise up against me. 12 The righteous shall flourish like the palm tree: he shall grow like a cedar in Lebanon. 13 Those that be played in the House of The Lord, shall flourish in the Courts of Our God. 14 They shall still bring forth fruit in old age; they shall be fat and flourishing; 15 To shew that the Lord *is* upright: *he is* my rock, and *there is* no unrighteousness in him.

Jesus: This, My daughter, I will do for My children. Behold, the hour draws ever near. Oh that My children would heed My call. I desire My Mother's work triumph with absolute swiftness and so it shall be. Oh daughter, the wonders and marvels that are even now being revealed. With time many will know and many others will be brought in these final moments.

You and all leaders, sources and brother messenger 'D.' **must** remain united in prayer and love. How I use each one of you is My own desire and there will be differences. But, rejoice one for another, for you will usher in one of the greatest moves of My Spirit. My hand is totally upon you.

Many will come to seek you and the others, but you must and can only be **love**, My love to all. I, Myself, will protect you from deceivers - for the enemy knows his time is over!

Do you desire your day of joy?

(S.J.) Oh yes, My Lord, for only then will your words to me be complete.)

Jesus: Do you accept your call?

(S.J. You know I do My Lord.)

Jesus: A fortnight will pass and many things will be revealed and changed. The hearts of many will burn with love for Me and My Mother.

Your aunt will be resting with Me soon (within this fortnight). 'J.' will be converted. My plan will go from "plan to action."

My daughter, read now in the book of Isaiah, Chapter 40.

My blessings and peace to all.

Queen of Peace and Lady of All Nations

January 13, 1993 - 8:05 P.M.

(S.J. - I hear a voice and ask: "In whose name do you come?")

Mary: I come as your Queen of Peace and Lady of All Nations, the Mother of The Son of God, Jesus The Christ, Savior and Lord of all.

Thank you for responding to My call.

I want you to tell My children of the great outpouring of love, prayer and sacrifice that was so soothing to My wounded heart. The hearts of all My children, their tears, sufferings and burdens were seen by My Son, as I their Mother interceded for them. I enfolded so many in My arms, indeed all. And I do not tire of comforting My children.

How I wish that My sigh could be one of assisting all My children, that they would in their cross see that I, their Mother, am leading them along the way of their cross as I did for My Son on His walk to Calvary. In the three times My Son fell, when inwardly His Agony was touching My pierced heart, I agonized with Him also. With each step, all I wanted to do was see Him, encourage Him, assist Him, for He was also submitting to the will of the Eternal Father.

Submitting one's will, to allow the will of God blindly to happen in My children's lives, is fought so hard against by My adversary. To know the will of the Father, one must communicate with Him. Through Jesus, the Father grants all. And through Me, Jesus intercedes to the Father for them and their needs.

I am preparing the way once again for the coming of My Son. His triumphant reign will come through the triumph of the Immaculate Heart of Mary.

Many of My children feel that I am 'optional'; that devotion to Me is something that you can or cannot participate in. For one born into **Catholicism,** the true faith of God, one must know that devotion to the Mother of Jesus is the first devotion attacked by the enemy for his defeat will come by Me. This has been revealed many times, in scripture and in many messages previously given to many of My chosen.

These are indeed My times and I continue to perform the works allowed Me by the Father, through His power, His Spirit, My Beloved Spouse.

The foundation has been laid. Events are even now unfolding. Have faith! Believe in all that has been said. I am lifting up My chosen messengers and if they remain obedient, they will continue to be used. You have been set apart to lead and guide. Your mission is, and will be different. Know that this already has been said.

Be of faith My little child. As you cried before My image, I indeed was caressing your head and kissing you. It gave Me great pleasure to hear the cries of your heart. I know you are sorry for thinking that My image was just a picture, while you gazed upon Me in Santa Maria.

There will be many more activities planned, and all will happen if you move when I say to move. If a plan or instruction or measure is given, then it is to act on. Remain obedient and humble, this was most pleasing to Us. Fight and remain alert, for the enemy is ever near and vigilant looking for the smallest of cracks to enter and spread his errors.

I am calling you and My other children to nine days of intense fasting and prayer. This is most important that you respond to. Pray whatever novenas My children are led to, but I desire that the novena prayer of **Jesus King of All Nations** be prayed as a body. It will avert a destructive force that is coming.

Many false prophets are arising! Pray that the Spirit of God will help you discern those, and remove them from your midst.

The events leading up the hill will happen in due time, after this nine day period of fasting and prayer. Gather as often as possible and pray in unity as always in love, and only then can My plan be completed. No one is leading this army of Mine other than Myself.

Walk in faith, as little children and you will see great and wonderful things for the glory of God and of My Son Jesus and by the power of My Beloved Spouse, The Holy Spirit, in which I dwell in their midst.

Many blessings to My children of light.

55

Remain Constantly in Prayer

January 16, 1993 - 8:05 P.M.

(S.J. I have heard Our Lady since early morning. However I did not respond because of the beginning of Her message. I tested and She continued.)

Mary: Daughter of Mine, daughter of Mine, I call to you. Would you not come? How I have called you today. I desire you to know I bestow on you the name of the **"little sorrowful rose"**. This is My gift to you for your faithfulness. The messages that come from now on , I address to you as My little sorrowful rose.

Do you not remember our first conversation? Did I not ask you to share My sorrow? You are My little rose for your love for Me and desire to obey every mandate from Me and Our Lord. You are chosen to do the will of the Father and at My request, I convey all that He desires for you.

Beware of many false prophets arising! Again I say to you pray, that the spirit of discernment will quicken to your spirit and keep you in the way of truth.

Remain always and constantly in prayer with Me. Our hearts beat as one, for you have opened wide the door to your heart. You have been most soothing to Us and with your faithfulness comes reward.

Much of My plan here is coming to light for it is My desire to honor the prayers and sacrifices of so many here. Where My children of simplicity and faith are, I can intervene to the eternal Almighty God and work My works of prodigy, for this is to bring hope to the hopeless, light to those in darkness, healing to the sick, uplifted spirits where there is despair.

I continue to work for the many souls of My lost children of the United States of America, and in particular My children here in California. Materialism and money are the gods that reign here.

They see their brother and sister in need and it does not move them to pity. There is no care for the least of My children.

On this day you remember your encounter with My Son, who in the likeness of one of the least of your brothers extended to you the opportunity to prove true Scripture.

"When you do these things for the least of your brethren, you do them to Me." The love you remember in His eyes does not begin to reveal truly the totality of His love for mankind.

How many of My children measure their good works on their scales, but woe to them who place those good works before God on the day of judgment and find them lacking. Your good deeds will be as filthy rags to those who had not the love of Christ in them. For all I have done for My children, can another lost soul see you and see only love? If not then, the works will be found lacking.

And I say, repent of your false pride, those who are guilty, for the God of all sees the innermost thoughts and actions of men. You fool only yourself if you are judging as this world judges, for this world is held bound by the prince of this earth and enemy of God.

Down with your pride! Down with your lack of trust in God's love and forgiveness, and turn to the One True and Holy God and His true church for your healing.

I bestow upon you My blessing, My little sorrowful rose, where you rest in My sorrowful heart. Do not be amazed at the completion of what has been foretold. Neither try to anticipate how, or when. Just pray and wait to see God's marvels in your life, for you will be used to touch many.

Again I bless you, and bid you rest. Continue in your prayers and fast. I love you, My little sorrowful rose.

The Rosary Is Your Weapon

January 18, 1993 - 5:00 P.M.

(S.J. I heard a voice and commanded it to go, in the name of Jesus, if not of God.)

Mary: My little sorrowful rose: Thank you for responding to My call.

I desire you to call Monsignor 'B.' and convey to him all that has been happening. Tell him I desire you begin distribution of messages and that as each step in My instructions are taken, more will come to light.

I desire that My messages be told and shared. You must proclaim loudly and boldly the matter of urgency.

As the events already indicate, the beginning of God's fury and justice has been released. Those who up till now have laughed and ridiculed My chosen, will now know and be given a chance to truly repent of their sin of pride and will acknowledge this truly is God's justice.

Those who would criticize God, should know I have been constantly pleading and praying with and for My children, for many of your years. I am tireless in My efforts to reach My children, to call them to sincere repentance and to return to their God; to acknowledge the might and glory of His Omnipotence! But to no avail!

Here in your nation, greed, power, money and love of material things matter. Men's and women's lives are dictated and governed by the time clock, the hours spent working for what will not stand in God's fury!

My children need to know this: Nothing, I repeat, nothing is of any value in God's kingdom to come, but the souls of My children. Oh, can't they see, can't they see, that I leave My signs over and over again, I manifest My presence for My children to believe. But what oftentimes happens, is they only look to see how big is the sign, and never heed the message always accompanying My presence.

Repent children of Mine! Do not remain hard hearted and in your love for Me, try to reach to as many of the lost, so together, we can go to the boundless ocean of mercy of My Son, where sins will be forgiven and you will be given a peace not of this earth.

My children, the clock approaches its set mark. There is no turning back. But this is My assurance to you, that up to the last chronicle of time, I will be working to bring all My children into the gift of life everlasting!

Prayer, prayer, and more prayer!

The Rosary is your weapon, pick it up and pray with fervor. I have need of your prayers. Invoke the aid of the celestial court, saints and angels to assist you in this final hour of battle.

Peace and blessings to all who have responded to My call.

These Are My Times

January 25, 1993

(S.J., I tested and Mary answered me.)

Mary: Today, my little sorrowful rose of Mine, I manifest My presence more strongly than has been felt up to now. Continue in obedience to Me and My Son. This is most pleasing and soothing to Our Wounded Hearts.

Now you must tell all, I choose to come to even more of My children of faith. I have claimed the hill in Piru as a sign of the truth being revealed. These are my times and I, though to the point of frustration and disappointment in many of My children, continue to work tirelessly for My children. I have been able to

59

work because of the faithfulness of My children. Pray daughter as you know how and rebuke the enemy from My work. Offer the walk today for My stated intentions and behold the wonders you will see today.

(S.J., I heard a voice and rebuked it in the name of Jesus.)

Jesus: Praise be Jesus Christ who I am.

Continue little one to follow the way of My Mother. She points the way for you and all. I grow weary. I see My world wandering aimlessly, being led by the prince of this world to their destruction. Oh children, when will you return to Me? Why do you continue to work for those things that will not stand in the day of judgment?

Indeed, I instill in the hearts of My chosen, the sense of urgency and of impending justice! It must be this way. This world is dire need of purification of the filth in their lives.

Woe, to those who live in lust, and those who choose unnatural acts and those who annihilate the innocents! Say woe! Again woe!

Pray, while yet there is time! Pray, repent and pray more!

(S.J. This message was given on the first day being called to the hill in Piru after the January rains, and wanting to go back up to see Our Lady's image on this hill.)

I Am the New Ark of the Covenant

February 1, 1993 - 5:30 P.M.

(S.J., I tested and Our Lady answered.)

Mary: Praise be Jesus and I am His Mother. Listen, My little sorrowful rose, to the stillness your heart. In the quiet you hear the things I confide in you. You are chosen because of your insignificance and total dependence on My Son and Me, His Holy Mother, who leads and guides you.

60

Tell all My children I claim the hill in Piru for the glory of God and Triumph of My Immaculate Heart! I desire this to be known as the "Hill of the Way". Therein lie many Truths, but I will explain the obvious. The Word is what I carried in My Womb. That same Word, The Word of God, says, "the Way, I Am the Truth, and the Light". All who follow, must follow Me.

The summit is the cross, on which the price of redemption was paid for dearly, by My Son's obedience. As He struggled with His Cross, I want My children to know theirs becomes less burdensome when they follow in His footsteps.

And as My children make this ascent up the mountain they will remember the Passion of My Son and His painful unto death crucifixion. All of you who suffer, when you meditate on My Son's death and passion, can you compare your sufferings to His? Indeed not. All pale in comparison, and therein lies the comfort; Comfort of His victory over death. Triumph with Him by allowing Him to come and lift you up.

As I am the New Ark of the Covenant, I carry, the Son, this second time, by preceding His very soon return. He desires to remain merciful; but alas, there is no one to respond with his whole being. Convert totally, My children, see the way of My Son and imitate it in your lives.

Jesus: Woe! Woe! Woe! My children do not know what they bring upon themselves by refusing to turn to Me. How I anguish over those who remain hard of heart. But I must bring about My hour, that which will cause the bowels of the earth to tremble. I will shake this nation to its very core. This nation once blessed by the Eternal Father, but now so shunned, for in the place of God, many molten images have risen; but I, the True God, the Great I Am, will show those hardened hearts that I will no longer allow the sins of mankind to go unpunished.

My child, do not worry, just take one step at time and allow Me to lead you. Those barriers will be removed by My very hand. This is the last hour of Mercy, and all will receive the opportunity to hear the glorious message of salvation. Be bold in Me, my daughter and do not fear.

I receive with great love the prayers and sacrifices of My children. But the scales of justice have been weighted down and demand the release of God's justice, for this affront to God the Almighty Creator.

Woe! Woe! Woe! to you men hardened of heart!

And those who chose to ignore the warnings will bring upon yourselves your own worst fears. For when you hear you are quickened to believe; but realizing that it would mean paying Me more than lip service, you choose to reason away those warnings. You along with many of My priests will suffer eternally!

Hear the little and the lowly who are risen to warn My people!

Pray little one! Pray, I love you. Peace to all.

(S.J., Our Lady begins to speak again.)

Mary: Do not worry My little sorrowful rose, you will be moved quickly and swiftly, by God's hand. Much will be revealed, continue in prayer.

The hands of time are almost up!

Cease not your prayers and remain in the silence of My Heart. God's love and peace to you, and I bless you this day to go forward in the power of My Son's Holy Spirit.

See What They Have Done To My Son

February 3, 1993 - 8:30 A.M.

(S.J., I tested and a voice continued.)

Jesus: Daughter of Mine, write down everything you have been shown in vision.

Vision: Today, after arriving for morning Mass at 8:30 A.M., I close my eyes for prayer and all of a sudden I hear a very majestic and angry voice that I know to be Our Father's. I see the Father holding the crucified body of Christ, like the Pieta, (I can't see His face) and I hear "See what they have done to My Son!"

All of a sudden I see the crucified body of Jesus laid atop the Capitol in Washington D.C. and from the dome of the capitol building there is a lance or spear going through His body, from His back protruding through His chest. Again I hear, "See what My children have done, they have turned their backs on their God!. Now I will turn My back on this country!"

Then I see a map of the USA with seven angels hovering high above, with coals or something glowing that they hurl down toward the earth. As this glow hits the earth, I begin to feel devastation, destruction and confusion.

And I see this one face, full of anger and hate, turn his face toward the heavens and shake his fist toward God. And I hear, "I will shake this country to its very core and mankind still will turn and curse their God."

(S.J., And I understood that even with all the destruction, man could and should begin to think about the God he has forgotten and affronted with all his sin and turn to Him and plead for mercy. But he will not. He will remain obstinate and hard of heart.)

Vision: And then on the map I could see glow of little lights all over the map.

(S.J., I understood this to be the believers of all the messages, and response to Our Lady's request for prayers and sacrifice and praying the Rosary.)

Vision: Then I saw more angels, lower than the ones who were hurling the glowing objects toward earth.

(S.J., I understood they were protecting the believers.)

Vision: Then I saw this thick cloud of black rise from the coast of New York, and it was no longer the map of the USA, but a picture of the globe of the world. And in a second it was covered by this blackness and I heard, "See the darkness they say will not come."

Jesus: Pray My daughter while there is still time.

Sins Of The Flesh

February 17, 1993

(S.J., I heard a voice and I tested. The voice was Mary.)

Mary: My little sorrowful rose: My greetings of peace and blessings to all My children of light. I come to plead for urgent and profound prayer of the heart. It is only by means of My cenacles in prayer, that My work can continue. Much has begun to fulfill prior messages. But this is not where it stops.

This is where the intensity of My children in prayer will bring about different levels of accomplishment. I am much comforted and pleased when I hear the rosary of the children, the little buds of My heart. Their prayers pierce the ceiling of heaven and fall into the whole of the celestial court.

These prayers are received also by the little souls of My annihilated babies, the babies lost to the sin of abortion. They joyously join in prayer with the children and rejoice at the voices of the innocents being taught to praise their God!

My children are suffering and perishing in their own filth by continuing to live in sin. I revealed to My children of Fatima, more souls fall into the flames of hell for sins of the flesh than any other sin.

Today, that sad truth is evermore true, many, many times over. Today I announce a serious period of time in which, as you spoke by My leading, My children can make a difference. The simplicity of truth is this, that where there is much prayer and sacrifice, there can be Our works of mercy. Where there is pride and refusal to live the totality of the messages, Our graces are in essence, sent away.

It is as if My Son and I would be knocking, with all His blessings and graces ready as a gift at the door, and the door once opened, is the only act given, such receiving the messages from My true chosen, and then we are not invited in, and that would be not living the messages totally. The love is not shown. The joy is not expressed.

And so, even though We wait for that invitation, after a sufficient amount of time, We can only leave, to knock on another door and wait for that invitation to enter. The signs of confusion, lies and discord run rampant among My children of light; it is the wolves among the sheep. Pray for unity. Pray for protection. Pray for the many who reason humanly away, God's Spirit, who is leading and trying to pour out the gifts over God's children. There are many events to come, as yet unrevealed, but quickly and swiftly they will be.

Many will ascend the mountain of Piru, The Hill of the Way. Follow it My children, imitate the Way of the Cross in your lives.

Christ suffered much to purchase this unconditional gift of salvation. Allow His Love to redeem you, by simply being a holy people of God, by imitating His life, imitating as He suffered, with Him in total union, so that you are consumed by Him.

Man's Own Sins Call For Justice

February 18, 1993 - 3:00 A.M.

(S.J. I heard a voice and commanded it to go in the name of Jesus, if not of God.)

Jesus: Get up My daughter and pray, for God's mercy is in the final hour. Pray to call as many as will respond to His mercy.

(S.J., At this point I prayed the Chaplet of Mercy and as I finished Our Lord speaks.)

Jesus: (The following transcripts are the Scriptures found in the book of the prophet Jeremiah. Our Lord tells me where to read as He dictated the verses. He then tells me to type up the transcript of those verses.)

"The word of the Lord came to me thus:

Before I formed you in the womb, I knew you, before you were born I dedicated you, a prophet to the nations I appointed you. "Ah, Lord God!", I said, "I know not how to speak; I am too young". But the Lord answered me, Say not, "I am too young". To whomever I send you, you shall go; whatever I command you, you shall speak. Have no fear before them, because I am with you to deliver you, says the Lord. (Jer. 1:4-8)

Two evils have My people done: they have forsaken Me, the source of living waters; they have dug themselves cisterns, broken cisterns, that hold no water. (Jer. 2:13)

Your conduct, your misdeeds, have done this to you; how bitter is this disaster of yours, how it reaches to your very heart! (Jer. 4:18)

I look at the earth, and it was waste and void; at the heavens, and their light had gone out! I looked and behold at the mountains, and they were trembling, and all the hills were crumbling! I looked and behold, there was no man; even the birds of the air had flown away!

66

I looked and behold, the garden land was a desert, with all its cities destroyed before the Lord, before His blazing wrath. (Jer. 4:23-26)

Because of this the earth shall mourn, the heavens above shall darken; I have spoken, I will not repent. I have resolved, I will not turn back. (Jer. 4:28.)

Shall I not punish them for these things? says the Lord; On a nation such as this shall I not take vengeance? (Jer. 5:9)

Your crimes have prevented these things, your sins have turned back these blessings from you. (Jer. 5:25)

Shall I not punish these things? says the Lord; on a nation such as this shall I not take vengeance? (Jer. 5:29)

The prophets prophecy falsely and the priests teach as they wish; Yet My people will have it so; what will you do when the end come? (Jer. 5:31)

Therefore My wrath brims up within me, I am weary of holding it in; I will pour it out upon the child in the street, upon the young men gathered together.

Yes, all will be taken husband and wife, graybeard with ancient. Their houses will fall to strangers, . . . For I will stretch forth My hand against those who dwell in this land, say the Lord. (Jer. 6:11-12)

Small and great alike, all are greedy for gain; prophet and priest, all practice fraud. (Jer. 6:13).

Thus says the Lord: Stand beside the earliest roads, ask the pathways of old which is the way to good, and walk it; thus you will find rest for your souls. But they said, "We will not walk it."

When I raised up watchmen for them, "Hearken to the sound of the trumpet!" They said, "We will not hearken."

Therefore hear, O nations, and know, O earth, what I will do with them: See, I bring evil upon this people, the fruit of their own schemes, Because they heeded not My words, because they despised My law . . . Therefore, thus says the Lord: See, I will place before this people obstacles to bring them down: Fathers and sons alike, neighbors and friends shall perish. (Jer. 6:16-21)

The following message came to Jeremiah from the Lord: Stand at the gate of the house of the Lord, and there proclaim this message: Hear the word of the Lord, all you of Judah who enter these gates to worship the Lord! Thus says the Lord of Hosts, the God of Israel: Reform your ways and your deeds, so that I may remain with you in this place. Put not your trust in the deceitful words: "This is the temple of the Lord! The temple of the Lord! The temple of the Lord!" Only if you thoroughly reform your ways and your deeds; if each of you deals justly with his neighbor; if you no longer oppress the resident alien, the orphan, and the widow; if you no longer shed innocent blood in this place, or follow strange gods to your own harm, will I remain with you in this place, in the land which I gave your fathers long ago and forever.

But here you are, putting your trust in deceitful words to your own loss! Are you to steal and murder, commit adultery and perjury, burn incense to Baal, go after strange gods that you know not, and yet come to stand before Me in this house which bears My name, and say, "We are safe; we can commit all these abominations again"? Has this house which bears My name become in your eyes a den of thieves? (Jer. 7:1-11)

See now, says the Lord God, My anger and My wrath will pour out upon this place, upon man and beast, upon trees of the field and the fruits of the earth; it will burn without being quenched. (Jer. 7:20)

This rather is what I commanded them: Listen to My voice; then I will be your God and you shall be My people. Walk in all the ways that I command you, so that you may prosper. (Jer. 7:23)

But they obeyed not, nor did they pay heed. They walked in the hardness of their evil hearts and turned their backs, not their faces to Me. From the day that your fathers left the land of Egypt even to this day, I have sent you untiringly all My servants the prophets.

Yet they have not obeyed Me nor paid heed; they have stiffened their necks and done worse than their fathers. When you speak all these words to them, they will not listen to you either; when you call to them, they will not answer you. (Jer. 7:24-27)

Cut off your dedicated hair and throw it away! On the heights intone an elegy; for the Lord has rejected and cast off the genera- tion that draws down His wrath. (Jer 7:29) (Elegy means a sad song or poem.)

Thus says the Lord: Let not the wise man glory in his wisdom, nor the strong man glory in his strength, nor the rich man glory in his riches;

But rather, let him who glories, glory in this, that in his prudence he knows Me. Knows that I, the Lord bring about kindness, jus- tice and uprightness on the earth; for with such am I pleased, says the Lord. (Jer. 9 : 22-23)

The Lord is true God, he is the living God, the eternal King, Before whose anger the earth quakes, whose wrath the nations cannot endure: He who made the earth by His power, estab- lished the world by His wisdom, and stretched out the heavens by His skill. When He thunders, the waters in the heavens roar, and He brings up clouds from the end of the earth; He makes the lightning flash in the rain, and releases stormwinds from their chambers. Every man is stupid, ignorant; every artisan is put to shame by his idol: He has molded a fraud, without breath of life. Nothingness are they, a ridiculous work; they will perish in their time of punishment. (Jer. 10: 10-15)

Jesus: Daughter prepare a script of previous Scripture. I would have My children know I am a loving and merciful God but man's own sins call, call for justice.

Pray daughter. You are consecrated to Me for your prayer.

Pray, pray and I receive all through My Mother's mediation.

Peace.

Sound the Trumpet

March 9, 1993 - 4:45 A.M.

(S.J., I tested and the voice answered me.)

Mary: The exodus of My children will be accomplished in an extraordinary miraculous way, for I am with all. My mantle will be your shield. Pray much, My children who have taken these messages to heart. It is not a time of fear.

My heart is heavy with sorrow that not enough have converted to stay the Fathers hand any longer. This administration is an abomination to the Eternal Father and thus has brought about this time.

But just as I work My miracles to help convert humanity, now My work will continue and I begin to bring My children of light protection.

You must disband the cenacle after tonight and meet in the mornings. Pray much before the tabernacle, plead that God will be merciful and swift. Have all prepared before hand, then there will be no precious time lost.

After a time people will return, but there will still be much to go through. It is so that My children can be spared much even after the big strike, that I have called all to be together.

Be of courage and strong spirit, as I have raised up My chosen to "sound the trumpet." My children will be spared and this will be part of My triumph.

70

Peace, blessing and much love to all who have responded to Our call.

God's Children Have Been Warned In Advance

March 12, 1993 - 7:30 A.M.

(S.J., I heard a voice, I tested and He answered.)

Jesus: My daughter take My message: I the Lord, your God have heard the cries of the innocent, the oppressed, the downtrodden and all My children of light, who have cried out in agony at the state of this world.

Many unbelievers have said to believers, "Why does your God allow this?" He is God, He could change this, never knowing it was their opportunity to minister and meet the needs of these beloved children of Mine.

So each one has gone about, oblivious to the needy, only striving to acquire more material goods. But now the God of all will show these unbelievers that there is a God!

They will fall to the ground and cry from the very depths of their souls and in that instant they will know There is a God!

For God's justice is upon the world in an instant, and My children of light who have always acknowledged and lived for their God will be received into their glory.

In the end the unbelievers will know that God's children have been warned in advance so as to show the world left behind that all prophecy is fulfilled!

Lift up your hearts for your redemption draws neigh!

Peace and blessing through My Mother's mediation!

71

Very Soon Much Will be Fulfilled

March 16, 1993 - 12:00 A.M.

(S.J., I tested and Mary answered.)

Mary: Daughter go to your **Father Gobbi** book and read message 73.

(S.J., Mary continues with the same message for 273, 373, 423, 430, 450, and 472.)

Mary: Now My daughter and little sorrowful rose, I have led you through very significant messages of My Marian Movement of Priests. All give hope and it ends with the very essence of God's work: faith.

Have faith My children and do not doubt. Soon, very soon, much will be fulfilled. This is the uplifting grace I give to all Our chosen, for being "good and faithful servants", up to the fulfillment of prophecy. Be at peace and know beyond your preparations, lies part of My glorious triumph.

I am, once again, accepting God's will, as justice now falls. But I am now dressed in the fullness of My battle array and lead My faithful children of light into protection.

Be at peace and know I am with you all.

(S.J., At 12:50 A.M. I heard the voice of Our Lord. I tested and He answered.)

Jesus: Behold, My daughter, I your Lord God, King of Kings and Lord of Lord's, Jesus the Christ speaks:

Be at peace My children, for I your God am with all My children. It gives Me great delight and comfort to see My children move in faith.

Do not doubt. Do not ask, "What if?" (such as, "What if this does not happen," etc.) Look at the prophecy being fulfilled daily, and know that I grant My Beloved Mother all Her requests.

We cannot however, obtain any more postponements. Though Our hearts are heavy with sorrow, we also rejoice at the release of the captives of Satan's reign. He would destroy all, if Divine intervention did not proceed. Be at peace, be at peace, be at peace. And rejoice for new life awaits all My children. I love you all and Give all My blessings.

(S.J., C. twice now I have received that the destruction of or the final coastline of California, has something to do with the shape of Israel. Mary asked me to share this with you.)

(Poem written by Sadie Jaramillo)

March 17, 1993

(S.J., 'C': I was in the process of packing and asking Our Lady to show me what I needed to take, and I was lead to a notebook, where I had begun a souvenir book on the Cross of Peace.

I found a poem that I was lead to write after the first initial visit, and a letter that I was prompted to write when I arrived home.

The poem goes as follows:

I've been to the Hill again,
many times, I know I will return,
and when I do,
there will be someone return to you.
Hail, Most Holy Queen,
Our lives you came to redeem,
back to Our Lord and Savior.
In whom you have so much favor.

The Cross of Peace will appear to draw all,
far and near, for Jesus' return is close at hand.
So you've come to dwell in our land
until the appointed time
when Mercy flows no more

and all who have shut the door
will be left behind
and know in their hearts
It was God's plan fulfilled,
right from the start.

(Written August, 25, 1991, when I returned home to Fillmore. I was asked by Our Lady to share these things with you.)

Pray God's Justice Passes Swiftly

March 21, 1993 - 3:00 A.M.

(S.J. I tested and a voice answered me.)

Mary: It is I, the Queen of Heaven the Mother of your Jesus Christ, praise His name.

Very soon now will the fulfillment of His words come to pass. Encourage all who come to you, share the words of comfort and peace.

Father C. will come to you at the appointed time. Share that which I have revealed to you. He will listen and hear. Be of strong faith and have courage. Do not fear.

The hand of God is heavy upon you. Do not fear for your family. I have bestowed upon them abundant graces and blessings for their pilgrimage in faith.

Do not worry about your son, or the father of your children. A new era is at the door. Pray God's justice passes swiftly and quickly.

Read message #415 of the Marian Movement of Priests, page #671. Call 'C.' and tell him this message and to read #415.

Tell them to pray also for Father 'C.' with novena prayer to My beloved spouse Saint Joseph. I am present and among all of you. Be at peace and do not doubt. For we bestow many blessings upon all our children.

74

Woe! Woe! Woe!

April 12, 1993 - 4:45 A.M.

Voice: Arise My daughter, I would have you take a message.

(S.J., I hear a voice and rebuke it. "Who speaks to Me? In whose name do you come?")

Jesus: I come in the name of the great I Am; your Lord and Savior, Jesus the Christ.

Do not be troubled My little one, the attack of the enemy is as all My children are undergoing. To all who have embraced the Truth and are preparing, those who look on and scoff and disbelieve My patience grows weary!

(S.J., Our Lord's voice was very angry sounding here.)

Jesus: You laugh in the very face of your God! Did I not of old send you all the prophets and messengers of God? Did I not warn My chosen people? Set them free? Do you not believe the Creator is able to do the same today?

Is it because the Word of God today is only a book to be read about olden times? To ceremonially be held aloft, high above the heads of these ministers of Mine who profane the very Word they hold high? They hold My Word high, yet, do not acknowledge My presence in the tabernacle. They hold the Word high, yet they allow abominations to go on all around My table of sacrifice! They no longer care if they consecrate My Body and Blood with hands and hearts stained with their own iniquities!

No more! No more! No more!

People of God and His priests know this: By your own actions you call down upon you My holy wrath!

Thus says the Lord your God!

75

You have forsaken Me, your God; you have belittled My Chosen and ridiculed My Words. You have turned your backs and your hearts away from Me. You did not recognize your time of visitation!

Woe! Woe! Woe!

Prepare to see and feel My holy wrath! It is upon you! You say you don't believe there is a God who would be this cruel and vengeful. Is it because you have not cared for the truth to reign in your lives and now the appointed time arrives you have not made your peace with Me?

You are stained with your sins and reject My complete blood sacrifice to forgive you, now before My holy wrath comes! And you remain in your obstinacy and continue to disbelieve.

Why Do You Recrucify Me

April 16, 1993 - 4:45 A.M.

Jesus: Now will you believe? To your own decree of eternal damnation!

My priests, My priests, My priests, why do you recrucify Me? Why do you play the part of the angry crowd and yell, "Crucify Him again! Crucify Him again."

My Blood runs again and this time it is My priests who have led Me once again through the agony of Calvary. Now will come the time of all times. It is so called and the decree comes from the throne of My Father. He can stand no more.

We tire. The gates of hell would prevail, if Divine intervention does not come. Be at Peace My little precious children. Your time arrives, redemption comes. No longer, no longer, will this go on.

Pray vigilantly, prepare your lamps, for it has come.

The just, holy wrath, of God Omnipotent, Everlasting and Almighty. Our blessings upon all the just and holy people of God.

(S.J., At 3:00 P. M. that same day, I tested and Jesus answered.)

Put on your armor.

Sound the trumpet.

Put your hand in Mine, all is to come quickly!

I give you My special blessing and anoint you in My Name, I guard you jealously as Mine, for you fight bravely for Me.

Peace to all My children.

The King of All Nations, who judges.

Silence In Heaven

April 16, 1993 - 11:00 A.M.

(S.J., I heard a voice and commanded it to go in the Name of Jesus, if not of God.)

Jesus: It is I your Lord and Savior Jesus Christ, whom you praise and whom I have received unto Myself, who is My beloved little victim.

I come to share many things with you as you are pulled out of your exhaustion. Now, My little one, our work continues.

You ask about My messages to the priests. Your director is dealing with My request to him. Share with Father P. This is so My words will be documented.

My words fall on hardened hearts and deaf ears! My words are truth and all who truly seek Me - for I am truth, will hear them and put them into action. My words will not bring confusion!

But those who are deceived into using My name for their own gain, will always bring confusion and division. **Woe** to them! My Words will bring the type of separation that cuts oneself from this world's lies and the persons who refuse to live for Me.

This is as it is to be and has always been. Those who trust greatly in Me, receive abundantly the graces for their burdens, answers to prayers and yes, miracles, because they come holding the hand of My Beloved Mother whose time has arrived.

Be consoled and trust.

The Cross of Peace will not be completed with mere human hands, but will come to Divine completion for all eternity. Trust Me. Believe what you hear is Truth.

(S.J., I retested whose voice and words I was hearing, to which He answered.

Jesus: Thank you, My daughter, for testing. Now write the words I give you and hear. I will speak again later.

Jesus: Yes, My daughter, we will continue.

(S.J., I tested again, whose voice was I hearing.)

Jesus: It is I your Lord and Savior Jesus Christ whose name is praised. My Mother will speak to you.

Mary: My little sorrowful rose, I come to you with words of serious consequence. So that you will understand:

The grains of sand no longer fall through the hour glass! You must fast again and pray constantly. Be totally in the silence of Our Hearts. I am going forward now to lead all My children and cover them with our protection.

It is vitally important for all My children to remain in a state of grace and peace. Only then will My interior warning to My children be heard.

The silence in heaven continues, and is heavy as all look upon the events that will transpire. The chosen who are being lifted up and used, will be for the glory of God and the triumph of My heart, and all are an important and integral part of God's plan. There is no more time left.

The messages have been distributed and fallen on deaf ears and hardened hearts, as My Son has said. So be it. What is being done now is to let all know that this was pretold, predicted and prophesied by all our chosen. My beloved priest sons who did not respond, how much agony you have caused My Son. You forgot God is the same yesterday, today and forever, and what was done in ages past, is able to be far and above repeated again in this sorrowful point of all humanity.

Now, as never before, has the need of divine intervention been needed. Mankind can no longer, of his own, lift himself out of the mire of iniquities, lies of the evil one; and more importantly, the deception of the priests whose sacred holy duty of souls entrusted to them, has been literally forgotten. So be it.

Most of My efforts were met with cowardice, for those who recognized the truth, would not fight and defend Our chosen, or outright ridicule. So be it. Or misplaced anger. So be it. Now, all will be known and revealed. All of what will happen is not coincidence, but exact timing of God's providence.

You are to become an important link to My Cross Of Peace project. Thus you have been led to 'C.' and 'C;' and 'S.' too, has been confirmation in the very depths of your soul and spirit to what is being revealed.

But none can comprehend the immensity of what is coming to pass; how all are loved for your faithfulness, for your perseverance, for your suffering. You will shine great in the Kingdom of God and will be rewarded accordingly.

These things are revealed beforehand to those of little faith, and to doubters and unbelievers; how they missed the same opportunity presented to all. Few have said "Yes". Few have said, "Not my will, but God's will in my life". Few have trusted, completely and totally on My Son's words. So be it.

Now share this with those I lead you to. The time is now. More will be revealed at the appointed time. I love you My children. I guard you My children. And I bless you in the name of the Father, and of the Son, and of the Holy Spirit. Amen.

Turn to Him Now!

April 22, 1993 - 6:20 A.M.

(S.J., I heard a voice and commanded it to go in the name of Jesus, if not of God.)

Mary: Only to those who enter. This was foretold to the children of God and all the lost. All had opportunity to believe. God's children were led to Santa Maria, City Of Peace, and were protected from the experience, fear, devastation and destruction of this earthquake.

They will be protected from all that will follow. This has been, and is, the holy just wrath of God, for the refusal of men in this nation to stop the running of the blood of the innocents killed in abortion, and your refusal to acknowledge, and repent, and turn to Him. Turn to Him now!

(S.J., I was told by Mary to leave this message in my apartment. I then realized that people will be searching after the earthquake trying to determine those who were lost and those still missing. Mary then told me that I was to share this message with those that Mary would lead to me that day. About eight people showed up that day. Mary instructed me to give to them copies of this message, but they were not free to copy it or distribute it.)

Note: On May 2, 1993, 'C.' called Sadie. Jesus and Mary told her to wait for his call and then share this message with him. Mary also told Sadie that she could share with C. and 'S.' at the appointed time.

Vision of Cross of Peace

April 28, 1993

(S.J., this vision happened during prayer while I was telling Jesus how much I loved Him. However, I was also telling Him how agonizing it was living out of suitcases packed for the trip to Santa Maria, but at the same time thanking Him for His mercy and extending the time of the earthquake so additional souls could receive His grace and be saved.)

Vision: Sadie could see Our Lord Jesus standing next to her. He was comforting her with His arm around her shoulder. They were looking towards the horizon.

Sadie could tell that this was the exact place where they were encamped at Saint Joseph's church in Nipomo, in the large open field next to the church. Sadie could see the same meadows and hills just full of people.

Off to the left side of the vision, Sadie saw the Cross of Peace. Jesus and Sadie were looking in the same direction, that is south along Thompson Road, towards the hill of the future Cross of Peace.

Sadie saw rays coming from the Cross of Peace and masses of people. She felt that they were in conversation and that Jesus was consoling her. She could see the Cross from the encampment in front of the classrooms.

Rays were just beaming from the Cross and all around the whole area Sadie could see masses of people. Many, many people. Sadie was overcome with an incredible feeling of peace and she felt very happy. Sadie saw many rays coming through the arms of the Cross. The rays were gold. The vision was not one of color, but these rays were gold.

Pray Chaplet of St. Michael

April 29, 1993 - 11:15 A.M.

(S.J., I was praying and asking for help from Mary in the messages from the Marian Movement of Priests book. Mary then gave me the following nine references. They were, 52, 158, 451, 452, 453, 454, 203, 318, and 166. Mary then reminded me to take down the following message.)

Mary: This great silence that you reflect on prepares you for the coming of momentous events.

You have been told by the Father, "Do not fear." I tell you now, again, do not fear, just remain in prayer with Me and with My Son. The silence will end soon. Events will happen quickly. You must pray for your son, the sin of pride deceives him. Continue praying the **Chaplet of Saint Michael**.

I love you and I am closest to you now.

(S.J., Mary then gave me a blessing.)

Decide For Me Now

April 30, 1993

(I tested and Jesus answered.)

Jesus: I speak to you My daughter, I Am, Who Am, Lord and Savior over all, Jesus the Christ who is praised.

Oh, My children, do not falter from the path that is laid before you. Do not become apprehensive if events do not fall in your

82

path in your time expectations. For every moment is grace, grace to bestow on My lost, mislead, and those who truly are working to spread My Word. There is no more time.

Though these words are said over and over in Our time frame, which is different from yours; but believe, there is no more time. To impress upon all the faithful, do not be caught sleeping, in indifference, disbelief, but at all moments be prepared and ready to flee.

To My children, who are faithful, there is no reason to fear. To My lost I extend to you My Mother who will lead you straight to the Truth which is Me. To My priests, give up the folly of your erroneous beliefs. You make a mockery of those things that are true and holy and cause My Blood to flow once again. Are you in line on every point of truth handed to you by My Vicar on earth? Woe to you from the greatest in this world to the least who speak against Me. Again, I say; woe to you if you cause one soul to be lost on account of your error.

There are many who are neither hot nor cold. Decide for Me now and fight bravely against the enemy who has already been defeated. Behold, I come quickly to deliver My children. Behold, I am even at the door.

I am your Lord and Savior and I love you and bless you and I keep you.

(S.J., Jesus told me to go to the book of **Obadiah** (Abdias) and read verse #15, 17 18.)

Douay Rheims Bible: Prophecy of Obadiah Abdias

#15 "For the day of the Lord is at hand upon all nations: as thou hast done, so shall it be done to thee: He will turn thy reward upon thy own head."

#17 "And in Mount Sion shall be salvation, and it shall be holy, and the house of Jacob shall possess those that possessed them."

#18 "And the house of Jacob shall be a fire, and the house of Joseph a flame and the house of Esau stubble: and they shall be kindled in them and shall devour them; and these shall be no remains of the house of Esau, for the Lord hath spoken it.

New American Bible: The Book of Obadiah

#15 "For near is the day of the Lord for all nations! As you have done, so shall it be done to you, your deed shall come back upon your own head."

#17 "But on Mount Zion there shall be a portion saved; the mountain shall be holy, and the house of Jacob shall take possession of those that dispossessed them."

#18 "The house of Jacob shall be a fire, and the house of Joseph a flame; the house of Esau shall be stubble and they shall set them ablaze and devour them; Then none shall survive of the house of Esau, for the Lord has spoken.

Signs of Warning

May 11, 1993 - 11:35 A.M.

(S.J., Our Lady tells me I am about to receive extraordinary graces, graces to serve God's people. Prepare by prayer and fasting. Then She begins to give me the following readings from Father Gobbi's book: #66 - "The Seed is beginning to Germinate" and #47 - "The Prayer of the Priests".

Our Lady says as I am reading the title, "The Prayer of you, for My Priest". In between the readings Our Lady answers what I had asked in prayer, whether I was going to receive permission to copy and distribute the messages. She says to me:)

Mary: You are to remain anonymous, except for those I give permission for you to share. The words we spoke will go far and touch many, who they come from is not important.

(S.J., I praise her for this, because Our Lord and Our Lady both know I prefer anonymity. Our Lady continues to lead me to messages - #132 "Love Always" - #133 "My Property" - #172 "Your Liberation is Near" - #193 "Offered to the Glory of God" - #8 "Watch and Pray". As I finished reading I begin to hear Our Lady and I test.)

Mary: It is I, The Mother Immaculate, Sorrowing Virgin, Mother of All Humanity and Mother of your Lord Jesus Christ. With the last words of the titles of messages from My Beloved Priests, "Watch and Pray", for you My little sorrowful rose, watch and pray with Me. I come to ask you to pray and suffer for My priests.

For this purpose, Father 'P.' is placed in your life. To help and guide you in your mission, that is to become a victim soul for My priests, the consecrated sons of My Son, who grieve Him so at this sorrowful point of all humanity.

He (Father 'P.') will become an even greater instrument used in the renewing of the Holy Church on earth; The Church that will shine for the glory of God by all that **has** been foretold by many faithful servants and saints. He will pray for you and by his prayer the fulfillment of prophecy will come. You, in turn, are to share with him all that you receive. In one sense, I have appointed him your spiritual guide. At My leading he is directed to (call) you.

All for the perfect fulfillment of God the Father, for you and for Him (Father P.). I desire you to inform your director, Msgr. 'B.' of My request. Again I say, for now you are to remain anonymous for the messages that have come since the last ones you received permission from Msgr. B. to distribute.

Sharing is to be done as I dictate to you.

(S.J., I heard the voice of our Lord and I tested.)

Jesus: It is I, Jesus Christ, Lord and Savior of All! Look to the heavens My child. Many are the signs of warning for My children. Only those walking in grace and trust can see mother nature's wrath. *(New reports on the various weather happenings referred to the wrath of mother nature.)* Do they not know Who created mother nature? Can they not see the signs of fury that are only the beginning of the birth pangs of labor? Even My priests who know My Word, disclaim the truth.

(S.J., At this point, our Lord tells me to read 2 Thessalonians and points out 2: 3-17, then Genesis 12 and points out 12: 1-3, and Genesis 3 and points out 3: 15.)

2 Thessalonians 2:3-17

(3) Let no one seduce you, no matter how. Since the mass apostasy has not yet occurred nor the man of lawlessness been revealed - that son of perdition

(4) And adversary who exalts himself above every so-called god proposed for worship, he who seats himself in God's temple and even declares himself to be God.

(5) Do you not remember how I used to tell you about these things when I was still with you?

(6) You know what restrains him until he shall be revealed in his own time.

(7) The secret force of lawlessness is already at work, mind you, but there is one who holds him back until that restrainer shall be taken from the scene.

(8) Thereupon the lawless one will be revealed, and the Lord Jesus will destroy him with the breath of his mouth and annihilate him by manifesting his own presence.

(9) This lawless one will appear as part of the workings of Satan, accompanied by all the power and signs and wonders at the disposal of falsehood.

(10) By every seduction the wicked can devise for those destined to ruin because they have not opened their hearts to the truth in order to be saved.

(11) Therefore God is sending upon them a perverse spirit which leads them to give credence to falsehood.

(12) So that all who have not believed the truth but have delighted in evildoing will be condemned.

(13) We are bound to thank God for you always, beloved brothers in the Lord, because you are the first fruits of those whom God has chosen for salvation, in holiness of spirit and fidelity to truth.

(14) He called you through our preaching of the good news so that you might achieve the glory of our Lord Jesus Christ.

(15) Therefore, brothers, stand firm. Hold fast to the traditions you received from us, either by our word or by letter.

(16) May our Lord Jesus Christ himself, may God our Father who loved us and in his mercy gave us eternal consolation and hope,

(17) Console your hearts and strengthen them for every good work and word.

Genesis 12:1-3

(1) The Lord said to Abram: "Go forth from the land of your kinsfolk and from your father's house to a land that I will show you.

(2) "I will make of you a great nation, and I will bless you: I will make your name great, so that you will be a blessing.

(3) I will bless those who bless you and curse those who curse you. All the communities of the earth shall find blessing in you.

Genesis 3:15

(15) I will put enmity between you and the woman, and between your offspring and hers: She will strike at your head, while you strike at her heel.

(S.J., Jesus then took me to the book of Revelations and as I read, He gave me to list the following verses and once again, told me to type the manuscript as one continuous message.)

Revelation 3:10-11

(10) Because you have kept my plea to stand fast, I will keep you safe in time of trial which is coming on the whole world, to test all men on earth.

(11) I am coming soon. Hold fast to what you have lest someone rob you of your crown.

Revelation 5:10

(10) You made of them a kingdom, and priests to serve our God, and they shall reign on the earth.

Revelation 7:9-10, 13-17

(9) After this I saw before me a huge crowd which no one could count from every nation and race, people and tongue. They stood before the throne and the Lamb, dressed in long white robes and holding palm branches in their hands.

(10) They cried out in a loud voice, "Salvation is from our God, who is seated on the throne, and from the Lamb!"

(13) Then one of the elders asked me, "Who are these people all dressed in white? And where have they come from?"

(14) I said to him, "Sir, you should know better than I." He then told me, "These are the ones who have survived the great period of trial; they have washed their robes and made them white in the blood of the Lamb.

(15) "It was this that brought them before God's throne: day and night they minister to him in his temple: he who sits on the throne will give them shelter.

(16) Never again shall they know hunger or thirst, nor shall the sun or its heat beat down on them.

(17) For the Lamb on the throne will shepherd them. He will lead them to springs of life giving water, and God will wipe every tear from their eyes."

Revelation 8: 3-5

(3) Another angel come in holding a censer of gold. He took his place at the altar of incense and was given large amounts of incense to deposit on the altar of gold in front of the throne, together with the prayers of all God's holy ones.

(4) From the angel's hand the smoke of the incense went up before God, and with it the prayers of God's people.

(5) Then the angel took the censer, filled it with live coals from the altar, and hurled it down to the earth. Peals of thunder and flashes of lighting followed and the earth trembled.

Revelation 14:6-7

(6) Then I saw another angel flying in midheaven, the herald of everlasting good news to the whole world, to every nation and race, language and people.

(7) He said in a loud voice: "Honor God and give him glory, for his time has come to sit in judgment. Worship the Creator of heaven and earth, the Creator of the sea and the springs."

Revelation 15: 1

(1) I saw in heaven another sign, great and awe-inspiring: seven angels holding the seven final plagues which would bring God's wrath to a climax.

Revelation 16:5-7

(5) Then I heard the angel in charge of the waters cry out: "You are just, O Holy One who is and who was, in passing this sentence!

(6) To those who shed the blood of saints and prophets, you have given blood to drink; they deserve it."

(7) Then I heard the altar cry out: "Yes, Lord God Almighty, your judgments are true and just".

Revelations 21:2-4

(2) I also saw a new Jerusalem, the holy city, coming down out of heaven from God, beautiful as a bride prepared to meet her husband.

(3) I heard a loud voice from the throne cry out: "This is God's dwelling among men. He shall dwell with them and they shall be his people and he shall be their God who is always with them.

(4) He shall wipe every tear from their eyes, and there shall be no more death or mourning, crying out or pain, for the former world has passed away."

Revelation 22-11

(11) Let the wicked continue in their wicked ways, the depraved in their depravity! The virtuous must live on in their virtue and the holy ones in their holiness!

Revelations 22:20

(20) The One who gives this testimony says, "Yes I am coming soon!" Amen! Come, Lord Jesus!

Zephaniah (Sophonias) 1:3

(3) I will sweep away man and beast, I will sweep away the birds of the sky, and the fishes of the sea. I will overthrow the wicked: I will destroy mankind from the face of the earth, says the Lord.

90

Zephaniah 1: 6-7

(6) And those who have fallen away from the Lord, and those who do not seek the Lord.

(7) Silence in the presence of the Lord God! for near is the day of the Lord, Yes, the Lord has prepared a slaughter feast, he has consecrated his guests.

Zephaniah 1:12

(12) I will punish the men who thicken on their lees, Who say in their hearts, "Neither good nor evil can the Lord do."

Zephaniah 1:14-17

(14) Near is the great day of the Lord, near and very swiftly coming; Hark, the day of the Lord! Bitter, then, the warrior's cry.

(15) A day of wrath is that day, a day of anguish and distress, A day of destruction and desolation, a day of darkness and gloom, A day of thick black clouds,

(16) a day of trumpet blasts and battle alarm against fortified cities, against battlements on high.

(17) I will hem men in till they walk like the blind, because they have sinned against the Lord; and their blood shall be poured out like dust, and their brains like dung.

Zephaniah 2:1-3

(1) Gather, gather yourselves together, O nation without shame!

(2) Before you are driven away, like the chaff that passes on; Before there comes upon you the blazing anger of the Lord; Before there come upon you the day of the Lord's anger.

(3) Seek the Lord, all you humble of the earth, who have observed his law; Seek justice, seek humility; perhaps you may be sheltered on the day of the Lord's anger.

Zephaniah 2:7

(7) The coast shall belong to the remnant of the house of Judah; by the sea they shall pasture. For the lord their God shall visit them, and bring about their restoration.

(S.J., the Lord tells me what to omit from certain passages.)

Zephaniah 2:9,11

(9) . . . The remnant of my people shall plunder them, the survivors of my nation dispossess them.

(11) The Lord shall inspire them with fear when he makes all the gods of earth to waste away; then each from its own place, all the coast lands of the nations shall adore him.

Zephaniah 3:6-9

(6) I have destroyed nations, their battlements are laid waste; I have made their street deserted, with on one passing through; Their cities are devastated, with no man dwelling in them.

(7) I said, "Surely now you will fear me, you will accept correction"; She should not fail to see all I have visited upon her. Yet all the more eagerly have they done all their corrupt deeds.

(8) Therefore, wait for me, says the Lord, against the day when I arise as accuser; for it is my decision to gather together the nations, to assemble the kingdoms, in order to pour out upon them my wrath, all my blazing anger; For in the fire of my jealousy shall all the earth be consumed.

(9) For then I will change and purify the lips of the peoples, That they all may call upon the name of the Lord, to serve him with one accord.

Zephaniah 3:11-12

(11) On that day you need not be ashamed of all your deeds, your rebellious actions against me; For then will I remove from your midst proud braggarts, And you shall no longer exalt yourself on my holy mountain.

(12) But I will leave as a remnant in your midst a people humble and lowly, Who shall take refuge in the name of the Lord:

Zephaniah 3:18-20

(18) I will remove disaster from among you, so that none may recount your disgrace.

(19) Yes, at that time I will deal with all who oppress you: I will save the lame, and assemble the outcasts; I will give them praise and renown in all the earth, when I bring about their restoration.

(20) At that time I will bring you home, and at that time I will gather you; For I will give you renown and praise, among all the peoples of the earth, When I bring about your restoration before your very eyes, says the Lord.

Jesus: I tell you once again I use My Word to speak to My people. Oh, that they would believe. I use My Word to answer your questions of the New Jerusalem, Santa Maria, for this time in humanity.

Many will come and many will know the fulfillment of prophecy. There will be much work to do amongst My children. Life will change, but it will be for the betterment of God's children.

NOTE: Message Number 6 of "A Cross Will Be Built.", 4-20-88. "Do not worry. The size is important that all may see. Many will come and many will stay in My City of Peace."

This was Jesus response to my question, "What does the New Jerusalem have to do with the city of Santa Maria, California?" C.W.N.

(S.J., The Lord then continues with my ongoing lesson from Him.)

93

Jesus: Open the Bible to the Book of Haggai.

(S.J., Jesus tells me to read. Again as I read, He tells me which verses to write down and then instructs me to type it as one continuous manuscript.)

Haggai 1:2-4

Thus says the Lord of Hosts: This people says: "Not now has the time come to rebuild the house of the Lord." (Then this word of the Lord came through Haggai, the prophet:) Is it time for you to dwell in your own paneled houses, while this house lies in ruins?

Haggai 1:9-11

You expected much, but it came to little; and what you brought home, I blew away. For what cause? says the Lord of hosts. Because My house lies in ruins, while each of you hurries to his own house. Therefore the heavens withheld from you their dew, and the earth her crops.

And I called for a drought upon the land and upon the mountains; Upon the grain, and upon the wine, and upon the oil, and upon all that the ground brings forth; Upon men and upon beasts, and upon all that is produced by hand.

Haggai 3:4-9

Who is left among you that saw this house in its former glory? And how do you see it now? Does it not seem like nothing in your eyes? But now take courage, Zerubbabel, says the Lord, and take courage, Joshua, high priest, son of Jehozadak, and take courage, all you people of the land, says the Lord, and work!

For I am with you, says the Lord of hosts. This is the pact that I made with you when you came out of Egypt, And my spirit continues in your midst; do not fear! For thus says the Lord of hosts: One moment yet, a little while, and I will shake the heavens and the earth, the sea and the dry land. I will shake all the nations, and the treasures of all the nations will come in, And I will fill this house with glory, says the Lord of hosts. Mine is the silver and mine the gold, says the Lord of hosts. Greater will be the future glory of this house than the former, says the Lord of hosts; And in this place I will give peace, says the Lord of hosts!

Haggai 2:14

So is this people, and so is this nation in My sight says the Lord; and so are all the works of their hands; and what they offer there is unclean.

Haggai 2:21 I will shake the heavens and the earth.

Haggai 2:22 I will overthrow the thrones of kingdoms, destroy the power of the kingdoms of the nations.

Jesus: These are My words about My holy church and My priests who should regard the holiness of their consecration.

I set My priests apart, to serve My people; to pray and offer the sacrifice of the Mass that I, their God, would be merciful to My people. To stand in their (the people's) place and plead My mercy, love and blessings upon all My children. To counsel according to truth and tradition. To defend its stand in a world that takes no stand. To be in front of My Real Presence keeping company with Me, seeking My wisdom.

But where are all My priests?

They no longer stand apart from the crowd, but have become part of the crowd. They no longer lead, they are following lies of the enemy, and philosophies of all sorts, that are not truth. Their hands and hearts are stained with the guilt of their own iniquities of which they confess not. How can My priests bring conviction to My children; a conviction they neither know nor preach?

Oh My priests! Embrace Me, comfort Me once again. Serve Me with clean hearts that I may receive your offerings for My children.

Return to the truth and devotion of old, that is unchanged; that is the same yesterday, today and forever!

Repent and run to Me. I Am there to cleanse you. Consecrate yourselves and your priesthood to My Mother. She is who disburses the graces; I will have it no other way. Humble yourselves with true contrition.

Woe! You serve a Mighty Omnipotent God who is releasing the just holy wrath of God eternal.

See the signs and know that all will come to pass. I have raised many of the littlest children in the kingdom of God, many to speak and spread My words. Listen to them. Let go of your pride and allow My peace and blessings to descend upon you.

Walk in the power of My spirit and defend My truth.

Always Remain Humble

May 13, 1993 - 9:30 A.M.

(S.J., I heard a voice and commanded, in the name of Jesus, "In whose name do you come".)

Mary: I come in the name of My Son Jesus. I come to greet you on this day of the anniversary of My appearance at Fatima. I am the Queen of Peace.

My child, little sorrowful rose, be expedient and joyful, for you are about to receive extraordinary graces from Me; graces that will confirm you greater still in the power, love and service of Our Lord.

Remember always to remain humble. This is an endearing quality you have. It is why We use you. You must always receive whomever We lead to you, no matter the hour or what is happening with you that moment. Duties with your children notwithstanding.

You will suffer much for the glory of God, but know that I am and will always be with you.

I give your on this day My special blessing, and soon, very soon, events will break forth. Be vigilant and prayerful.

I love you, My little sorrowful rose.

God's peace and blessing upon you this day.

The Victorious Queen of Peace

May 14, 1993 - A.M.

(S.J., I heard a voice and tested, "If not of God, be gone in Jesus name.")

Mary: It is I, the victorious Queen of Peace, Mother of Jesus, King of Kings.

My child, little sorrowful rose, you are destined to suffer and work much to bring glory to God the Eternal Father. You receive these words to remind you gently I am always with you. I will never fail you. In your despair, in your agony, you gain many souls.

There are many events about to unfold and be revealed. Even so, mankind still refuses to acknowledge its Creator. You are destined to suffer for My beloved priests; the consecrated sons who much offend God the Almighty.

Soon you will be called to reveal all that has been spoken by My Son. Be of strong spirit and do not fear. Those people who are to be instrumental to you and your call are in place. The fulfillment of words spoken will be your credentials that you are called and sent by us according to the will of God Eternal.

You must know child, even after this punishment, the work will be even greater for all My children, to remain steadfast in prayer. Do not anticipate anything further than the present moment.

For with all My children, as with you, daily take My hand, and allow Me, your Queen and Mother to lead you. At every moment, in everything you do, pray and love. Love is the binding element to our hearts.

I bless you today and give you a measure and a double portion of My love.

There Will Come A Great Sign

May 19, 1993 - 2:40 A.M.

(S.J. I heard a voice and tested: "In whose name do you speak?")

Mary: I speak in the name of the great I Am, Jesus, whose Mother I am, Mary Immaculate, Refuge of Sinners.

The doorway of all humanity has opened; for in a moment, events will cause the passing of everyone though, in particular, here in the United States of America.

Thus you continue to see heaven's door.

Many will pass through the door that has been opened. Some will be prepared, some will not. All will be brought together.

My priests are no longer responding, thus My littlest chosen are also starting through this door for the task entrusted to each one. Different in purpose, all for the same end.

You, too, My little sorrowful rose, will be sent. Do not be afraid to speak what we give you, for it is what My Son would have you say.

You will see great events continue to unfold quickly!

Remember we are close to you at all times.

You will call those people entrusted to your care.

98

You will not see the manifestation of what My Son has spoken until after the earthquake.

He is about to visit you and with His wounds.

Go to Msgr. 'B." today.

(S.J. Here I started testing the voice again, because this message is so serious and even frightening.)

Mary: I thank you My child for testing.

There will come a great sign; a sign to preclude all others.

You and all My children will know deep within their spirits that it is sent by the great I Am.

My son 'P.' will call you and confirmation will come through him.

Do not wonder at how you will be used. Just remain at all times in the presence of My Immaculate Heart.

Thus, I protect you at all times and remove the desire to do all other insignificant activities.

My Son and the Father guard you as their own!

The Saints, St. Michael and the Holy Angels, at all times assist you!

Thus, know you are embarking on a very important mission.

Events cannot be stopped! However, I now lead My army into safety and battle!

This sign will have to do with the elements of nature. No lives will be lost at this time.

Do not be concerned about your financial state. I provide through My Son. Have all preparations complete. Look high in the sky to the west. There take My picture. Believe and trust you stand vindicated.

I Bless you this morning in the name of the Father, Son and Holy Spirit.

The Enemy Rages

May 25, 1993 - 2:47 P.M.

(S.J., I heard a voice and rebuked it to go, if not of God, in the name of Jesus.)

Mary: My daughter and little sorrowful rose, it is I your Mother and Mother of all humanity, Mary Immaculate and Sorrowing Virgin, praise My Son, Jesus.

Tell My children this spilling of My Son's blood, by Cardinal Posadas is not in vain. He has died a martyr's death and it will bear just fruit. It is also a very significant event for the Holy Church on earth.

Indeed, a black cloud has rested over the church. The enemy rages against those consecrated to Me, but, in this his rage, lie the keys of My triumph. That remnant that perseveres in prayer, through faith, are justified. You will have one more cenacle in the morning. You will be in Santa Maria by June 6.

(S.J., I had been taking Polaroid pictures and getting the door, and what I perceive as the dome in Washington, D.C. I saw in a vision, during prayer yesterday, that building in the photo with a large hammer head appearing over it.)

Mary: The vision you saw is the Capitol Building in Washington. The State of California and Washington D.C. will be struck simultaneously. For then it will be impossible to explain its happening.

Many events will begin to happen quickly. You must walk with faith and trust and do not fear. All that has been spoken will come to pass. Rest in the graces of My love and blessings.

(S.J., I struggled with this message most of the day. Then in the evening, at 6:10 P. M., while meditating and praying, I began to hear our Lord's voice. I commanded it to go away and rebuked it several times in Jesus' name, until I demanded, "In the Name of Jesus, in whose name do you come?")

Jesus: But it is My name Jesus, in whose name. I come, and I bow down and worship God Eternal. Amen.

My child, know and believe all words spoken to you. All that has been told by My Mother is true; for where She dwells, in the midst of the Trinity, She receives knowledge of those events foretold. Thus, She works tirelessly to bring more of My children to conversion.

I tell you now, child, continue to prepare by your complete and total abandonment to the will of the Father. Pray at all times. It is most soothing to My wounded heart.

My Priests Will Know: I Am

May 25, 1993 - 6:10 P.M.

Jesus: The moment is near and can be seen on the horizon. That which I will cause, the innermost bowels of the earth to give in vent to the justice of God. My angels prepare to go forth according to the decree of God Almighty, and all will know:

From the greatest to the least, I Am.

(S.J., His voice became very majestic and very forceful.)

My priests will know: I Am.

My people will know: I Am.

Humanity will acknowledge, nature was commanded by the great I Am.

My remnants will be brought together and acknowledge and praise: I Am.

My peace and blessing descend upon you.

101

Do not doubt but believe for your sons, your father and your 'J'.

I seal this promise to you with My Precious Blood, shed for you.

I am the way, the truth and the light. I cannot lie.

I love you.

Fear is From the Enemy

May 26, 1993 - 10:20 A.M.

(S.J., I heard a voice and I tested.)

Mary: Know that, I Queen of Heaven, Queen of all Angels, and Queen of earth, the Mother of Jesus whose name is praised, pray with you today as the moment spoken of, rapidly approaches. You must believe and act on your faith.

You are truly mine and truly sent. Do not despair or fear. Fear is from the enemy. Because you have prayed not to know, we in heaven know that there is no guile in your heart. Therefore, We entrust to you this message. Type it out and mail it to My beloved son P. Call S. now. I will lead you as the day progresses.

(S.J., She left me with a beautiful message.)

Warn My Children

June 1, 1993 8:40 A.M.

(S.J., I heard a voice and commanded it, "In whose name do you come?")

Jesus: Yes, My daughter, it is I, your Lord and Savior, Jesus Christ who does bow and worship God Eternal.

Yes, I, your Lord and your God am going to strike this nation from one end to the other. I tell you My child, My hand is about

102

to fall for the great strike. Do not be afraid of what I reveal to you. Warn My children, tell them to be prepared for the appointed time has come.

I have raised My chosen to lead My children. At Our guidance and word, they (the chosen) are moved and guided in all they say and do.

I, your Lord God, have allowed the mockery to My chosen for they have chosen to drink of the same cup I drank, they have submitted their wills, their lives for the glory of God's kingdom.

But now I leave My throne and will strike and strike and strike and defy their understanding. God will no longer be made a mockery, for what they have done to My chosen, they have done to Me.

I am in a state of constant sorrow at seeing My children oblivious of My presence in their lives. My only consolation comes from the small remnant who have heeded My Mother's call for prayer and sacrifice. Do not be afraid, We are with you. All these events spoken of will, and are, happening in a very rapid sequence.

Do not be caught off guard, My children! At all times remain ready to flee. My angels, My holy angels surround My children, do not cease your prayer and sacrifices. We are with each and every one of you. Praise Jesus, praise God Eternal, praise The Holy Spirit. (Mary repeated this three times.)

(S.J., After testing, Our Lord continued.)

Jesus: My child, do not block Me. Those who have remained steadfast are entrusted with more. My people, My priests need to hear the voices we have raised up, thus I tried to tell you of correction needed.

There is not a cenacle that has not been hit by strife and division and discord of the enemy. The root is always pride. Do not compete. My children, in all things remain united. United in prayer, love, all with the glory of God as the uppermost thought.

103

Each one should ask; "Would this glorify My God? In that (question) each would know what is being revealed to each and every one of My children. Those who are the greatest must be the least.

My peace to you, My little sorrowful rose; pray for all visionaries. Call down the Holy Spirit upon your group. There will be special graces and blessings. Give thanks to God for all His blessings and mercy.

Give thanks to God for His deliverance of His children.

We bless you in the name above all names, "Jesus"; In the name of God Eternal Father, in the name and power of the Holy Spirit.

Release All To God

June 2, 1993 7:44 A.M.

(S.J., I heard a voice and commanded it to go, in the name of Jesus, if not of God.)

The Holy Spirit: The Spirit of God who praises Jesus and God Eternal, who is anointing God's children in His power speaks:

The word of the Lord came to me thus:

My child know that in your suffering, much is being accomplished for the glory of God. Your suffering of heart, shows you the pain of the Savior at the rejection by His children.

When He desires only to bring eternal life to His children, they choose death. This causes Him profound sorrow. Thus He became a man of sorrows. You too, have been chosen, for the sorrow in your life redeems many.

Soon however, your suffering will change. I have come to seal upon you God's anointing power. Thus you will become God's instrument through whom He will touch many of His children.

104

I come to verify and testify that which has been spoken in regard to 'J.' He is a man crushed in spirit, only now can he allow God's love to work and move in him.

Do not despair. Rejoice, pray and fast. Release all to God, thus in your release, you trust God ever more.

The spirit of love grows dim and cold in many of My children, thus I am sent to enkindle and fan those flames to a burning fire of love. Now is My time come; hold fast to the hands of your Mother. She leads and guides you to the hearts of the Trinity, the Father, The Son and Myself.

You are the delight, of all of us, for your childlike abandonment to our will. You have found favor with God; draw ever near to His Love. Great is your reward. But know that soon, as all warnings given have stated, God the Father's justice will rain upon mankind. There are those souls chosen and predestined to work tirelessly for God's kingdom until the final battle.

Do not fear. Trust, draw closer to the fire of Our great love. Pray for those entrusted to your prayers, rejoice for the fulfillment of God's words come.

Amen!

And I bless you as the whole heavenly court looks on, in My Father's name, in the name of my Son, Jesus, and My Holy Spirit.

Before Every Storm There Is A Calm

June 11, 1993

(S.J., I hear a voice and I tested.)

Mary: Behold, My little sorrowful rose, I, your Mother and Queen of Heaven, speak in the name above all names, Jesus, My Son, Lord and Savior of all.

I come to tell you the Son shines down upon you today. Believe your suffering is gaining many souls, but especially souls of His consecrated sons, who cause Him to be wounded again. Become more and more childlike. Do not doubt; do not get caught up in the lies of the enemy. He rages against you because of your yes.

The words I spoke through My son P. are truth and My source of consolation for you. Soon you will be placed in front of many to speak as the Spirit of God prompts. For now your hiddenness is necessary, but as equally important. I love you and bless you. Your Mother who enfolds you in My arms.

(S.J. - I tested and He answered.)

Jesus: I Jesus who am, and who worships and praises the Father, say to you the words of My Son P. are truth. The periods of abandonment are converting and saving many souls. We are teaching you and training you for the work that will continue until that time. Do not get caught up in the deception of not believing. Indeed, as My consecrated son, (Father P.) spoke the words of My Mother, "soon the Father's hand will fall", I tell you before every storm there is a calm.

Soon many of My children will be forced to bend their knees, and I tell you this, justice is mercy. Pray for the souls that will perish in an instant, but have died with the hope of everlasting life. For the innocents (babies and small children) who will immediately be with Me and who will be spared what is to come. I ask you trust Me as your children trust you. Trust Me ever more, for your welfare in every way concerns Me, so much do I love you. I never tire of hearing you tell Me of your great love, thus I have imprinted My wounded Face deeply in your soul.

Live every moment in peace and preparedness for the wrath of God reaches its appointed target. Trust, love; and your offer of life at every moment is most pleasing to Us. I chose you as you are, who you are and as you are to become. Do not argue with My plan for you, everything told will come to pass.

(S.J., Personal. I asked about the conversion of the father of my children. Our Lord answered me as follows:)

Jesus: Even 'J.', especially 'J'.

(S.J., will you give me a sign?)

Jesus: Yes! (S.J., Soon?)

Jesus: Yes, I will flood you with My graces. Now be at peace, go about your day and know I am with you.

(S.J. Jesus then blessed Me as He does after most messages.)

I Will Confound The Wisdom of the Learned

June 14, 1993 10:15 A. M.

(S.J., I heard a voice and I tested.)

Jesus: My dearest little daughter, I your Lord and Savior of all, Jesus, the Christ, desire to give you these words: Your days of hiddenness and preparation are coming to a close. Soon is the time you will speak with the power and anointing of My Spirit. You must not fear or doubt, but believe.

Your burden is lifted, I promise with My sign for you. Soon the feast of My Sacred Heart approaches, as does the day to remember the one who preceded Me in My walk on earth. Who has preceded Me at this time? My Mother, and just as in those days, they refused to believe. I have told you that all storms are preceded by a calm. Do not let this calm deceive you.

For the time has now arrived and events spoken of, will be revealed quickly and swiftly.

107

I cry for My souls. I weep tears of blood for those who do not bend their knees. But many are the souls of the faithful, the innocents, the suffering who now demand an accounting of justice. And justice shall be rendered.

This, too, is a sign of My love and mercy. For the many who have heeded My Mother's pleas for reparation and sacrifice, this has been a time of extended mercy, obtained by the implorings of My Mother.

However, that time of mercy has ended. Pray and fast, pray at all times. You will soon be brought together as My remnant people.

(S.J., Our Lord blessed, and He asked me to bow my head and I heard:)

Jesus: "Father, I, Your Son Jesus, ask You to bless your servant with the fulfillment of Our words for Your glory, and I bless you In the name of My Father, In My name, and in the power and name of My Spirit.

(S.J., Words received after I was praying and praising God.)

Jesus: Thus speaks the Lord, your God: "There is a darkness fast approaching the earth. The sun will lose its brilliance. I will lower mankind's intelligence to nothing. They will predict one thing, I will send another. I will confound the wisdom of the learned with the faith and words of children. So be it."

Chaplet of the Seven Sorrows

June 23, 1993 - 1:30 P.M.

(S.J., I heard a voice, I tested, "In whose name do you come?")

Mary: My child, little sorrowful rose, I your Mother, Queen of Heaven, Mother of Jesus, praise the Father for His great love. Love for His children and all He has created, has allowed the One predestined in the beginning to be graced with special favor, to be the Ever Virgin, Mother of God, to grant Me My pleading for My children.

On this day I ask you to recall our first conversation. I identify with your sorrow, I am the Sorrowful and Immaculate Virgin whose Heart will triumph.

I want all My children to know that I meet them with their sorrows, I help them with graces to carry their crosses, just as I helped My Son. Yes, much has been granted to Me.

I ask you to pray a novena for nine days for all souls living, especially here in California. I want you to offer **My Chaplet of the Seven Sorrows** for all these souls that will die. I ask you to continue to fast for them. I ask for your "yes" once again.

I want you to look neither to the left nor to the right but only straight ahead, on Me. Know that I am leading you and preparing you for your mission. I have obtained a sign that will confirm deep in your soul all that has been spoken of J.

The time for signs will end, the time for fulfillment begin.

These nine (9) days will bring signs in the weather and all will wonder, few will respond anymore.

Plead for My children, my little sorrowful rose, through the holy face of My Son.

My angels surround you, as I bless you in the name of My Son, the Father and My Spouse, the Holy Spirit.

Remain open at all times to My leading.

I Am Mourning For All My Children

June 29, 1993 - 7:20 A.M.

(S.J. I heard a voice commanded it to go in the name of Jesus, if not of God.)

Mary: It is I child, your Sorrowful and Immaculate Ever Virgin Mother and Mother of Jesus. Praise the name of Jesus!

(S.J., Inwardly, I see Our Lady dressed in black, being to the upper left in my vision, bending down, and holding in Her arms beautiful roses. I see a rose appear and She places it with all the rest, in Her arms. Jesus is comforting Her by placing His arm around Her shoulders.)

Mary: Now, I tell you, I appear to you in mourning, for I am mourning for all My children. The stubborn and prideful who resist the calling of the Holy Spirit. The lukewarm and indifferent, who see the whole of what is happening throughout this nation and the world, and continue as though they are unaffected.

For the "scribes and pharisees", who go through the motions of fulfilling the law of God, yet they know not God; for they know not My Son, they know not My place, they know not love.

For the ones who choose the lustful pleasures of this world, deceived by Satan, who make not the least effort to break the bondage of his hold, and run headlong to the damning and eternal fires of hell.

For My priest sons, consecrated to My Son, who no longer believe the tradition and truth of the Holy Mother Church of God,

110

Catholics, who have not stood for the truth, but have watched with no word uttered against the abominations committed against My Son.

Who has gone "on record" to defend, speak up, and decry these outright offenses to My Son and their God?

Today, My Son consoles Me, for the moment has come to "behold, all you peoples, the mighty power of God, His holy just anger! His righteous judgments are just!"

Woe to you My children, who did not listen to your Mother. For that which I tried to tell would come is upon you. Prepare those of you who have become lax.

Prepare My beautiful little children who have offered Me, by means of your prayers, those roses I hold; to be led by Me to your protection.

(Personal.) I tell you My child, little sorrowful rose, believe the words of My Son. You have not the time to move. Save your efforts and preparations for the "great move of your life," to My City of Peace, Santa Maria, California.

And now My child, My beautiful little sorrowful rose, I bless your works this day, in the name of My Father, and of My Son, and of the Holy Spirit, My Spouse.

Chapter Three

Where Are My Priests?

Messages From July 15, 1993
To December 29, 1993

Ark of Refuge

July 15, 1993 - 11:54 P.M.

(S.J., I heard a voice and commanded it to go, in the name of Jesus, if not of God.)

Mary: I, your Mother, Queen of Heaven, Queen of all Humanity, Queen of Angels, Mother of Jesus, desire you write these words:

I see your littleness as I do in all My children. And for all My children, I am always at their sides. Oftentimes they have only but to gently call Me, and I am there. Sadly, even those consecrated to Me, do not call, do not reach out for My hand.

These are the ones who, while gathered in a group of prayer cenacle, are so in love with their Mother and the Son; however, once removed from this group prayer, they return to the desires and will of their flesh. These grieve Me so, for I truly desire to be seen to all as the model of submission. I surrendered totally and completely My will to My Father. I am always near, but not always called upon.

My dear children, the time has now arrived when the wills of most will be destroyed and broken. Up to now that choice has been one hoped and prayed for by all the faithful. But see, My little children, the hand of the Father's justice all around you. Listen to Me deep within your souls, I desire to lead you all to the safety of refuge in My Immaculate Heart. Your decision can no longer be put off or you will suffer the painful truth of eternal damnation! You must now decide whom you will serve totally and completely.

Because the punishment will be so severe for this state, the Father has allowed other parts of this nation only to begin to suffer His wrath for their own sins and choices to live oblivious of God's presence in their lives.

Their choices of living only for the material things of this world, as they are finding out, will not stand through the justice of the Father.

My children, My children, pray to discern My messages. But do not continue in your disbelief. As in the days of Noah, there were those predestined, because of the choices made in their lives, to be taken into the ark of refuge.

Today, I am that Ark of Refuge, and all who consecrate themselves to Me will be as secure, through the destruction of evil in this world. In My plan, I have raised the little to give voice to My words, and all who have the faith to believe as little children, believe and trust, will be led. I have raised you, along with 'S.' and others to lead My children.

You must be like Noah and proclaim the wrath of God comes, and all must now decide whom they will believe and serve! To choose not to believe in the mercy and love of God, in My Son, in the Holy Spirit, in the Mother of God, means, My children, you condemn yourselves. For there is nothing unforgivable in the lives of any of My children.

The Time Grows Short

July 15, 1993 - 11:54 P.M.

Mary: Beware of the biggest sin of all, pride, pride not to believe in God's forgiveness. The battle is well under way, My children. My children, run, confess your sins like little children. Pick up the weapon of heaven, your Rosary, and pray all you families! Consecrate yourselves, and I will gather you into the ark of My Immaculate Heart in which there is refuge!

Priest sons and brothers of Jesus, My Son: shake from your feet, your hearts and your minds, the lies of Satan! There is but one church! There is but one truth!

115

Return to the God who gave His only begotten Son as ransom for all humanity! The Son who instituted every sacrament for grace bestowed upon His sheep! They (His children) are in your keeping, do not share in the choice of Judas, to betray the Master, and lead these entrusted to your care to be lost eternally forever.

The messages of My Son were simple. They were truth! They struck as a two-edged sword in the hearts and souls of all who heard. Do not speak lies any longer. Go back to the Gospels, align yourselves once again with the truth spoken by My Son's Vicar on earth!

For quickly, the day comes when all you who, by betrayal, serve Satan, will receive the judgment by the Father. Woe unto you who have not taken your consecration with the duty, love and care of prayer it deserves. Submit to the desire and will of God, instead of the lies of Satan! Repent, cleanse yourselves of your sins and disbelief. Become as little children, consecrate your priesthood to Me, Your Mother, and I will lead you too, along the way of holiness and growth.

The time grows short for you My sons, whom I love so. Listen to the voices of the little. You can no longer hear your God. And now My child, I tell you that as you were told not to be deceived by the calm, know the storm arrives! It is even now at the door.

Trust, speak the words you hear. Those who rage against you, those who do not believe, listen! For not to believe does not mean it is not true. I, your Mother, Queen of Heaven and all Humanity, have been warning for many of your years.

Now I tell you it is here. And I bless all who receive My words into their hearts.

My little sorrowful rose, I desire you get permission from Msgr. 'B.' to distribute this message. Share with 'C.' and 'C.', 'S.' and all those close to you.

116

I bless you, My little sorrowful rose, in all your work this day. Know I protect your children, and you are correct in sparing them the influence of evil that comes from the lies of their father.

Pray more for him; soon My Son will touch him.

(S.J., It is my understanding that we here in California will experience something significantly greater than anything we have seen or ever gone through. God's mercy and love is allowing us to see what is happening all around us, perhaps to make the right choice that Our Lady is referring to.

The choice to repent, turn to God, consecrate to Her Immaculate Heart, you and all your family, that more will be saved for the glory of God's kingdom.

These words come immediately after Our Lady's message and were tested.)

Jesus: I, your God, Lord and Savior, Jesus, behold the words spoken by My Mother.

She dwells in the midst of the Blessed Trinity and She has been given the title Co-Redemptrix of All Humanity. She obtains the distribution of My graces, for it is through My Mother, I wish My children to come.

Listen, My children, to Your Mother. She was My gift to you before I died on the cross.

I came into the world and was held by My Mother, and I held Her tenderly to Myself before I left the world.

You must all come to Me through My Mother.

The hour is late and has been allowed to be so, to usher all those through the door of secure refuge in the Ark of My Mother's Immaculate Heart.

The last have gone though.

117

The rest will be forced to see and feel the justice of God Almighty. After that time, those remaining will also be given the good news of the gospels, thus the last will be first and the first will be last.

You will go forth, My child, as My "herald of truth." Do not fear, for We are with you.

(S.J., then the Lord blessed me, as He does after giving me a message.)

Prepare, Daughter, Prepare

July 26, 1993 - 4:40 P.M.

Mary: My daughter, My daughter, would you not listen to the voice of your Mother?

(S.J., I had been invited to go out of town with my daughter for a weekend. Our Lord had once already said to me, "I ask you, My daughter, not to go;" to which I did not want to pay attention. I tested and Mary continued.)

Mary: I, your Mother, and the Mother of Jesus who is praised and glorified, ask you, My daughter to listen to the voice of your Mother.

Has not the Father spoken words of comfort to you?

I come to ask you to not get distracted by the diversions of man, but rather remain focused entirely on your Mother, your God, your call. I ask you not to go with your daughter. I ask for your total cooperation in prayer, fasting and even in living your life in isolation as you have.

Yes, He is holy, He is mighty, He is wonderful, and He is sorrowing at that which must happen.

(S.J., I had said, "If this is not of God I command in the mighty, holy, wonderful name of Jesus begone!")

Mary: I ask you to remain totally focused. Do not be concerned. That which awaits you first is God's word fulfilled.

"Before the great punishment," you will see, all will see, everything come to pass. Prepare, daughter, prepare.

These are not times to spend in frivolity. Offer Me everything on the altar of your life in solitude, for it is over. Your hiddeness is over. You must be brave and go forth as your Lord's "herald of truth".

(S.J., at this point my children called.)

Mary: "Go tend to your children, we will continue later."

I Am the Mother of All

July 29, 1993 - 5:15 P.M.

(S.J., I heard a voice and I tested.)

Mary: My dear child, am I not your Mother who has guided you along the path the Father would have you walk? Praise My Son Jesus! Was I not your "Angel of Consolation" in your fear and heartache?

Do you not know the enemy, My adversary, rages intensely against you? This is because of your submission to the will of the Father. This is because of your great love for souls that is drawing you deep into the depths of Our hearts.

But I tell you, little sorrowful rose, he, the enemy, is defeated! Look how I warn you of this and other traps he lays for you. You alone are nothing, but because of your yes, We become your all.

These are moments of intense preparation daughter. Take not your eyes off your source, your vindicator and your deliverer. Jesus is all these things to you.

(S.J., I am drawn by the fragrance of a crimson red rose on my dining table. A moment later Our Lady asks me to look at the rose.)

119

Mary: See the crimson red color of My rose. The color, symbolizes the Precious Blood of My Most Beloved Son shed for all humanity. There is a fragrance so sweet that emanates from My rose, the fragrance of all holiness, the fragrance of graces bestowed, the fragrance of love and peace.

When one desires to pick one (rose) to smell its fragrance, oftentimes they are pricked by the small thorns. Sometimes these thorns cause the most intense pain. They would almost crush the desire of holding and smelling and drawing close to the beauty, (of the rose).

The thorns of sins do not have to be big to feel the pain. These are the pains of My children, their thorns of sin. But to those who persevere, remove the thorns first from their fingers, then from the stem, will at last, enjoy the fragrance of peace and of holiness.

The stem is their (My children's) life.

At times My children remove the sin from their souls, but do not remove it from their life. Consequently they wonder why they always fall into that same sin. Many times children by themselves cannot remove the thorns. But then comes their Mother, who will pull the thorns and clean the wound, hold them and kiss them. Then, the Mother with the child, will cut the rose, clean the stem and give the child the rose they wanted.

This is My role. I am your Mother. I am the Mother of all. I will draw you to the fragrance and lead you to the Precious Blood of My Son, who will clothe you with holiness. And you will know love. And you will know peace. This has been given to Me to obtain whatever is needed to pull the thorn of sin from My children's lives.

(S.J., At this point Our Lady's voice changed and became very old sounding. Like Our Lady of Sorrow's picture, where she looks very worn because of all the sorrow She feels.)

Mary: I tire, I tire, I tire. To you My sweet little sorrowful rose has been given the grace to console Your Mother, to share with

120

Me My sorrow. You pour gentle balm on the wounds of My Son. Do not despair. Only look forward to your Mother. I am guiding and leading you.

My adversary, who rages against you is defeated.

Trust your God.

Trust your Savior.

Receive the power of His Holy Spirit, which will move you in the direction you should go.

I tire. Try daughter, as much as you can, pray, offer reparation, fast.

I tell you, My child, be expectant on the 1st of August. Look to the anniversary of Our first conversation. There will be abundant graces and blessing bestowed upon you.

I bless you and tell you soon you will go forth.

In the omnipotent name of God and of My Son and of My Spouse the Holy Spirit, you are blessed.

The Blood of the Innocents

August 11, 1993 - 12:30 P.M.

(S.J., I had an early appointment this morning. At 11:30 A.M., on the way, I pray the Rosary with my two children. On the way home, I hear the voice of the Father, which is distinctly different from those of Jesus or Our Lady. It is very majestic and forceful, yet loving.)

God the Father: Sadie?

(S.J., after I hear my name, I test, then He continues:)

God the Father: I call your name, I, God Omnipotent, who gave My only begotten Son, Jesus as ransom to be praised!

My little one, do not fear, I call you by name, I call you to lead My people. If you are not known, it is because you have not reached your appointed time. There is an appointed time for all, for everything.

But I, the great I Am, call you to greatness in My Kingdom. None of My chosen can glory in themselves, only I am glorified, and when I am glorified, My Son Jesus is glorified. This glory is preceded by My Spirit, for it is My Spirit, the Spirit of the living God that calls My Children...

> First to repentance and sorrow....
> then to purification and expiation.....
> then on to the glory brought by
> the redemptive suffering
> for more of My souls......
> created by Me.....
> to be loved by Me.....
> to be filled with Me.....
> to be moved by Me.........

but, I cannot withhold My justice which will fall in recompense for all these who offend Me greatly!

You who live with no thought or thanks for your God, for your life, your day, your blessings; who have allowed the proud one to close your hearts, eyes and ears to the call of your God. I have allowed My daughter to plead, to plead, to plead for them. (Referring to Our Lady.)

I have allowed Her to manifest signs and wonders as Her credentials for being sent by God! To no avail!

Now, My daughter, you will lead My small faithful according to My plan. Do not be fearful or doubt. There will be many signs given.

(S.J., I asked, "Soon, My Father?")

God the Father: Soon. Be vigilant. Be prepared. Be prayerful. Be not concerned for your own situation, each day will be taken care of by Me, your Abba.

You are called. Be obedient, remain humble. Humble yourself even more. The time of all times continues. There will be more storms. There will be cosmic phenomena. There will be confusion.

I will show Mr. Clinton there is a living God!

For his answers for this nation once blessed by Me, there will be more disasters. I will avenge the blood of the innocents for which he and all who follow him have no regard. (Aborted babies.)

Each victory (of Clinton's government) will be followed by My justice!

Gather all you people of God, led by My Immaculate Daughter (Our Lady). Take refuge in Her Heart. Consecrate yourselves to Her.

She leads all to the very depths of My Son's heart.

Together They will triumph!

I have decreed this!

Behold My daughter, I bless you in the power of My Spirit, and in the name of My Son. I am your Father.

The Time of Suffering Increases

August 26, 1993 - 9:30 A.M.

(S.J., My children have just left with their father to go to the fair. I have been in extreme turmoil, from attacks of doubt and not responding to the calls of the Lord or Our Lady. My eyelids are heavy and puffy from crying. I say a prayer asking God what He wants of me. I lay on the couch to rest and contemplate. I am looking out my front living room window, and looking up at the second story of this apartment, I hear the following:)

123

Jesus: The angels of the Lord will hold up this apartment as a testimony to the servant of the Lord. Yes, My daughter, it is I, your Lord, Jesus the Christ who is praised. You have been running from Me, but where can you go? Did you not hear the word of the Lord that, if you go up, He is there; if you go down, He is there? Where can you go to hide from Me? But I have given you a contrite and obedient spirit, and you understand whose voice you hear. Indeed I have arranged the time to be spent with Me.

You come into the silence of your heart and you will not allow any other thing to fill your day; for you know that I am the Good Shepherd and My sheep hear My voice, they know My voice. I am leading and guiding you along the way the Father would have you walk.

I understand your pain and sorrow. I have felt the same pain and sorrow magnified many times. In your prayer you asked not to look at or feel your own pain, but to see and feel mine. Then you would forget your pain and sorrow. But all is coming to pass as the Father would have it. What you look at as **delay** is only mercy for many of My children who otherwise would not have the opportunity to hear the message of repentance, mercy, love, and now, impending justice of the Father.

For all My chosen, the time of suffering increases; for they are the ones who are bringing many who otherwise would not be granted the graces of that opportunity. Many do not understand the meaning of redemptive suffering, and indeed, if they are not close to My body and My Blood, will never have an understanding.

I ask for your contemplative prayer and life. I ask you to continue even when you feel it is for nought. You will never understand the glory of God's work. All I ask is that you continue. I ask this from all My children. I ask that they not look to the left nor to the right, but keep their eyes on Me.

124

I am the Good Shepherd, who has come for His sheep. Lead all to the consecration of My Holy Mother, She leads all to Me. There can be no other way. Some, out of stubbornness and pride, will not heed the messages and warnings being given all over the world. This is their own condemnation. When they stand before Me, it will not be Me who condemns them, but their own actions, or lack of them.

I, the Great I Am, tell you to be at peace. Do not fear. Do not doubt. How many times must I tell you this? Be firm and steadfast, for when the time comes, all will be fulfilled. Be at peace and pray. Meditate on My passion. Go now, we will continue later.

Peace and blessings descend upon you.

My Herald of Truth

September 6, 1993

(S.J., I heard a voice and I tested. Jesus answered.)

Jesus: My child, I am your Lord, your God, your Jesus whose name is praised in heaven, on earth, and under the earth! Yes, the saints in heaven and the holy angels assist you in your daily walk with Me.

My child, I come to ask you once again to give Me your life as one of My beloved victim souls. Do you give Me your yes?

(S.J., Oh yes, Lord, forgive me my sweet Jesus, for faltering. For questioning the way My God would have me walk. Yes Lord, be it done to me according to your will. I believe Lord, help thou my unbelief.)

Jesus: No one is to know the merits of your suffering; of your giving your will over to the Divine. In your anonymity, you are assisting in the redemptive sufferings which are then turned into the salvation of many of My souls who otherwise would be lost eternally.

125

This time is coming to an end, the time of your anonymity. You have been prepared, you have been taught, and it will continue, but now you will go forth as My herald of truth.

The words you speak, will not be your own, they will be Mine. When they persecute you, fear not; for to whomever will follow Me so too will suffer the same treatment. As I was humiliated, as I was persecuted, as I was accused, I suffered all in silence, so too must My followers.

By meditating on My passion, My agony, My crucifixion, you and others, realize your sufferings fall short of what I suffered. But you share in the same glory of My life offered as the perfect offering for the redeeming of many when you unite your life, your will, your sufferings to Me.

Tell My children they must do this daily. Daily give Me your yes! Daily give Me your wills! Daily give Me the little you have to offer. It is not for you to understand fully the redeeming Glory of God's work! These are the days of great distress, they come upon My children as a thief. Unless My children of light do all I ask, they will falter, they will be deceived, they will fall.

My children, pray and unite in love. Do not judge what is happening with the next person, pray and love; these show they are Mine! Consecrate My children, to the Mother of All Humanity! The Queen of Heaven, Mediatrix of All Graces, Co-Redemptrix of all humanity. My Mother's triumph arrives!

Pray especially for My priests, child.

Do not worry about what is to happen, I your Lord God, solemnly tell you. Hold your heads high, lift your drooping hearts, your deliverance draws near and I, your God, will be in the midst of My people.

I will lead. I will protect. I will console. The time of all times continues. Woe to My children who have failed to heed the messages of preparation, of warnings. For to them the days ahead will fall as the thief in the dark. Only with much difficulty will they persevere, for the time of their visitation they knew not!

As the pharisees and scribes burned with envy towards the Prince of Peace and in the end, suffered the supreme price for obstinacy of heart, eternal damnation; so will My children know the error of their ways and know terror in their hearts.

I have spoken, I, the Great I Am, the Alpha and Omega, say all this is true.

My Mother arrives (to speak to you).

(S.J., I test the voice and Our Lady answers.)

Mary: I am the Queen of Heaven, ever virgin, born without the stain of original sin!

Yes, My little sorrowful rose, how I have prayed for all My children, with My children of light who respond to the requests of the Mother of all humanity!

The purification continues and will intensify. I adjure you to get and remain prepared, do not be lax. God the Father has been merciful to honor the request of the Mother.

Why are My children so blinded? They have eyes, but cannot see! They have ears but cannot hear! They have hearts but do not love. Their Mother, their God the Father, My Son, the Holy Spirit, My chosen, but indeed the time is here when all spoken will be fulfilled.

It will catch many off guard, unaware of the severity of this time, and at that moment they will know the truth and the Way. Only with great difficulty will they be able to manage the days of distress.

Be not afraid, My little sorrowful rose, I am with you and will always be.

127

Have faith, My children of light.

I am protecting you and I bless you in the name of the Father, My Son and My Spouse, the Holy Spirit.

Pray For My Beloved Priest Sons

September 9, 1993

(S.J., I heard a voice and I tested.)

Mary: I, your Mother and the Mother of Jesus, praise His Holy Name.

Yes, My little sorrowful rose, you must begin to look beyond the meaning of this event about to unfold. This earthquake will be significant in the occurrences that are to be. But there is so much more that is going to happen, pray My little sorrowful rose, that My Spouse, the Holy Spirit enlighten you.

I, who have come to give evidence of My place and My presence have been met with apathy and indifference. They (My children), come looking for a sign and not the Son; for miracles and healings and not the healer!

These hearts of My children do not soften to the promptings of The Holy Spirit. My presence and graces preclude those that still wait to be given.

The fire of conversion has been lit by My Beloved Spouse, the Holy Spirit, and will fill the entire world with His power and presence.

Pray, little daughter of Mine, for My beloved priest sons. Invoke the aid of My priest saints to help you; they await your prayers and request.

There is much work to do and so little time left.

Let the fragrance of Divine love emanate from your very being. The fragrance of holiness, of sanctity, of love is so pleasing to the celestial court.

(Personal message omitted here.)

Pray child for the many who will die. Pray they live and die in a state of grace.

This state will lie in ruins and only those places chosen as places of refuge will be places of protection. I am saddened that these events must now unfold. All could have been averted through the response to prayer, conversion, repentance and reparation.

Do not be fearful little one, for there yet remains, after the painful purification, the glory of being received by My Son's triumphant return!

(S.J. At this point my children needed tending, to which Our Lady said.)

Mary: Tend to your little ones, child. We will continue later. The work increases; the time of your rest is over. Remain in the peace of My heart and in the heart of My Son. **We Are One!**

Pray and Fast

September 13, 1993 - 8:48 A.M.

(S.J., I heard a voice and I tested.)

Jesus: But it is I, the Messiah, sent by God the Father, Jesus, His Son, whose name is praised!

Write little daughter of Mine, My words, the Great I AM.

(S.J., I had been watching the signing of the Middle East Peace accord, when I heard Our Lord say, "See the heads of these nations, they deal with deceit in their hearts.")

Jesus: See the heads of all these nations gather, even that one (Israel) chosen by My Father to make His covenant.

They glory in man's way, they do not acknowledge the Prince of Peace. They do not believe without the Son, the Father and the Spirit, there can be no peace. I will bring upon the leaders of these nations the wrath of God!

They who glory in themselves, who do not remember the ways of their ancestors long ago who gave thanks to their God. No, they will see and know what strikes them, will be God's wrath!

I tell you, My child, this day will dim during the coming days and they will be left in the darkness of their error. And all who do not acknowledge Me as the Lord and Savior of all, will know the most frightening terror in their hearts.

Pray and fast, little one, for My ways cannot be comprehended without the soul strengthening that come from fasting! I leave you My peace and bless your efforts this day in The Name of My Father, My Name and the name of My Spirit.

Messages of Preparation

September 20, 1993 - 9:00 A.M.

(S.J., I heard a voice and I tested.)

Mary: I am your Mother, Ever Virgin, born without sin. With you I praise the name of My Son Jesus!

My child, do not despair at your failures, at your shortcomings. Do not look at the way others before you have been used, for to each of My children called, the way to holiness is distinctly different.

(S.J., After reading several books lately on different saints, I was despairing that how could I have ever thought that I could be used.)

130

Mary: It is in spite of your weaknesses that you are used. It is because I have become your all, and through that, you give Me permission to enter the depths of your heart, whereupon I can lead you to a deeper relationship with My Son. Because you permit us, for We are one, to enter; We are able to mold you more to the likeness of My beloved Son Jesus! And no one can know the Father except through Him, and finally the Holy Spirit becomes a reality through which the power of God can spiritually strengthen His children.

My little sorrowful rose, tell My children do not try to understand My messages by what has always been, for what has always been is no longer, and in an instant all the signs can be made manifest. There are great days of distress ahead and only those who have heeded the messages of preparations and especially of prayer will survive.

My children, pray harder for My priests. They are to have a much stricter accounting because they will have led so many of the faithful astray. Put your faith in no man, but upon the Spirit of Truth, the Word of God. The faith and truth of tradition handed down through the ages by the visible head of the church on earth, My Son's Vicar.

Woe, Woe, Triple Woe, to My priests, bishops and cardinals. They will be cast eternally to the flames of hell for their lies, deceit, and love of materialism. Let the priests bring back devotions, devotions cast aside long ago; then see the blessings that will be loosed in heaven. They (priests) forget their duties each wanting the esteem of man rather than God. Time quickly runs out child. There is no one to pray and offer reparation for My priests.

The Holy Father, My beloved John Paul II, yet a little while, then he will be brought home. He suffers greatly at the hands of the wolves in sheep's clothing. There is **no more time**. There is **no**

131

more time. There is **no more time**. Prepare the messages. Pray. Continue your fasting. We will continue later.

I bless you little sorrowful rose in the name of My Father, My Son Jesus and My Spouse, the Holy Spirit. Amen.

September 29, 1993 - 9:30 A.M.

(S.J., I heard a voice and I tested.)

Mary: My little sorrowful rose: I ask you to come into the silence of your heart, that you may hear the words of your Mother. Praise Jesus!

Very soon now this day of destruction will be upon My children. Press the cross of My Son deep into your hearts and unite the sufferings that are coming to His on Calvary. Many events will simultaneously happen. They will begin in the East.

(S.J., I had arrived to do some work at school, Our Lady said to go; we would continue later. Next day, at the same time I began to hear Her and I tested. She continued.)

Days of Trial Are Upon You

September 30, 1993 - 9:30 A.M.

Mary: Do not fight against the Spirit of God, but submit. Remain open to receive heaven's words at all times. Pray for My poor children who continue in their indifference to all that is happening around them. Now the days of trial are upon you.

Pray My dear children! Pray with Me for the many who have chosen to disregard heaven's warnings!

My children are so loved, yet very few return that love. Come inwardly, My children, separate from the things and persons that keep you from hearing us. We wait longingly to hear you speak, so that then We may answer and love and guide. Come to Me and I will lead you to My Son. And He gives life to whose who ask, and He refreshes those who ask, and He strengthens those who ask.

He is the source of life-giving waters! Drink your fill, all My children who thirst! He will quench your thirst of holiness. And you shall know the truth. And the truth shall set you free. Those who seek, they shall find. Take heed of My words and warnings. The signs are all coming to the eclipse.

(Definition of eclipse used in this context: cutting off of light.)

Pray Children! Prepare! Love! Fast!

Do all in the name above all names: Jesus, and this will gain merit; merit and souls through His most perfect sacrifice of calvary.

Love and peace are our gifts to all. We bless in the name of the Father, My Son and My Spouse, the Holy Spirit.

Amen. Amen.

Day of Destruction Gets Nearer

October 2, 1993 - 3:00 A.M.

(S.J., I heard a voice and I tested.)

Jesus: An understanding will be given to all who have sought to follow Me. It will be clear. It will lead. As the day of destruction gets nearer, all My children of light, I your Lord God and Savior, Jesus give this assurance to all those who are mine.

They are the ones who read the messages and believed; who accepted like little children these warnings and messages of love. I tell you, My daughter, this day looms on the horizon. You must all prepare practically.

(S.J., "Materials, Lord?")

Jesus: Yes, as much as you can. The rest will be done divinely with love.

Take heed, see what has happened by the first blow of justice (India). Those numbers are small in comparison to the magnitude of loss of life here in California. Know these places of refuge will be spared the fears that are being spoken of.

(S.J., Decomposing of mass number of bodies, cholera, disease, water problems etc.)

Jesus: Pray, daughter, pray. You and all My children who have responded are much loved and kept in the hearts of My Mother and Myself.

(S.J., Here Sadie drew two hearts, one overlapping the other, without any thought in the original dictation, but to repeat the drawing a second time was difficult.)

Jesus: See how they overlap and are in actuality one. (Referring to the two hearts.) She has worked tirelessly to warn. **Woe** to those who have dismissed Her warnings!

Pray, Child.

I leave and give you My blessings, Father, Son and Holy Spirit.

(S.J., I begin to pray the Rosary, and in the third decade, Our Lady comes. I tested, "In whose name do you come?")

Mary: I am the Mother of Jesus! Praise His Holy Name!

The Cross of Peace project will bring together many of My children of light. They will be needed to help minister to God's people who have escaped from unbelief to belief.

Many of My children will settle in My valley where I have shown My presence for these years. Eventually a religious community will evolve from the gathering of so many of My

children. **There will be peace. There will be love. There will be harmony.**

C. and C. have worked diligently for this "labor of love". They will see the fruits of their love and labor. Soon you will be brought together.

(S.J., I continued to pray the Rosary, for I felt that since Our Lady had not given me Her blessing, She wanted me to continue praying. As I was praying I thought about a certain priest. I then heard Her say:)

Mary: Do not worry about him. He is being purified. He will be brought back and will shine and bring much glory to God. He along with other (priests) are being placed.

Tell My children I love them and am leading them. Pray, that is all I ask. Pray. Fast.

Peace and blessing of My Father, Son and Holy Spirit.

Community Centered Around Your Eucharistic Lord

October 12, 1993 - 8:15 A.M.

(S.J., I heard a voice and I tested.)

Mary: Yes, My little sorrowful rose, you are correct in understanding the meaning of My messages, messengers, apparitions, and love.

Yes, I am the Queen of Heaven and, with you, I praise My Son's Holy Name and bow down to worship the Father and through My intercession, send forth My Spouse the Holy Spirit.

Yes, I have and continue to try to reach My children, My children who don't want Me or will not listen to Me, so that My children can understand My love.

135

As a mother sometimes your own children say the most hurtful and hateful things to their mother. This causes great tears of agony and pain, but it does not stop the love.

So it is with Me. No matter who you are, no matter what you are, no matter what you have done, no matter what you have said, I love you, with the unconditional love of a Mother, the Mother of God. . .

God who also loves you unconditionally, who loved you so much, that His Only Son willed to be born of a woman ever virgin, born without the stain of original sin, who became One with Him through His conception, birth, life, death and resurrection.

What the Son feels, the Mother feels, and what the Mother feels, the Son feels. We are One. He knows My pain and I know His.

It is for His lost children. It is for His shepherds on earth, who are leading the flock to mass destruction. Destruction of their faith, destruction of their morals, destruction of their lives, destruction of their eternal life.

So you understand the tears of agony of your Mother. Pray My children. The time quickly approaches. Love and Peace descend upon all here today.

I bless them all, in the name of My Father, the name of My Son, the name of My Spouse, The Holy Spirit.

Jesus: Let Me interpret the vision. It is a community centered around your Eucharistic Lord, with great devotion to My Mother. You will serve one another, and you will be clothed in the purity of holiness that comes from centering life around Me, the source of all life. The familiar things you saw and feel comfortable with, means it will be your home.

I Am Your Jesus, Your Lord.
I Am Your Jesus Who Is Praised.
I Wish To Reign In The Hearts Of All.

136

Write what you saw in the vision.

Write My words.

Amen, Amen I Say To You, It Shall Be.

Vision

(S.J., I was praying and had the following vision: I could see this very long banquet table with many people sitting around it. I was (as everyone was), dressed in a long, white gown. I was serving it seemed, pouring a liquid into glasses. Everyone had a feeling of warmth, love, happiness, something almost not in this world. I turned and could see at the end of the room through a doorway, Our Lord standing; and sitting off to one side, Our Lady. Around them were many more people.

I saw items that I have always wanted to have as a home. It has been my dream to have an old-fashioned home with a long porch, double hung windows with lace curtains, and especially a large old-fashioned kitchen. I saw all these things in this vision. But I did not understand what it meant. This vision was given to me about three weeks ago.)

You Will See Your Country In Ruins

October 19, 1993 - 5:20 P.M.

(S.J., I heard a voice and I tested.)

Jesus: I come in the name of the great I Am, Your Lord and Savior Jesus the Christ, whose name is praised! I tell you My child, the great schism spoken about is upon My children. My sheep will scatter and be hard-pressed to find a church that still has one of My consecrated sons true to his consecration, true to the faith handed down through the ages.

You (traditional believers and followers of Our Lady) will be ostracized and held in ridicule by most. They will no longer hold back many of their abominations. For this reason, My

137

Father's hand will fall and His justice will be mercy for My children, My flock.

Your deliverance is near, but a little while and I will be with you. You will gather and know, My remnant flock, there will be a few of My priests who will gather My sheep. Behold they strike and My sheep scatter. But there is no snatching from My hand what My Father has given to Me.

Those who stand against Me will be lost in the slaughter. For it is not the strongest, or mightiest, or the wealthiest, or most well-known who will stand. No, it is the ones chosen by God, My Father—those who do His Will who will stand. They will know His protection. Look to My holy word and know this is true.

My small flock, be prepared, you do not know all that is about to fall upon mankind, fall on what remains of My Church. The blows of My hand will move the very bowels of the earth! Woe to mankind! You cannot stand in the slime of your filth any longer.

My innocents annihilated before any chance of life! The perversion of man's wanton desires! My religious have become the cesspools of iniquity! No, it will not be without their just reward,

The Justice Of God, Omnipotent And Mighty!

He created all things good, and good there are, but only a few. For you, My little flock, will walk and be led, and you will see a thousand fall on one side and ten thousand on your other, yet on you will be My protection!

You will be prepared to live in Eucharistic communities. For you will see your country in ruins: economic ruin: civil unrest, threats of attack by foreign nations and natural disasters. It will be very difficult for those who believe they can stay behind. (Once communities begin forming.)

138

Be warned, prayerful and alert. Pray. My peace to My children, in the name of My Father, in the name of My Son, in the name of My Spirit, holy and just.

Pope John Paul II

November 5, 1993

(S.J., I have been praying, for it has been relatively quiet, and have not received any messages for a while. It is the first Friday, November 5, 1993. During the Holy Mass, as I prepare to receive Communion, I see the following vision: I see a wide winding road on which there is massive procession of cardinals, bishops and priests. I know by their headpieces, the mitre cap, red cap and priest's stole.

Then I see a very small rocky path going up a hill. I see the **Holy Father, John Paul II**, with a cross on his back. He has fallen and I see as if the picture frame is frozen. He is about to get up and proceed, and he is almost at the summit of the hill. There are very few cardinals, bishops and priests following him.)

Where Are My Priests?

November 8, 1993 - 11:00 A.M.

(S.J., I heard a voice and I tested.)

Jesus: I am the great I Am, the Lord and Savior of the world and soon just judge.

The gospel of the Lord does, indeed, preach "good news", reconciliation, and peace. But it is also a two-edged sword that will cut and separate. The gospel proclaimed uncompromised will pierce to the soul by the convicting power of My Spirit.

139

Where are My priests, to stand and take back and bring order to My church? They must begin to teach the true tradition of teaching in regards to My Sacrifice in the Holy Mass. There must be reverence! I am King!

There must be modesty. My Mother is the epitome of purity and modesty. She teaches by Her example. I am King!

My priests must not turn over their duties to lay persons in regards to My Sacrifice in the Holy Mass. To their consecrated hands I have given this privilege! I am King!

I tell you through certain movements the most abuses are incurred, for they wish to place the women of the Lord in the place that was intended for none. (Women that is.)

This is not to lower My love or their place, but to give the worship instituted long ago, to the priests of the Lord, consecrated and set apart to pray for My people. My Mother who brought Me to the world and who today is still bringing My children back to Me was, and would be, the first to teach this. Where are My priests? I am King!

There must now be a movement of traditional teaching for My children. Do all, My children, to teach by example, that which has been revealed to you for: I am King, And soon will return to separate the sheep from the goats!

Where are My priests?

Be vocal, be strong, though you may have to undergo persecution. For but a little while and My vicar approaches His calvary.

(S.J. In regards to the November 5th vision.)

For soon I lay on this nation and others the blows of My justice! My people, hearken to the pleas of your God and My Mother! The remnant church will be built from those who will follow only the truth. They will be few.

My child, I tell you to tell 'C.' and 'C.' to prepare, prepare for all that has been told. Preparations for the gathering must go ahead. Do not be concerned about time and when. The gathering will be as it is to be. My people must be taught, My people must be told.

Amen, Amen I say to you, it shall be! Peace and blessing descend upon all of My children of light.

(S.J., I wish to explain in the message, Our Lord calls the women, "the women of the Lord" recognizing their love for Him and desire to serve Him. However, He is very clear in making statements that this is not the place for feminists who insist on their place on the sides of the altar.

Prior to this message I was instructed to read the book of Deuteronomy on the first day of November. Moses is instructed to proclaim to all of Israel the commandments of the Lord and the manner in which they will serve him.

He is instructed to tell the people over and over, "teach this to your children and your children's children". He is then instructed to proclaim the blessings and the curses on God's people, for following the Lord, or sinning against Him.

People of God listen to the cries of your God through this message. He is proclaiming that He is King! He is proclaiming that He is about to lay on this land His just punishments. The word of God says, the world's way and God's way are at odds. They do not mix. They are like water and oil.

There are a few who will be touched by what they hear. Others will scoff. So be it. I pray if you do not believe the words spoken to me, perhaps then someone else. We are running out of time.)

Remain In Prayer

November 10, 1993 - 9:30 A.M.

(S.J., I heard a voice and I tested.)

Jesus: My child, I tell you, I am with you and soon will take you as My bride. Will you be all mine?

(S.J., Yes Lord, your know my heart, you are always foremost in my heart.)

Jesus: Peace

(S.J., Our Lady comes and I test. She answers:)

Mary: My daughter, My little sorrowful rose, I, the Mother of Jesus, Counselor of the Afflicted, tell you do not despair. I am with your son 'R.' and in the coming days will surround him even more with My presence. Believe and stand fast for him and all your family.

Soon My Son will take you as His bride. Hold nothing back from Him now. The Father lays His hand heavy upon you and soon all will see, for He send signs as your credentials as being sent by God.

Remain in prayer for it is not important to go here or there, but always be in a state of prayer as you unite your day and actions to Me and My son. Your whole day becomes a prayer.

Father C. prepares to come home, and home he will stay.

You would do well to take your trays (t.v.) they will serve you well. Do not worry about clothes, you have prepared well there.

(S.J., this is in response to my going about wondering what else I should take when the time comes, I was cleaning and packing things over.)

Mary: You will soon have a new home and will be about the work of My Son. I love you, My little sorrowful rose, as I do all My children. C. and C. soon will see the fruit of many prayers.

142

But the work will increase. My little links in the great master plan will be brought together, and together We will prepare to receive My Son's coming in glory!

(S.J., I heard a voice and tested and Our Lady answered:)

Mary: But, child, I dwell in the midst of God!

The cross will be made manifest for now and all eternity, the signs granted by Me, through Me and with Me.

By My pleas the Godhead has heard the cries of the Mother entrusted to the world by the Son on Calvary;

Through Me: I have been the Mediatrix between My Son and men and bestow all graces:

And with Me: for I pray, plead and cry with My children. You know My great love for you as evidenced last night.

I will always be with you, and the enemy rages for you speak the words of God. Remember, daughter, he is defeated. Offer all to Me as you do, pray and fast. And I bless you today in a special way, In the name of the Father and the Son, and the Holy Spirit.

Amen.

WOE, WOE, WOE, TO YOU MY PRIESTS

November 16, 1993 - 11:30 A.M.

(S.J. At the M.M.P. cenacle prayer group, towards the end of the Rosary, I see a vision. It is an angel. He is on a black horse and he himself is dressed in black. He looks fearsome and large. I don't understand this vision, and so I pray for discernment.

The next thing I see is the **Holy Father, Pope John II** at a window, much like the one that he stands at when he is blessing the crowds at St. Peter's. He is standing at this window looking upwards and he is holding onto a sword that is impaled into his chest. I don't understand this vision either and have been praying for discernment.)

(S.J. I hear a voice and commanded it to go, in the name of Jesus, if not of God.)

Jesus: I, your Lord God, interpret the vision for you, My daughter. I am Jesus who is praised!

You see before you the Angel of Death about to go forth and at My command will slay all evildoers. There is still but a short time for My mercy to fall, but very little. I am King and yet My priests make a mockery of the Alpha and Omega! My people chose to follow those who tickle their ears, so be it.

For the sake of the just, I will deliver My people, My chosen few. I will shake the very foundation of My Church! My priests will know the error of their ways, and the souls of their flocks, the blood shall be on their hands! They think the God of all does not see every abomination they allow and participate in!

My flock has scattered and will continue to do so until that time when My Eucharistic Communities are formed and God is truly worshiped as He intended from the beginning of all ages. Woe, Woe, Woe, to you My priests. You give Me the kiss of Judas and betray Me!

For this reason, My little victim, I grace you with suffering, that you and others may save these souls of My priests, of My children, of all called to salvation. Pray for My faithful priests, that they may be strengthened, and remain solid as rock.

The vision of My vicar, John Paul II, he stands holding onto the Word of God, the two edged sword! He will die to defend this Word! This Word that has been since the beginning with God, in the presence of God, and made incarnate, Word dwelt among men through the fiat of the purest lily of heaven, My Mother, the Virgin, humble servant of God.

Hold fast, My children of the light, that you may recognize the hour of your deliverance, for it draws near.

The blows of My hand will deliver justice and all will know the mighty hand of God. Many though, will remain obstinate and persist in their belief. The evil one in this world has permeated them with their belief in "mother nature", "sciences" and the belief that man is his own deity and can control and manage through the disasters being made manifest through My hand! Now Woe, Woe, Woe, to you men hardened of heart.

The signs have been given, more intensely than any other time, and yet you persist in your disbelief! My Mother pleads for all Her children, images cry tears and tears of blood. This is not only to bring her children into the truth, but to warn and protect them, to counsel them to remain in Her Immaculate Heart through consecration, that She may oversee their protection.

For the time of all times is here and yet they scoff. They say My prophets are carriers of doomsday predictions; for they do not want to give up the ways of the world. They want to continue in their sins, for who is there to call sin, a sin anymore?

None from the greatest to the least want to acknowledge their sin, and that now is the time to turn to their God! My house lies in ruins and there is no one to be disturbed and cry.

I cry.

But soon My appearance will cause all men to fall on their knees and beat their breasts and lament. But My angels have their orders and know the ones with the seal of My Mother, and the mark of the beast.

Pray, My little victim, pray and continue to offer Me all you are, and all My children who unite with Me. You soothe My wounded heart and comfort My agony once again.

Share with those who are to be shared with.

145

Peace and blessing fall upon you and all My children.

(S.J., just an added note of the vision of John Paul II. The sword is not just an ordinary sword, but a very ornate and gilded sword made of gold. The Holy Father himself is dressed in white vestments trimmed in gold.)

People of God, you serve a royal King. If we built a temple, (church) with all the precious metals and stones contained in this world, it would still not be worthy of who Jesus is!

The King who died for all of us and reigns in heaven and who will shortly reign here on earth. He is King. Pay Him homage that is due to Him. And give Him the temple of your heart, it is there He wants to dwell.)

The Great Sign

December 5, 1993 - 6:00 P.M.

Jesus: Little daughter of My Heart! Would you be in silence with your God?

(S.J., I turn off the radio as I had been listening to Christian music, soft music.)

Jesus: I am Your Redeemer, your Savior, the lover of your soul. To Me and Me alone you abandon your thoughts, words and actions. Because of your great trust in My mercy you receive great graces.

(S.J., a personal message.)

Jesus: I have spoken, Amen.

Soon all is to be fulfilled, the signs and great sign are about to be revealed. From one end of this earth to the other, My children will know there is a God who loves them, and chooses to deliver them from the evil in this present age. There will be no other signs after the ones spoken of down through the ages.

146

Let all who would believe, believe now, while there is yet mercy. Let them approach the fountain of life-giving water that they may be sealed with the seal of great protection. This seal can only be placed by, and through, the mediation of My Most Holy Mother. She dispenses all graces, for God's children are all Her children.

Soon the time of darkness approaches. Let those who are strong console and encourage the weak. Prepare for the glorious reign of the Immaculate Heart of Mary's triumph and the reign of the Sacred Eucharistic Heart of Jesus!

Eli, Eli, lema sabacthani.

(S.J., Our Lord led me to the book of Matthew chapter 27: 46, for these words are the words I heard. I understand Our Lord himself to be crying out these words in regards to His children, i.e. "Why have you, in gospel forsaken Me?")

Do not forsake Me any longer My children! Nor My priests. Dare they dip of the same bowl as Judas? Then they will reap the same consequences!

You, My little daughter of My Heart, and My children must see My wounded face and My pierced heart in all and My prayer must always be on your lips and hearts,

"Father forgive them for they know not what they do."

Doors are opened only I can open and shut, only I can shut, for My Father's Glory.

Pray and be at peace! I lay My hand heavy upon you and bless you.

Love is Jesus, and I love you.

Soon My Times of Apparitions Will Be Over

December 9, 1993 - 10:05 A.M.

(S.J., I heard a voice and tested, it was our Lady.)

Mary: Behold, My little daughter, My little sorrowful rose.

For the moment your joy replaces your sorrow. Do not fret or worry about what is to be. That you submit your will to the Heavenly Father is all that is required.

Pray My Immaculate Conception.

(S.J., here Our Lady told me to read the latest message entered for the day of the Immaculate Conception in Father Gobbi's book for the cenacle.)

Mary: The gift of heaven, I am. To the Father's will I said, "I Will?" To My Son's plea, behold thy Son, I said, "I Do."

I do behold the beloved of the Lord at the foot of the cross and all My children near the cross today. And I go searching for those far from the cross. Ponder what I say child. I go searching for the lost as My most beloved Son did. So many do not realize the wonder of this gift.

I am totally pure, conceived without the stain of original sin, so that I could encompass the Diving Man-God in My most pure womb. I am heralded by the angels in heaven. I am given by the Father to man. Just as He gave His Son to redeem mankind, He gives the pure vessel used to bring the Prince of Peace forth.

Soon My times of pleading and apparitions will be over. I have been granted many times over a stay for mankind. This cannot be any longer, but I will now, as the Woman clothed for battle, moon at My feet, clothed with the sun, crowned with the stars, lead, protect, and guide My children through this most painful purification.

148

Live each moment in peace, live as if you must flee, from one moment to the next. This way you do not become caught up in the way of the world. Rejoice, the deliverance of God's people is at hand.

I lead the battle, to his has been given the Most Pure Lily dwelling within the Trinity.

My triumph arrives.

Pray, be vigilant, watchful of the signs given.

My Immaculate Heart enfolds each one gathered here today.

We bless you, for My Son is present also, in the Name of the Father, of My Son, and of My Most Chaste Spouse, the Holy Spirit.

The Walk of Faith

December 13, 1993 - 11:15 A.M.

(S.J., I heard a voice and commanded it to go in the name of Jesus, if not of God.)

Mary: Beloved little sorrowful rose, I your Madre Querida (Beloved Mother), Virgen de Guadalupe praise the name of Jesus as you do!

Do not despair, My little one. Can you not see you have been chosen to bring glory to God's kingdom through your suffering? Everything needed to be said was in that letter.

(S.J., I had sat down to write 'R.' a letter this morning.)

Mary: They are not your words, but the words of the Mother who wishes to bind up his pain and fears. You are corrected in understanding the fulfillment of the Father's words to you. Be patient and wait for your Heavenly Mother to complete the work started for you. You are merely an instrument that is used; for none of the credit, glory or praise, can go to anyone but the Father.

You have been separated into silence for a most heavenly reason. No one is to be leaned on but God only. He is the source of all. Through Me, the Mother, I ask for, am granted and distribute those graces asked for or needed by all My children. Separations bring growth; spiritual growth to believe in God for everything. The feeling of walking without seeing is the walk of faith.

Growth comes for all those who will be brought together soon. C. and C., S. and all those being woven by the heavenly desires.

(S.J., I heard the name 'Erlinda', but I'm not sure. I don't know anyone by that name.)

Mary: This is a small moment of rejoicing to remember the true meaning of the Christ in Christmas. Are not your phone, T.V., anticipated gifts only the superficial? Is not your silence a time of deeper reflection, prayer and listening? Listen for the true sounds of joy, the health in families, peace and not fighting, food and not hunger, warmth and not cold; love in people around you who believe as you.

Rejoice in each moment for soon, very soon, the trial is upon you. Mankind will shudder in his fear, and God will reveal His awesome might in a most terrible way. Continue in your faith walk. In everything give praise to the Father and consecrate all to My Most Immaculate Heart.

The time of restoration begins for you. In but a moment many things will come to pass for you. Your St. Joseph, the partner to support will be told.

Rejoice, little sorrowful rose, your Christ loves you. The Father blesses you, and the Holy Spirit leads you.

Your Mother enfolds you in Her most loving arms.

Godless Will Fall to Their Knees

December 28, 1993

(S.J., For about two weeks I had seen this vision of Our Lord standing in a profile position, dressed in His resurrection gown, extending His Heart in His hand, as in some of the Sacred Heart pictures. He then turns to show me a frontal position, and when He does, I am shocked to see the other half of His person, bloody, welted, and in the form of the crucified Jesus.

I had not received any messages of understanding of this vision, but because of the profound sorrow and pain in His eyes, it affected me very much.

At the cenacle on Tuesday morning, during the Rosary, Our Lady asked me to give a message verbally. I argued with Her, "I don't like to do this," and then, She said:)

Mary: I have need of your voice for My words. Do you deny Me My request?

(S.J., Prior to the cenacle for about two or three days, I had been hearing Our Lady begin to speak to me, with the following words:

Mary: Shortly after the first of the year, there will be an intense shaking. This will not be the earthquake, but rather a cosmic nature. I come that you may warn My children in advance.

(S.J., I didn't want to hear anymore, so I would not open to receive the message. Then I heard Our Lady at the cenacle. She began the very same way.)

Mary: I am Mary, Virgin Mother of Jesus the Christ, the Savior, whose birth brings salvation to the world. I come to tell My children once again, I receive the love and the prayers, for indeed, they pierce the very throne room of heaven; for indeed the prayers of the innocents are received into God's throne room.

151

(S.J., This day was the Feast of the Holy Innocents, and the Rosary was led by some of the children, as they were home for Christmas vacation.)

Mary: As for the souls of the innocents being slaughtered they also are seen by God. I come to tell My children to remain very close to their Mother, through their consecration, for I come to the remnant few who have believed and persevered; to warn them of all that is about to happen. God's children will see and know, but the godless will fall to their knees in fear, and My children will walk unscathed by all that is to happen.

(S.J., She then gave everyone there a blessing, and I cannot remember all that was said. This has been given to me as I prayed to remember what God wanted, to document Her message. Since this has only happened a few times, I have not made the arrangements to ask anyone to write the verbal messages as they are being given.)

Oil in the Lamps

December 29, 1993

(S.J. I was in prayer on the 29th, praying the Rosary, and arguing with God as I feel so assaulted by doubts, that I didn't want to see anything anymore, or hear anything. I just wanted to be a servant who loves Him, hidden, alone. Then I heard Our Lord, and He said, after I had just finished giving Him a long list of why I didn't want to be used:)

Jesus: But you know My voice and I know My sheep. Would you tell Me no? Little daughter of My heart, I am Jesus, Son of God, to be praised . . . (personal message).

My child, you see your Lord and Lord of all wounded once again. This scourging comes to the resurrected Jesus, who passed once through agony on Calvary. (Referring to the earlier vision of Crucified Jesus). How long must this go on? How long do My children think God the Eternal Father must stand?

(S.J., I understand this to mean, how long do My children think God The Eternal Father must stand without acting and sending His Justice.)

Jesus: Those who wantonly remain obstinate in their sins? Those who slaughter my little holy ones once again (aborted babies)? No, My Mother's little sorrowful rose, this will not continue. She indeed comes to those who are the remnant to warn, to comfort, to lead.

This shaking will be the hand of God; it will be of a cosmic phenomenal nature.

(S.J., Lord, I do not understand?)

Jesus: Then just write My words, for there will be no explanation. They (the scientists) will try to explain but only My children will know and understand. Others will fall to their knees in fear. It will be shortly after the new year.

(S.J., Lord? Time? Shortly could means days, a week, a year?)

Jesus: Do not concern yourself, My children, with guessing, with fearful anticipation. Know the parable of the ten virgins, and the oil in the lamps. The oil is symbolic of material preparations. They then returned and waited, peacefully, prayerfully, for the groom.

My Mother's time approaches an end, indeed, She has said all She could. You and My children are prepared and will go to your place of physical refuge (Santa Maria). My Cross (Cross of Peace) will beam the light of grace, much grace for My people.

I bid you My Father's peace, love and blessing from heaven above. Remain prayerfully vigilant.

In His Name, Abba. In My name, Jesus. In Our Spirit Most Holy. You are blessed.

Chapter Four

The Time Is Here When All Will Be Fulfilled

**Messages From January 4, 1994
To June 16, 1994**

Storms—The Beginning of God's Fury

January 4, 1994 - 6:00 A.M.

(S.J., I was pondering the first part of the message, I had received. It seemed similar, or the wording seemed very similar to the ones that I had received last year, when She told me about the flooding and She was addressing those thoughts. Referring to the messages of January 6, 1993, one year ago at the beginning of the rain storm. "These storms are the beginning of God's fury unleashed on mankind." I was thinking about the similarity of those words and the words of "shortly after the first of the year".

Mary: My daughter, My little sorrowful rose, I am your Virgin Mother and Mother of Jesus, who's name is praised. I come to console you. Be not concerned for any of your children. I enfold them in My Immaculate Heart. (Personal message.)

"Shortly after the first of the year." You ponder upon these words. They are the same as the ones received by you and others last year. "These storms are the beginning of God's fury unleashed on mankind." Thank you for hearing My request for your prayers. For the deaths and devastation that occurred, indeed would have been much higher and worse, but for the responses of My remnant few.

Woe to mankind. For the time quickly approaches, and is here, when all that has been foretold in many of My apparitions, and prophesied since the beginning of the ages, will be fulfilled.

Once again I request your prayer, fasting and sacrifices. Once again I implore My children to pay heed to My messages and requests. Once again I am intervening in these last days for all My children.

For I am Co-Redemptrix, and through My requests the Triune God can refuse Me nothing, when it is in accordance with God's will. My children request so many favors, many of which do

not concern their spiritual well-being, but rather the frivolities
of this materialistic society by which mankind has been bound.

I desire, more than ever before, an intense attitude of prayer, fasting and sacrifice to help Me battle the forces of evil, and snatch
many souls from My adversary, that would otherwise be damned
eternally. And most importantly, the attitude of love towards all
that are placed in your lives.

God's love, My children, must prevail. God's love is merciful.

Be yourselves merciful towards others. God's love is forgiving,
when approached in sincerity. Be yourselves forgiving of all, in
any who come against you. Let all know of His great, merciful
love. Through your consecration you are sealed as Mine. As the
Woman Clothed with the Sun leading My remnant through the
battle, I am protecting those sealed as Mine.

God's peace cannot be obtained other than by submitting **all** to
God's will. God's peace is His gift through the terrible days ahead.

My children I bless you, in the name of the Father, of My Son,
and My Spouse the Omnipotent Holy Spirit.

The Blows of Divine Justice

January 19, 1994 - 3:30 P.M.

Jesus: Little daughter of My heart, I am the Great I AM, Jesus,
whose blood was poured out for all humanity; whose name is
praised, always and forever.

No longer will I hold back My Father's justice. He is in Me and I
in Him from which goes forth Our Spirit.

The earth will give vent to the anger of God and is being prepared
to do so. I call all to the refuge of My Mother's heart. Those who
follow and are the remnant, felt and will know My protection.

157

(S.J., I understood this protection referred to this last earthquake of January 17, 1994 in Los Angles, California, and for any future events.)

Jesus: Those who will be called from this earth will be latter day martyrs and will wear the crown of martyrs and their blood will redeem many lost souls for My kingdom.

Prepare and remain alert for you know not the Father's hour. There will be no rest for this earth from the blows of Divine Justice. Woe to the godless - Woe to My priests who have not lead their flock in truth. The desecration of My sanctuary continues and increases.

Heed My messengers for they have hearts to hear their God. They are the lowly, but have hearts to hear, and have recognized the time of their visitation.

Sound the trumpet, little daughter of My Heart. Warn My children. Pray, remain vigilant.

Peace is My gift to all. Blessing descend upon you.

Signs Will Confirm

January 21, 1994

Mary begins in Spanish. These words are translated here into English.

(S.J., I tested and Our Mother answered.)

Mary: My daughter, My sorrowful rose. These words are given by the Virgin of Guadalupe, and with My sons and daughters I sing praises to My Son, Jesus. Glory to God.

I give you these words in your language to show you that I am the Mother of all. My children do not know of the mercy of God. They do not know that the justice of God is coming.

158

Some do not believe, because the ones that should prepare God's children, are My Son's, the priests of Jesus, but they do not believe. They have left the road of Jesus, and they are on the road of error.

That's why I have chosen those who in this world are nothing, but who have hearts to hear the Mother and God. Very soon you will go to proclaim these words and all that we have given you. The signs will confirm that you have been chosen by God and these words come from Him.

That all would put themselves under My mantle. That all would consecrate themselves to Me, to know My protection. The time not to believe has finished. Blessing in the name of the Father and of the Son and of the Holy Spirit. Amen.

Mary: Now My child I tell you that all will be fulfilled, as to prophecy and time. Do not cease your fasting and pray in your heart through your most mediocre actions in your day. Do them in Love. Do them by Him who is love, Jesus. There will be more tremblers of the earth. They will come from all directions, and they will have all learned minds in total confusion.

Fears will increase, so will violence. From all natural elements devastation will come. But, to Mine I say, prepare as God's chosen people to go forth and be lead to refuge. Now, My children of Santa Maria, at all times be ready to receive this exodus of God's children.

Peace remains, and is My Son's gift to you and all. In Him, and by Him, and through Him, and with Me, your humble servant of God, Mary Ever Virgin, We bless you and all. In the name of God Eternal, God the Son, and the name of the Omnipotent Spirit. For the glory of God's Kingdom.

(S.J. Understanding received with above message. Moses went to Pharaoh for the release of God's people. The people had to go through many plagues and things that would bring fear. I understand from this that there is no fear for God's people. We can be prepared and pray, and know that He will protect us.)

The Fury Of God's Justice

January 28, 1994

Jesus: I am Jesus the Christ, who is praised. I come to the daughter of My heart and My Mother's little sorrowful rose. Now will this world know the fury of God's justice!

The heaven and the earth will convulse under the weight of God's justice! One year of mercy has been given to My children. All that has been foretold and was to have happened already was averted through the power of prayer. But in this year,

Who Has Believed?

My priests, to whom I come and send My Mother, they have not responded!. With scorn, ridicule, disbelief and indifference they have received My prophets!

My sacrifice on Calvary, given to My Church, built on Rock, has become little more than the breaking of bread among mankind. My priests allow the deception of Satan to ensnare and hold them bound.

Who Has Believed?

The little, the lowly, the broken, the weak, the captives set free, the small remnant of God's people who truly enfold all the teaching of the Gospel and of the teaching set forth by My Holy Vicar on earth! To these does the Spirit of Truth quicken. To these do the imploring and shedding of tears of My Holy Mother fall deep in their hearts and lives. This small remnant carries with them the true light of My Gospel.

I Am The Same! Yesterday! Today! And Forever!

Just as My own rejected Me when I walked on earth as man. I was accepted by the lepers, called unclean, by the prostitutes, by the beggars, by the pagans. To all I came, but was rejected by My own. . .

As I Am Today!

Therefore the signs will be unleashed and dispatched one after another, and I say: Woe to you hardened of heart! Woe to you My shepherds! WOE to you godless! Now will the loss of life be as never before.

I will cause man to be broken and unable to lift himself out of the chaos and destruction! Heed My messengers, people of God. Return to your God who has tired of waiting, but will yet receive you.

In twenty days there will be another earthquake.

(S.J.: Lord, will it be **the** earthquake).

Jesus: Be ready to flee.

(S.J.: Whom do I tell this to?).

Jesus: Tell it only to C. and C.

(S.J., Lord, can this be averted?)

Jesus: No! Pray that the justice of God pass quickly and swiftly!

(S.J., I was having tremendous difficulty receiving this part of the message and was rebuking in Jesus' name and He answered.)

Jesus: Listen to me, My child! I speak. To you will be given a clearer understanding. To you will be given much for you have remained steadfast. Do not fight My Will for your life. God's hand is heavy upon you. Heaven rejoices. The innocents will be avenged. Pray child, at all time. Be not vexed at your situation.

This will be brought to completion. You are blessed! My Father blesses you. I bless you. Our Spirit blesses you. Amen.

(S.J. After I received this message from Our Lord, I began to cry and feel a tremendous weight. I asked why did I have to know how many days, and perhaps this was just me? I felt led to go to the calendar to count out the twenty days from this date.

The date would be February 17th, a Thursday, which would be fulfillment of S.'s messages. February 16th, is Ash Wednesday. After this I went and fell before my statue of the Virgin Mary and began to implore Her to tell me this wasn't true. I kept saying this is just me? Then Mary came and said:)

Mary: I am Mary, Ever Virgin, Humble Servant of God, **Praise Jesus**.

(S.J.: Mother, please tell me this isn't true)

Mary: Listen to My Son, My child. Have I not asked you to share My sorrow? This will be so you can pray with me, child, **intensely**! Be not afraid! All this will be for the glory of God! Do as you are told. Call C. and C.

Peace of My Son, and My blessing upon you.

Co-Redemptrix and Mediatrix of All Graces

February 3, 1994 - 8:25 A.M.

Mary: My little sorrowful rose, I am your Mother Ever Virgin and Pure, who soon will be proclaimed Co-Redemptrix and Mediatrix of all Graces. Along with you I bow humbly under God's mighty hand. Along with you I praise the holy blessed name of Jesus.

These, My child, are the days foretold by Me long ago. Now they are upon My children. It is imperative all be in a state of grace. I

162

call all My children to be reconciled to their God. You will see in the hours ahead many frightening events, but now is not the time for My children to be in fear, fear which is not of God.

My children will go forth to their place of refuge (Santa Maria, California) and then a thousand and tens will fall. The loss of life will be as never before. But Mine will know their security and protection under My mantle.

Those who have laughed and scoffed and ridiculed will, with difficulty, arrive. But only My own will know, see, and feel God's peace; for My Angels will be assisting all of My children. This is a message of hope and consolation. This is a message of warning.

This is the moment the trumpet sounds and woe to the inhabitants of the earth. For this nation that shows a way of error and lies, of murder and deceit, God Almighty has turned His back to you.

Now the lies will of feminism and atheism come tumbling down. All error and falsehood will be laid bare. Then and only then, will those caught in the snare be able to chose truth. There is given to you, My little sorrowful rose a week, a week to pray, to fast, to offer all to Me that I may dispose of these actions accordingly. At that time a sign, pretold to you will be made manifest.

You are to tell them simply what I have said. I call you to leave at 6 P.M. Ash Wednesday. You will go to Saint Joseph's. The doors will be opened.

(S.J. May I share this with C. and C.?)

Mary: Yes, with them only.

(S.J. May I tell my family.)

Mary: Tell them only that you have been called to Santa Maria on Ash Wednesday. Implore the Father for swiftness in administering His holy justice. Pray for the souls that will be lost. Pray they die in a state of grace. Pray for My priest sons who erroneously have led their flock and now God's justice finds the sheep unprepared. To these priests God's justice will be severe. Be at peace, little sorrowful rose. Know we are ever present and with you. Blessings of God The Father and of the Son and of the Holy Spirit.

My Justice Is My Mercy

February 16, 1994 - 3:45 P.M.

Jesus: My child, My little daughter of My heart. I Am Jesus, whose name is praised. Be assured I am ever near you. Have faith, do not doubt; have faith in Me and My Father who sends you. Very soon you will be confirmed as My "Herald of Truth".

My Justice Is My Mercy!

The hour is here and, as I marked you with My sign of mourning, very soon now the whole world will mourn. There will be death everywhere! Pray little one, pray for My souls who perish for there is none to atone and offer reparation.

My Priests!

Behold! Thus says the Lord Your God! Listen to the prophets who have been raised, for you no longer hear the voice of your God.

The little, the humble, the obedient will be lifted up by Me. Do not keep My children from their refuge (Santa Maria). This has been decreed by God Omnipotent!

I send My little daughter of My heart to pray. Be watchful, vigilant, the hour is here. I bless you in the name of My Father, My name, and the name of My Holy Spirit.

(S.J. When Our Lord said He signed me with His sign of mourning, He was referring to this morning as I had received ashes on

164

my forehead. I was totally unaware that the priest had spilled an extra amount of ashes down the whole of my face. I had ashes on my nose, behind my glasses and on my chin. When I looked in the mirror in the car and realized, I laughed and said "Lord, I must look like a fool. But its O.K., I will always be a fool for you." That is where I first heard Him say, "I have signed you with my sign of mourning. Very soon the whole world will mourn.")

February 26, 1994 - 9:00 A.M.

(S.J., I have been very tired and feeling attacks from the enemy concerning my failures, inadequacies and dwelling on my son. I am committing to the Lord my day and everything I am and will do.

I basically have been telling the Lord I will do anything He asks of me, but He is going to have to do all to get me to move, so tired do I feel.

All of a sudden I see in a vision like a floor raised high above me and there are people falling off the edge, like a human waterfall, falling downwards. I am overcome with a sorrow, a sorrow I know Our Lord feels.

I then see another floor off to the side of the other. It appears to be a round floor and I see people on this floor, holding rosaries. I am given to understand these are the victim souls and the remnant. (Those who are following the requests of Our Blessed Mother to pray, offer sacrifice and reparation). There are demons coming at these people, but I see St. Michael and other angels holding them off.)

Fulfillment of My Prophet Joel

February 28, 1994 - 9:30 A.M.

(S.J., I heard a voice and I tested. Jesus answered.)

Jesus: Be still and know I am your God, your Savior and your Lord. I am Jesus, I bow and worship My Father, I am the Alpha and Omega - I AM!

To you, My little daughter of My heart, you will never understand My great love. You have been tested and the enemy rages, but you trust. You persevere and you trust. How great is that virtue! I do not see your failures and weaknesses.

I see a humble spirit. I see your heart so full of love for Me. I see your willingness to put aside your desires for the sake of mine. But it is not great acts of proof I desire. It is the little ones that draw Me to you.

The desire to be meek.
The desire to be unseen.
The desire to remain humble.
The acts of your vocation done with love
These are what I see!
The testing remains constant and intensifies,
for the enemy knows his time is short.
This is for all My chosen and victim souls.

You see (in the vision) the immense number of souls falling into the flames of hell. You see the small number who offer prayer, reparation, and sacrifice for the sake of those lost souls who have no one to pray for them.

Because the remnant is (praying) there are vast numbers of souls being snatched from the enemy.

For My sorrow is, and always will be, for the many who refuse My love, My offer of everlasting life instead of eternal damnation. No, My children will never comprehend My great love.

These are not the days of ages past. These are the fulfillment of My prophet Joel! These are the last great days of mercy, such as this world has never seen. The last call has gone out.

My children do not lose faith. Do not lose hope. Trust in Me only, and persevere in faith, not feelings!

I love you, My little daughter of My heart and My Mother's little sorrowful rose.

I give you and all My blessings and peace. Amen.

Believe the Signs and Wonders

March 10, 1994 - 9:30 A.M.

Mary: My little sorrowful rose: You have not heard the voice of Your Mother. I am Mary Ever Virgin, humble servant of God, with whom I join all My children in singing the praises of God.

(S.J., I tested and rebuked and She answered:)

Mary: But I dwell therein the midst of God and I am sent by God! Now listen My child, you dwell on your fatigue, you dwell on your failings, you must continue to trust in the mercy and love of My Son Jesus. He is the one from whom I obtain all that is asked of Me.

You gaze upon My image and remember. Remember the first time you heard My voice, I said: "This is but a prelude of what is to come." You must believe in My words and My work. Even though many have refused the outpouring of messages of love, repentance and conversion, this is My time!

To some I give messages of love and teachings. To others I give prophetic messages of warning, but to all I give the grace to receive and believe the signs and wonders accompanying My work. I will continue until the last epoch of time to obtain all for all of My children and the good of their salvation.

These are indeed dire days, and the day of thunder will catch many like a thief in the night. Many will die in their fear. All will know the hand of God. No longer will they scoff at the words of My prophets. But these are messages of hope. For My children

167

will be at peace, and evil will be no more. There will reign once again true worship of God according to the Way.

My children are being gathered from every corner and being led, for the Mighty Hand of God has already fallen and these are the beginning of the chastisements. They will increase and will worsen. Only My own will be at peace.

The coming of the three days of darkness is closer than many of My children can realize. For this reason My warning and My prodigies have been granted.

You must strengthen yourselves to be strong for the weak. Many who perish in the preceding events will be mercy for them. My Son and all His glory and splendor await the receiving to Himself His spotless and cleansed remnant church.

Be at peace My little ones. I will always be at your sides, and as you enter My Immaculate Heart through your act of consecration, My covenant with you is My love, protection, and guidance so that My Son Jesus can receive you into the bosom of His Heart and be glorified by your love.

God's peace and blessing to all My children of light.

(S.J., Note: Our Lady addresses me this way because I was praying and was mentally wondering why I had not received any messages from Her and I was remembering the very first time I heard Her speak to me.)

My Own Despise and Turn Away From Me

March 15, 1994 - 9:21 A.M.

(S.J., I begin to hear the voice of Our Lord.)

Jesus: Be at peace My little one.

(S.J., I am led to test who is speaking to me and I say, I command you to go in the name of Jesus if you are not of God!)

Jesus: I am Jesus the only Son of God, My Father, who with the Holy Ghost is praised in heaven, on earth and to whom the demons must bow!

Be at peace little daughter of My heart. The increase of evil is prevalent all around and indeed one of the signs of this evil age! I will open doors, I will lead and you will know soon the Lord God has spoken and fulfilled! (Fulfilled all prophecy).

Events continue to unfold every day and yet the hearts of My children remain hard and obstinate. To their own condemnation!

I am Mercy!
I am Hope!
I am Love!
I am the Healer! (of souls and bodies)
I am the Source of All Good!

Yet, My own despise and turn away from Me.

(S.J., Here I began to wonder who Our Lord was addressing in this statement when He said My own.)

Jesus: Yes, I speak of sinners who have not opened the door of their hearts to the King of Kings, the Lord of Lords, the Prince of Peace!

But a sacrifice has been asked from you for My own, the priests.

(S.J., Here He answered me, He calls the priests His own.)

Jesus: I am a God of peace. They (the priests) have created confusion! They have caused division; they have brought down the wrath of God! If there are questions of faith, have I not said I would send the Holy Spirit and He would lead all to the truth? For I Am The Truth, the Way, and the Life, and Light of all.

This I ask of My priests: Be obedient, as I was obedient to My Father! He sees all. **He knows all, and in due time, He will cleanse and purify the filth, the stench and the rotten! And He will start in His own House. (The Church.)**

My Mother is the Virgin of the Way. For She brought Me to mankind. She walked the way. She shows all today the way: the way to walk, the way to suffer, the way to be humble, the way to love, the way to pray. For where I am, She is. Where She is, I am.

Once again child, I say be at peace and pray. For yet a little while you remain anonymous and in a little while you will speak Our Words and the credentials and the conviction will be given by God, to whom all glory is given!

I bless you (all) in the name of My Father, My Name and name of the Holy Ghost. Amen.

This Day of Thunder

March 24, 1994 - 9:00 A.M.

Vigil of the Annunciation. Sixth Anniversary of Cross of Peace Messages.

(S.J. Test "Will you bow down to Jesus and praise His Name.)

Mary: My little sorrowful rose. I am your Mother, The Virgin of the Way, The Mother of the Way, Jesus! Let us together praise His name.

This day of thunder is upon My children! To My own (the children of light), it is an awesome and wonderful thing! To the godless, their hearts will be filled with terror!

It is a type of second Pentecost. My Divine Spouse will descend and, in a swift but thorough sweep, convict those souls of the truth and those souls will be brought into the Mystical

Body of Christ. Others will know also, this is of God and though they resist, it will be a type of warning for them.

That gathering* will be as never before. I will once again inspire the hearts of My own and provision for every need will be met. Many will be touched profoundly and many will come to hear (the truth) for the first time. This is truly of God and all will be fulfilled.

Rest in the peace of My Son and I bless you from the heavenly throne. It shall be.

* (S.J., Gathering is the Cross of Peace Sixth Anniversary Celebration and Gathering in Santa Maria, California, March 26 and 27, 1994.)

Wonders of All Time

March 28, 1994 - 8:30 A.M.

After the Cross of Peace Celebration and Gathering in Santa Maria California, March 26 & 27, 1994.

(S.J. I command you in the name of Jesus, in whose name do you come?)

Mary: I Am your Mother, The Virgin of the Way! Praise be to Jesus, My Victim Son!

My Child and little sorrowful rose: I come to tell you many things. Indeed many graces were given freely and abundantly; many blessings bestowed on all My children for this gathering of celebration in My valley and My City of Peace.

You see once more a little, but a little, of the devastation and death that still awaits this humanity that refuses to see the call of God, the hand of God and the mercy of God. Very soon now, this day of thunder is upon you and will be the signal dispatched to the four corners of the world.

171

The Holy Spirit of God will be, once again, the power which will renew the face of this earth; will cleanse, and will purify. The children of light will be filled with wondrous awe at this advent of His arrival, and the godless will know their dread and truth of their souls! Have I not requested of My children, "Pray the Holy Spirit come?"

Rejoice oh little children of mine. The wonders of all time are about to be made manifest and you are called to be a holy people of God! Become little. Recognize this time of your visitation and rejoice! Gather in your families and in your groups and peacefully and prayerfully await the fulfillment of all prophecy! That which God has prepared for My children, no one can imagine or comprehend!

For C. & C. and the servants of My valley, the recompense will be the fruits of the conversion of many souls! Peace among My children, as they dwell at the foot of the cross, so glorious in its design, the designs set forth by God the Father! The Glory of the Cross is souls, for which every drop of My Son's Precious Blood was shed!

You will see the Cross in all its glory and glorious design at a time when defeat seems most immanent, just as the glory of Christ's resurrection came when all thought He was dead!

Do not cease your prayers of fasting or acts of reparation. They bear much fruit. Persevere oh, little children of mine, and know who calls you, who protects you, who comforts you, who strengthens you, by obtaining these graces for you from My Beloved Son!

It is I, your Mother, the Mediatrix of All Graces, the Mother of all Humanity, and servant, very humble servant of God.

In God's peace and love, I leave you.

The Earth Will Shake

April 7, 1994 - 10:10 A.M.

(S.J., I have been in prayer in the early morning and after praying I begin to do my housework and I hear Our Lady:

Mary: My daughter come before My image!

(S.J., Mother, you are here?)

Mary: My child, I am always with you.

(S.J., I go before my Pilgrim Virgin of Fatima. I test! Will you praise the name of Jesus and worship God in The Holy Trinity?)

Mary: My little daughter, My little sorrowful rose, I am the Mother of All Humanity, the Virgin of The Way, with you I praise The name of Jesus and worship God in the Holy Trinity!

(S.J., At this time, I begin to feel interference from the enemy and I rebuke him and send him back to the foot of the Cross of Jesus, then I hear Our Lady say, "Thank you My little one.)

Mary: I've come once again that you and all My children of light may be assured that I am with each and every one, that I hear their cries, that I receive their prayers.

Once again I tell you the earth will shake again, and again there will be immense devastation and destruction, it will happen at a different hour. This will precede the sign and strike given to My shepherdess by a very short time. (See footnote at end of message.)

Once again the hearts of many will remain hard and stony and refuse to see the hour of mercy; for there is yet time to open their hearts and receive Me and My Son, for We are One. But very soon that mercy will be through the justice that has begun to befall this poor humanity.

There is much speculation as to the state of My Pope, John Paul II, but none knows how heavy is the cross he bears. Yes, He will flee and be taken as a martyr. Pray much for him My child, for then woe to humanity. The door is open for the antichrist!

I place myself between the spirit of Antichrist and My children of light. My children who follow, My children who pray, My children who suffer, My children who take a stand for Truth, My children who worship with reverence My Son the Christ!

I beg you, pray much for much to be mitigated, but it cannot be averted any longer. And tell My children to trust in the Queen of Heaven, to trust in the Woman who stands on the head of the serpent! His defeat is done!

For God is constantly giving His Holy Angels bid about you, and when you consecrate yourselves, and invite Me in your hearts, I fulfill My promises! My pact with My children: at your cries, I am here, at your praise, I join in, in your dangers, I protect. With My Son, I am the vanquisher of demons! How quickly they take flight! Do not fear, My children!

C. and C. will know which door to go through, unmistakable and peacefully, for I have not started this work to let it end for nought! (See footnote at end of message.)

I address all these concerns of yours, My child, for they are My concerns too. And all across this network of mine, all will know and feel My presence. Pray one for another, My children. Continue your gatherings of prayer until that time we are gathered as one, in community, in My Valley of Peace. Peace is My Son's gift to you. From heaven's throne, I bless you today. Remain expectant and prayerful, you too are being led.

(S.J., My understanding is that once again Our Lady is telling us to remain at peace and not speculate as to time because She is not in the business of being a psychic and making predictions! She is

174

going about the business of warning God's children, as God has done down through the ages.)

(S.J., Footnote: **The sign**, is a glorious crucifix that will appear in the sky, which will follow a 5.5 earthquake in the Victorville, California, area. The **strike** is a 8.4 earthquake, equivalent to a 12 in death and destruction, for the California area, 5 hours after the Victorville earthquake. My shepherdess referred to is 'S'. This work is the Cross of Peace Project in Mary's "City of Peace", Santa Maria, California.)

I Am the Lord God, Almighty!

April 14, 1994 - 8:40 A.M.

(S.J., I command you in the name of Jesus, in whose name do you come?)

Jesus: I Am, My daughter, the great I Am, Jesus, slain for the salvation of many, praised in heaven, on earth and acknowledged by the demons!

My little daughter of My heart, I receive your cries of praise and worship through the hands of My Mother.

I ask this question of My children.

Do you believe this has been My Mother's work, gathering the cries of agony, prayers and supplications, and the songs of praise; and ever presenting this to the Eternal Father, so that the Father and the Son, long ago, would that divine justice be meted out to those who live and rule oblivious and obstinate of God's Omnipotence?

But, through the hands of the Mother I gifted humanity. She has always been before The Father interceding on behalf of all. Those who acknowledge Her, those who do not. Those who are in most need of My Mercy, forgiveness and peace.

175

But now, little daughter of My heart, I say this: Behold this moment of distress and extreme trial is even at the door and in but a moment all will be unleashed. Many are those who are called by Me; few who respond with the totality of their hearts.

But I tell you this: Humanity will see the divine justice of God and remain obstinate and hardened in their hearts. They will again drop to their knees in fear. And again they will rise in pride and obstinacy against the mercy of God's warning. My own little children, I gather you all to My Breast. I tell you now, more than ever, **Believe I Am The Great I Am And I Am Ever With You!**

I will assail the enemy who comes against you with My Holy Face! Those who receive the cleansing of My Blood over their offenses, will be held deep in the protection of My Heart. I never sleep, I do not lie! Your protection is guaranteed by My Word. Your salvation is guaranteed by My Blood. I too come, as with My Mother to calm your fears, reassure you of My love and bestow on you My peace!.

I Am Lord God, Almighty And True And I Say: You see evidence worldwide of the justice of God, but My children, this is but the beginning. Remain close to Me, draw ever closer with My Mother. We are come today to bestow great graces of peace and assurance of protection.

I tell you this: They will know Our presence!

We are present to bless each one in the name of the Holy Trinity and God's peace!

(S.J., Note: this is a wonderful message of assurance from Our Lord. There is nothing different here that we as Gods people have not known. He comes to warn and assure us and that is a great grace. Be at Peace, Gods children, for He is in control and knows all. Remain in a state of grace to have the Peace of His Protection!)

A Spiritual Battle Fought In the Heavens

April 20, 1994 - 9:20 A.M.

Mary: My little sorrowful rose.

(S.J., I heard a voice and I tested, in whose name do you come?)

Mary: I your Virgin Mother come in the name of Jesus, My Son, where He, Three persons in One God, is praised eternally!

Do not disdain yourself for your failure. I have chosen you as I have chosen all My remnant members of My heavenly army, of which, I am Queen. I am your leader, I alone am your strength!. It is through My Heart I obtain from Jesus graces, flowing from His Heart, for you and all.

I have chosen specifically those who are poor, simple, and who, the eyes of the world gaze upon as lowly and, of course, that is what you are. But all (My children) in My army have a heart that bends to the will of God, which is what I am teaching you all. They have a heart, not filled with pride, but one of humility and obedience.

My children believe at times, their own earthly attempts can stop the attack of the enemy. But My children, it is a spiritual battle being fought in the heavens! One fiercely raging between Satan and his demons and those bound in his power, against My own children and priests, angels and saints. All these are part of the heavenly cohort.

In heaven the power is obtained, through the most simple. Through them and their prayer. The beads of the rosary as they are guided through the hands of My children are heard in the nether world and Satan acknowledges the power of the rosary. It is one he fears most. That is why he furiously tries to silence the sound of the beads, by distracting My children, calling them away (from prayer). Putting obstacles in the way of prayer and especially the prayer of the rosary. It is through

177

these prayers I am afforded the most power to complete the plan which has been set.

And you My little ones, are being called to sainthood by being little. By your love and reverence of My Son, Jesus, ever present in the Eucharist. Draw close to My priest sons still celebrating that sacrifice obediently. Pray much for My Son's Vicar on earth, John Paul II. It please My heart that the littlest of angels should respond to the prompting of, "let's pray for the Pope."

(S.J., Our Lady refers here to My two children who have begun, by themselves, to say "let's pray for the Pope" and then pray an Our Father, Hail Mary and Glory Be, as requested by Our Lady of Father Gobbi, when we are saying morning and night time prayers.)

Mary: Rejoice My little ones, you have been chosen by Me, the Woman Clothed with the Sun, that My army would defeat once and for all Satan and all his evil followers.

You have been called. You have responded. Rejoice in the love this Mother has for each one of you. I have caressed and kissed each one and placed you deep in the well of My Immaculate Heart. There you will be protected and led deeper into the heart of My Son, Jesus!

Thank you for responding. Thank you for your prayers.

From heavens throne, you are blessed.

(S.J., Note to message of 4-20-94: After I received this message, I asked Our Lady to give me a message from Father Gobbi's book and She asked me to read message number 61. Please read this message to see how wonderfully it confirms to what Our Lady has said in this message. I was also shown how, when we are praying the Rosary, and the beads are going through our fingers, the demons beneath, (in hell) cower, and acknowledge that someone or some group is praying. And of course they hate it:)

I Call My People To Holiness

April 22, 1994 - 5:20 A.M.

(S.J., I was awakened yesterday morning, April 21, by the phase, "Seven times I was told of this war and seven times I was told to go to my place of refuge", being repeated over and over. I had been praying for discernment. All during the night of April 22, last night, I have heard alternately, "I call My people to holiness and I am come that thou would have life everlasting". I am awakened at 5:20 A.M., and I gaze into my picture of the Sacred Heart of Jesus and I hear:)

Jesus: Yes, it is I, your Lord and Master of your soul, Jesus!

(S.J., At this point, I test and rebuke the voice to go if it is not of God.)

Jesus: But, My little daughter of My Heart, I am the Second

Person of the Trinity that will always and forever be praised, worshiped and glorified.

Jesus: My daughter, you cannot know the deception and diabolical plan that is already set in motion, that will bring upon this country and world a scourge never before experienced on earth.

If My people will not bend their knees to their God, if My people will not bend their hearts to their God; then they will serve and be at the mercy of the prince of this world, who, though he holds many bound, is yet held at bay. But woe, to this hard-hearted people who do not hear, who will not change their hearts, who do not pray.

Prayer my child is the only weapon. Few are those who prefer to be with Me to console Me in My loneliness. The spirit of antichrist and his reign is close at hand. Do not My children know scriptures?

179

They (My children) are left without shepherds to prepare them. They (the priests) have left My Church as all others, empty with no presence or sign of My sacrifice. The Church is being nailed to the cross. But this Church will rise, resplendent and refined, purified; and once again bring glory to the Alpha and Omega, the Lord and Master of all, the True One.

(S.J., As I received these words I simultaneously saw a cross and to the left, a church that seemed to be falling apart as if it were being smashed by a large hammer. To the right of the cross, I saw a beautiful church, with very ornate carvings and very brilliant.)

Jesus: Then know when these things begin to happen, you have been shown, you have been warned. I desire you pray much, you console Me much and few are they who know how to flee from the world into the silence of their hearts, where I can commune with them. Pray much, My children. Those who have responded to My Mother's pleas, I hold you in My Heart.

I bless you and all in the name of My Father, My Name and of Our Spirit.

(S.J., I believe that these places of refuge are being revealed all around the world. How we are taken there will be different, but ultimately there will be protection from the reign of the antichrist. Much can still be lessened through conversion, repentance, prayer and sacrifice. The greatest prayer is the sacrifice of the Mass. Return to the sacraments. Pray the rosary and wear a scapular and sacramentals! The devil, yes there is a devil, hates them! And then pray, pray, pray!)

I Will Not Leave My Sheep

May 12, 1994 - 9:45 A.M.

(S.J. Test. In whose name do you come?)

Jesus: I Am The Great I Am, Jesus, Once Ascended To The Father, And Soon To Return.

(S.J. I have been receiving bits and parts of this message all during the night, and during Mass yesterday, when my two children were able to make their First Holy Communion. I was thanking the Lord for this special grace, and I heard Him tell me various things. During Mass yesterday:)

Jesus: I give the best that I have to these little ones, indeed to all my children. Myself! To those who believe, to those who recognize My Presence!

(S.J. I heard Him say during the night:)

Jesus: The time of tempestuous times is arrived! Tumultuous and tempestuous time for my people!

(S.J. I heard Him say this morning:)

Jesus: My little daughter of My heart, you must know that these words are coming to you and to others, that you might warn and therefore, prepare My children of this time. Indeed, the earth and galaxies mourn at what is to befall the earth. The sun does not shed its light. The earth is in turmoil and there is no explanation. But to My own they see it as a sign, and indeed that is what it is.

Remain steadfast to Me My children, and to My Mother. You will feel our protection in an unprecedented way. My children do not fear. There is no fear for those in a state of grace. Do not stray children, as sheep with no shepherd! **I Am Your Shepherd And I Will Not Leave My Sheep! My Sheep Know My Voice And I Know My Sheep.**

These **are** the times of all times. Do not persist in your disbelief and doubts My children. All has been planned according to the words of the Father, and **all will** come to pass.

Continue in your gatherings of prayer and cenacle. We are present in a most special way. Thank you, My children, for responding to the pleas of My Mother.

181

Heaven in all it's glory anticipates the passing through this moment of time.

I bless you all in the omnipotent name of My Father, My Name, and in the name and power of the Holy Spirit.

Amen.

My Justice Will Be Poured Forth

May 22, l994 - 11:15 A.M.

(S.J., I begin to hear the voice of God The Father, I test and He answers me.)

God The Father: My Daughter, listen, I am the great I Am, The God to be worshiped, revered and praised down through the ages!

Many are the gifts of My Spirit bestowed on you on this Feast of Pentecost. I confer upon you, My herald of truth, those graces which will be needed and used in this all-powerful and wonderful infilling of the Spirit, that is being poured in abundance on My own. For the words you heard were not from My Son but rather from Me.

(S.J., The Father refers here to words I had heard during the night, "time and mercy have come to an end." I heard this phrase several times and, as I know the enemy works to confuse, I had prayed that if these words were from God, then they be told to me in a message.)

God the Father: Mercy and time have been available to My children for their salvation. Now the time comes to an end and mercy without justice is over! My justice will be poured forth and all those who have lived in total ignorance of their God will be called to account. Those who live in obstinate hatred of God will be annihilated with the blows of My justice.

Look, you peoples of the earth! Majesty and creation is Mine! See, the stench of your sins fills the earth! The blood begins to flow and will rise higher still. I will purge the evil from all humanity and leave only the purified and refined; and heaven will be joined to earth and all will be fulfilled.

I tell you My child, these people have voted in a law, "three strikes and you're out." I have struck once, I will strike once again, then I will strike once and for all. (See footnote.) And those who have not heeded the words of My Son and of the most pure Lily of Heaven will be struck with terror!

Some, with much difficulty will arrive at all My places of refuge; but those who have walked in truth, walked in love, walked in obedience, walked in humility, I jealously guard. Not one of the evil one's schemes will steal them from Me. You have been placed in the crucible of My Son's Love and you have been purified, you have been purged of all earthly desires, that your desires may only be of fulfilling the Divine Will. Those tested and purified only rise to a higher brilliance and shine with holiness. Be holy as I am holy. You are a temple of the Bread of Life, the Body and Blood shed for you and for all. He it is who fills your being.

My peace, My grace, My blessing, My gifts of the Holy Spirit, that you will fulfill My divine will. Amen.

(**Note:** S.J., I am given to understand this is for us here in California.)

June 1, 1994 - 10:10 A.M.

Jesus: Behold the Lamb of God!............He comes!
Behold the Lamb of God!............He comes!
Behold the Lamb of God!............He comes!

I am Jesus! Praises be to God, the Father for the gift of His Son!

My child, listen! Little Daughter of My Heart, go to the book of My Book of Revelations.

(S.J., At this point I get my Bible.)

Jesus: Read from Chapter 18, until the end.

(S.J., Jesus then instructs me to include the following bible verses in this message.)

Apocalypse (Revelations) Chapter 22: 10-21.
Douay-Rheims Edition.

10 - And He said to me, Do not seal up the words of the prophecy of this book; for the time is at hand.

11 - He who does wrong, let him do wrong still; and he who is filthy, let him be filthy still; and he who is just, let him be just still; and he who is holy, let him be hallowed still.

12 - Behold, I come quickly! and My reward is with Me, to render to each one according to his works.

13 - I Am the Alpha and the Omega, the first and the last, the beginning and the end!

14 - Blessed are they who wash their robes that they may have the right to the tree of life, and that by the gates they may enter into the city.

15 - Outside are the dogs, and the sorcerers, and the fornicators, and the murderers and the idolaters, and everyone who loves and practices falsehood.

16 - I Jesus, have sent My angel to testify to you these things concerning the churches. I am the root and the offspring of David, the Bright Morning Star.

17 - And the Spirit and the bride say, Come! And let him who hears say Come!. And let him who thirsts come: and he who wishes, let him receive the water of life freely.

18 - I testify to everyone who hears the words of the prophecy of this book. If anyone shall add to them, God will add unto him the plagues that are written in this book.

19 - And if anyone shall take away from the words of the book of this prophecy, God will take away his portion from the tree of life and from the holy city, and from the things that are written in this book.

20 - He who testifies to these things says, It is true, I come quickly! Amen! Come, Lord Jesus!

21 - The grace of Our Lord Jesus Christ be with all. Amen.

(S.J., After I read and do as He tells me, He continues:)

Jesus: My daughter, I tell you all these things are to be and on the point of being. The words of My prophets have been, and always, there are those who refuse to believe.

I say to all: I am coming as a thief in the night! Do not let your sins and evil deeds be exposed by My light. I see all, I hear all, I know all. Heed the signs. Pray the discernment given to all by means of My Spirit. Be vigilant, I come. Heed the voices of My trumpets! (The messengers giving warnings.)

I bless you and all. Do not fear, those of you who are mine. I know you. Amen!

Pray daughter. Do as My Mother dictates to you.

(S.J., At this point I understood that Our Lady would give me a message, and I tested).

Mary: Child!

(S.J., I replied, Mother?)

Mary: Yes, It is I. I am Mary, Co-Redemptrix, Mediatrix of All Graces, that My Son Jesus may be glorified by all I bring to Him.

185

My daughter, you sorrow still, as I do. Remember when I told you . . . "but I am crying too. They do not know My Son's justice is on the way. There is so much to do and so little time left".

(S.J., This is part of my original testimony of hearing Our Lady for the first time, 8-1-92.)

Mary: I tell you, My little sorrowful rose, the time is **really** over. I emphasize because many have not understood the meaning of time as given in My messages. They have not seen the urgent use of the words to stir those into fervent prayer and change of life. They have only seen that they (prophecies) have not been ful-filled by their own interpretation of time. So they lose faith, they lose heart, they do not change.

So now, I, your Mother and Mother of all, tell you, My little trumpet, I empathize with your understanding of time. This, so that you may be as Noah, as Jonah, as Moses, as John, as all My prophets; for of them, I am Queen. Warn My children! All is soon come to pass and fulfilled.

Does it matter to you child, that you stand as an oddity to many? That you are misunderstood? That you are judged by others? That you are ridiculed or persecuted?

(S.J., As Our Lady ask me these questions, I reply no after each. I end with no, My Mother, no. She continues:)

Mary: Well said, My little servant. All this and more they did to My Son. Follow Him. I leave you in God's peace. Do not be fearful. I am with you and all who are mine. You are blessed from heaven!

186

My Apostles of Light

June 10 & 13, 1994:

Jesus: Behold, My little daughter of My heart, would you not tend to the call of your Lord? For I am Jesus, resplendent in all My glory, who is soon to return to all humanity! Sing praises to God The Father for the redemption of man is nigh!

Do you not see, My child, the call on your life is great? For you have responded with great love. My call for all My children is the same. I desire all to come to Me that I may immerse them in the fire of My great love. None knows or understands how great My Love is for each of them, that My Light, may, through all who respond, illuminate this very darkened world.

You and all who have answered the call of My Mother, have become My apostles of light for these last days. My Mother shows you the way to walk, which is in imitation of Us both. Silent, humble, in love, and totally obedient to the Eternal Father. To complete His will in your lives is all that should matter.

(S.J., At this point my children were in need of me.)

Jesus: Go child, we will continue later.

The Greatest Act of My Love and Mercy

June 13, 1994

(S.J., I am reading the "Life of Christ" by Saint Catherine Emmerich when I hear:)

Jesus: Sadie. Sadie. Sadie.

(S.J., I answered, Jesus?)

Jesus: Come to Me child, I call. I am your Savior and Savior of all.

(S.J., at this time I get my book and sit before Our Lord's image as I usually do.)

Jesus: With you I sing praises of God, My Father. I continue child with My discourse.

(S.J., This reminded me that we had been interrupted during the previous message.)

Jesus: You have been placed in the crucible of My heart's love. I am the lover of your soul, the delight of your spirit! I desire to be this to all; but the times are grave for those who have refused My call, My grace, My love.

The fulfillment of all prophecies is fast approaching. Man will see. Man will know. There is a God!

Jesus: The greatest act of My love and mercy is to pour in abundance once again My Spirit; that mankind can be convicted and repent! Those who are My faithful flock, strengthen yourselves, for the harvest is ripe, the laborers few. You will all be called to work in My vineyard, My apostles of light and of these latter days.

Strengthen yourselves by offering Me the simplicity of your lives, Everything that is done in My love, and in My Name, will be great in My eyes. I do not require great things; it is the littlest, simplest, done in obedience and love that attract Me to them.

Strengthen yourselves for this day is upon you. You will need to walk in love, obedience and humility for the coming days and this is My Mother's role. She is leading, She is guiding, She is at the head of the heavenly army!

The threat of war looms on the horizon! The plagues are! The cataclysmic events begin and this My own will know: peace, protection, and love; as the world, as it is known, comes to a halt. My own will walk through this valley of death, and I am with you.

188

Remember, little daughter of My heart, God's justice is holy! God's justice is true! God's justice will be! Pray child and all mine, that it (God's justice) pass swiftly. Pray children that **I come quickly**!

Prayer is the key. You must continue to pray. For in My Father's Kingdom, the prayers of the just move the hand of God. Peace to all My children. You are mine.

(S.J., I am given to understand that Our Lord hears the cries of His people who feel that there is no longer any call or need in any of their daily situations to pray. They take the attitude of, oh well, let's sit back and wait. Wait for the prophecies to be fulfilled. (Of this we know and feel, that everything will be fulfilled.)

But Our Lord is saying, pray harder, be constantly in prayer by offering your day to Him. It is our prayers that will govern the severity of all punishments, the number of souls won for Our Lord, and the sense of peace and security we will feel when everything begins to happen. There is no fear if one is spiritually prepared.)

June 14th, 15th and 16th, 1994

Mary: My daughter, the messages you have received to share with your prayer group and others have come to an end.

(S.J., This message was given in parts over three days and then repeated in full on June 16th, 1994. I am given to understand that personal messages for my mission will continue, but they would be private and not to be distributed indiscriminately.)

189

Chapter Five

The Triumph of
The Cross!

**Messages From July 1, 1994
To December 30, 1994**

The Sword of Truth

July 1, 1994

(S.J., I was awakened at 3:00 A.M. the night of June 30th with these words, "Make it known". The words were so clear that when I awoke, I thought someone was in the room. I rebuked and tested and our Lord answered.)

Jesus: I am Jesus. Praise be to the Triune God.

(S.J., I answered Him: "Now and forever.")

Jesus: I am coming with a vengeance never before known to man. Listen to these words, oh little daughter of My heart. I am coming through with all the words of My prophets. I am coming through the blows of Divine justice that will be unleashed through and through this nation and yes, around the world. I am going to lay to the root of all evil the sword of truth. I am going to lay bare every malice and trace of evil, every thought, action and deed.

Prepare, oh little daughter of My heart. Gather your belongings. You have sought hard My Father's will. You will not be here much longer, then you will settle in the distant land (Santa Maria). Prepare to take your leave. Prepare and pray and watch. The quiet before the storm is over.

Peace.

My Heart Remains Sorrowful

August 16, 1994 - 10:40 A.M.

Mary: Little daughter of My Son's heart.

(S.J., At this point I tested and Our Lady answered.)

Mary: But I am your Mother, most powerful, the Mother of Jesus and of all My children. Together let us praise the Son, the Father and the Holy Spirit.

Although this is My time, My heart remains sorrowful for the many who refused to heed My warnings.

My Father and My Son have given over to Me the power to bring about this plan (1), which **will**, in spite of the defeats of many of My plans, **will** be victorious!

When I called you to obedience of silence, it was just that the days which seem so long to you and all My children, are all part of what is offered to Me, that these instruments that have been used will continue to persevere. You have been set apart to give these warnings and now I tell you that this hour is here!

The upheaval of the earth will bring such death and destruction as has never been seen before! The blows of My Son's hand will strike and strike again and you My apostles of these latter days will be called to work tirelessly. Your days will no longer go in silence. They will be filled with those who have seen what their God sees, and be filled with repentance.

The refuge is given, My heart. Do not worry about anything else, the signs have been given to you (2). Only those who have stepped out and walked in faith will be led by Me to their safe havens.

Go child the day is blessed with your God's blessing of His peace, and Our presence! Amen.

(1) Cross of Peace Project

(2) and to all

It Is Now

August 18, 1994 - 5:45 P.M.

(S.J., This vision was received during evening Holy Mass. I am preparing to receive communion, with my eyes closed, when all of a sudden, I see this flaming object with a tail of flames, hurling through space downwards, in total blackness.

I then see the same thing a second time, only this time I can see a planet, way off in the distance, such as when they show shots from the moon of earth, depicting it very small, very far away. I see this object a third time, only this time the object and the point of impact (the planet) are as if only seconds away.

I was overcome with a sorrow and began to cry and I kept saying, Lord, what are you trying to show me? Along with, "No, no Lord, I don't want to see anymore. Please don't show me anymore. I don't want to know anything else." I was overcome, then after communion, during mediation, I began to hear the voice of Our Lord, and He said:)

Jesus: I am Jesus, whom you have received and made for Me a home of your heart. I have just shown you what will cause man to fall on his knees and know the dread of his soul.

(S.J., I continue to pray on the way home and then upon arriving, I know the Lord is going to give me a message. Approximately 7:00 P.M.)

Jesus: My little daughter of My Heart, I am Jesus, whom you have received and made for Me a home of your heart. I receive your praises along with those of all My children and I, too, present them to My Father. Do not fight the will of My Father for your life.

You have been called victim and you have said yes. The wonderful silence of your heart is where I find solace for My wounds, consolation for the lack of love from many of My children. I have shown you what is soon to bring many to the dread of their hearts, many of My children will repent yet.

Do not concern yourself with times. But know this: You have seen heaven's interpretation of time. It is **now**. I tell you this that you will continue to pray fervently!

Adieu, My child, And blessings!

(S.J., Then I asked what was I to do with this message and immediately came:)

Jesus: Share with C. and C.

(S.J., I was crying and inwardly I said, "Lord, I will do anything you ask of me, but you know that. Please increase my faith and confirm this is truly of you. Have C. call me." He did call that same night (8:30 P.M.), which is not unheard of, but highly unusual as we communicate regularly on Sunday nights. It is a long distance call.)

(Vision 5:45 P.M....Message 7:00 P.M. 'C.' called 8:30 P. M. Times approximate.)

August 20, 1994 - Early morning.

(S.J., all during early morning hours, during moments when I would awake, I would hear:)

Mary: I am Mary, Virgin of the Way. I have come to assume My motherly duties for all My children; to show them how to live the Way, to cover them with My mantle and place them in the refuge of My heart. Here they must be first to allow Me the permission to lead them along the road of safety, holiness and peace. [See 2/27/97 Message.]

Humanity Cannot Comprehend
That Which Awaits

September 1, 1994 - 7:42 P.M.

(S.J., I began to hear Our Lady, but I tested by rebuking the voice and commanded it to go away in the name of Jesus.)

Mary: My child, it is good to test. The enemy rages. But it is I, Mary, Mother of the Son of God, Jesus. Come and I'll pray with you.

(S.J., This is the first time, to my knowledge, that She has asked me to pray with Her. So I went over to my little altar and prayed a Hail Mary, Apostles Creed and a Glory Be.)

Mary: Now, My sorrowful rose, I come to console you, to comfort you as I wish to do for all My children. Your life bears much fruit. Do not despair. I hold you in My arms at your cries and sorrows.

Trust daughter, trust Me for everything. I tell you all humanity cannot comprehend that which awaits them. It is the prayers of the remnant, the true acts of reparations, that will allow many to be converted, though they would not have otherwise.

I have made reference to this day before to you as the day of thunder. It will be a day of reckoning, everyone with their sins in clear view, just as they are seen by God. No longer will the darkness, that has pervaded every inch of the world, be able to blind these souls.

My child, it is imperative that you remain open. Remain prayful and vigilant. The Holy Spirit is enlightening all who are now mine. There will be many, child, come to you and this extreme fatigue you fight through now, will be gone, and you will go forth as all My children will, to call the last through the door of refuge in My heart.

This will happen very soon, child, for the events that have seemed so long delayed have only been put in the place of God the Father's

196

perfect time. You will be guided and lead at all times through the next critical days.

As much as you can, fast even more. Let nothing disturb your peace. I am with you and all will be taken care of by Me. Do not worry about anything. You pray, you love, you lead your life in silentium. It is the smallest of your acts seen by the Father. He has great designs for your life. Trust, child, and love. I bid you a good and blessed night.

I bless you in the name of the Father, My Son, and the Holy Spirit. Pacem.

Grave Moment Arrives For All Humanity

September 10, 1994 - 3:00 P.M.

(S.J., I heard the voice of Mary, Mother of Jesus, and I tested.)

Mary: My little sorrowful rose: I am your Mother and the Mother of Jesus and all humanity. I am the Flo Carmeli.

(S.J., Flo Carmeli means Flower of Carmel.)

Mary: Child, I have brought you here and isolated you once again that you may receive great graces, for in a moment, the time arrives and you will minister to God's children. I tell you this grave moment arrives for all humanity, all My children.

The serenity of this day will be replaced by chaos and great reconciling of My children to their God, the Father. That His just and holy justice will pass swiftly by them. But very quickly now will events foretold come to pass. My Son....

(S.J., I knew that our Lord was present, and Our Lady was stepping back so He could speak. I said, Jesus? He answered:)

Jesus: I am, and I worship God, My Father and the Holy Spirit and receive the praises of My children! Little daughter of My

197

heart, in a moment's flash, the reality of this world will pass away and great confusion come upon the world though the world chooses to ignore the warnings that have been given. The great illumination of men's souls will cause grief, anguish and repentance.

There will be many to minister to, thus at our bidding, you have come to obedience in this weekend of solitude. But, therein, you are graced with fortitude and wisdom for the coming days.

Fear not little one, the great gifts and love we shower you with are for the distribution to others.

With My Mother, We are here to bless and guide you. Peace.

Days of Woe and Trial Ahead for All Humanity

September 14, 1994 - 6:34 P.M.

Today is "Triumph of The Cross." Tomorrow is "Our Lady of Sorrows."

(S.J., I began to hear Our Lady and after testing the Spirit, She answered me.)

Mary: I am your Mother and the Mother of all humanity that was given to Me at the foot of the glorious Cross by My beloved Son. I have from that time embraced this sorrow: that all would know, love and serve My Son and He has deemed that I be loved. Many do not know Me, many who do, do not love Me. But all is given to the praise and glory of God and My Son. For, by this wonderful cross, soon will come the fulfillment of Jesus' sacrifice on Calvary.

(S.J., here I will describe the vision I was shown during Mass today.

I saw the silhouette of Jesus' body hanging on the cross at the top of a hill and in between from where I was seeing the cross and where the cross was, there was an ocean of people. So the image of the cross was very small as if seeing something off in the distance.

Off to the left side, I also saw a bunch of demons huddled and cowering. They were bound together by a chain, like prisoners. As I continued to gaze upon this, I saw the cross lift up into the heavens and it was no longer on the ground, but in the air, at somewhat of an angle. Please bear with my descriptions as sometimes it is very hard to put what I am shown into words. The message continues.)

Mary: There are many of My children who do not know of My Son's love for them, or how great it is. So they live in ignorance and total rejection of the sacrifice on the Cross. Thus rejection of My Son's Cross, has made Me, **A Mother of Sorrows.**

But little one, all will soon, so very soon, know the complete fulfillment of Calvary, that God would reveal to all the state of their soul; so that then, they will accept the triumph of the Cross! That cross held high in the heavens will be to all humanity their last opportunity for conversion.

You and My remnant will have long days and endless nights before you. Thus you will usher in the last of those who would believe by your love and prayers, embraces and explanations. "The harvest is ripe, the laborers few." Count everything joy and peace of Our love and protection. This is Our gift to the remnant.

Days of woe and trial ahead for all humanity! But to this very end, all of God's plan has come to the completion.

(S.J., at this point, the enemy was interfering and I had to rebuke him.)

Mary: You are graced and loved, however, no more than any of My children. But your response and sufferings have counted greatly in God's eyes. Be at peace all. In your Mother's love you are held and blessed!

(S.J., I continued to praise God and Our Lady at this very wonderful and awesome message. As I did so, I was meditating and looking at my statue of the Pilgrim Virgin. Her countenance seemed so sad and sorrowful. I began to converse with Her and the following is the conversation we had:)

Lady, you truly are a Lady of Sorrow. Why did you ask me to share your sorrows?

Mary: You have been no stranger to sorrow. I wanted you to respond to the call of the Cross, that united, We would win more souls for My Son. For in comparison to everything you have suffered, when you took it and measured it to the Cross of Calvary, yours was sorely lacking. But you allowed your sufferings to become engulfed by My Son's passion and sufferings. Therefore, that surrender united and sealed your call.

(S.J., Lady, I feel your presence even stronger than before.)

Mary: Child you have been infused with grace, so that in the coming days, you will feel My presence even stronger. I am letting all My children know through signs and dreams, signs in the heavens, that I am with them. There is no need for anyone to worry or fear. But you must stay close to the "shadow of the Lord."

I have pointed the way: repentance, conversion and return to frequent confession and communion, prayer and silent prayer, and a knowledge that by your sufferings you are being purified and strengthened; so that in your meeting with My Son, you will stand spotless without stain or wrinkle and He, Your Lord, can say to you: "Well done, good and faithful servant."

But before that day the final ascent of Calvary by My Holy Church must be completed.

Be at peace little one.

200

(S.J., I love you, Mother!)

Mary: My child, you and yours are loved and protected.

(S.J., Good night, Lady.)

Mary: Good night, daughter!

Woe to You, My Shepherds

September 29, 1994 - 8:30 A.M.

(S.J., I heard a voice and I tested.)

Jesus: I Am Jesus, Lord And Savior Of All Who Call My Name !

Praises are sung by My remnant, but soon, little daughter of My Heart, I tell you, every knee will bend! Every knee will fall and acknowledge their God, their Lord and Savior. The heavens will shake, the earth will tremble, all of creation will resound with this knowledge. In the light of mercy all will see the darkness of their soul. The moment is here.

The act of mercy comes before the blows of justice, for I tell you, though all will see and know their God, not all will embrace Him or receive His tender mercies. They will instead rage at the revelation and remain ever hard of heart. To their end.

I am, with the Father, ready to receive these last, and ready to give vent to the just anger of God!.

Look to the nations and see, abomination on top of abomination! They are all there for God to see! The cries of the helpless, who cannot defend themselves, from the womb to the aged.

But abomination of all abominations is here! The Holy Sacrifice of the Mass, My gift to mankind, left in the hands of My shepherds. They have left their flocks to be devoured by the wolves, for they no longer offer with blameless hands! Woe to you My shepherds, for your flocks have been scattered.

But, I am the Good Shepherd, I hear their voices, and I will not leave one who cries out for Me without means of receiving Me into their hearts and lives. I am Creator and all creation will give testimony to Me. Your love must increase through Me!

There was great significance to P's visit.

As to those who pray and meditate, God reveals His wisdom and understanding (of) some of God's plans. Do not worry for the meaningless (things) in your lives.

I know all, I leave all for you according to your strength to endure, to increase your faith, your trust and your love for Me. It is all obtained through the hands of My Mother, your Mother, My gift to all. I love you and all My children.

Continue to allow Me to lead you, with My Mother. We are always at your side.

Peace and blessings.

Chaos and Confusion for Those Walking in Darkness

October 4, 1994 - 8:15 P.M.

(S.J., The voice was Our Lady's, as I began to hear Her, I tested.)

Mary: My little sorrowful rose, I am your Queen! The Victorious One over **all** evil, who dwells in the midst of the most Holy Trinity with all My children and the angels and saints. I praise Jesus, My Son, My Father, and My Beloved Spouse, the Holy Spirit. From the wounds of My Holy Son, will come forth light, mercy and grace to penetrate the darkness that covers the whole of creation.

I am here to receive the praises and prayers of My children. They fall like so many roses at My feet which I gather and present to the Father for the continuous intercession on behalf of all humanity.

Twofold are My requests: First, that the justice of God would be mitigated and lessened. Secondly, for more souls of My children.

My children who wander aimlessly as in a desert, with no one to lead them. They do not turn to their God and Creator. They do not drink from the source of living waters that they might have life and peace. They choose instead every kind of perversion, thirst for power and money and are driven by greed. They live daily, unaware of the presence of God, and give Him lip service instead of their hearts.

My Son has spoken of His displeasure and anger towards His shepherds. They do not hear the little ones who speak the words of God. They have chosen for themselves to drink from the cup of God's wrath!

For they, the priests, glory in themselves and bring no glory to God. They enjoy their consolation now, in this worlds by their choices of worldly recognition, possession and pastimes.

They forsake their pastoral duties! They forsake truth for error! They betray their Jesus and give Him the kiss of Judas! My Heart is laden with sorrow. I weep and weep tears of blood at what will befall this humanity.

But I come to you, little daughter of My Son's heart, to tell you the moment of all moments is here. Be not afraid and know My angels have been around every one of My children walking in this hidden army of mine.

There will be much chaos and confusion for those walking in darkness. For My own, all that happens will be greater confirmation of signs already told.

The preparations have been made. With a grieving heart, I now take My army through the most intense and painful moments of these years of trial and tribulations. I am leading and guiding all who will listen and give Me permission to enter into the abode of their hearts.

203

The time for merriment ends. The only joy will be the joy of the Lord, even through these most painful moments!

Be not afraid. We are with you.

There awaits, for those who persevere, My promised era of triumph:

The triumph of the Cross!
The triumph of the Two Hearts!
The triumph over all evil in this world!

Continue children, continue, be ever ready and constantly in a state of grace.

And now little daughter, I bless you and lay My hand upon you, that you will be blessed in all you are led to do.

In the name of My Father, My Son, Jesus and My Spouse, the Holy Spirit.

(S.J., Note: The joy Our Lady refers to is that during all the moments of trial, the children of God and Our Lady will marvel at the wondrous ways we are to be protected. We will see it and know it is the hand of God. Also, Our Lady instructed me to read Revelation from Chapter 8 until the end. I suggest all do the same. It is all there.)

The Warning

October 10, 1994 - 8:40 P.M.

(S.J., I tested the words I began to hear and Our Lord answered me.)

Jesus: My child, I am the Second Person of the Trinity, Jesus your Merciful Savior and Lord.

My child, you try to silence the words of God within you, yet in the silence of your heart they reverberate until you respond. I am the Living Word!

Through all things that come to you, I give you best of what I have; tender mercy and love for you. I am always with you. You do not know the consolation your love brings Me. I hear at all times your cries, your sighs of love, your sufferings; and always you have My name in your heart and on your lips.

This plan of God's for all humanity cannot be contained in one soul! Thus I bring together those who will confound the wisdom of this world.

(S.J., Our Lord speaks here of all His prophets and messengers.)

Jesus: Because you draw deeper and deeper into My heart, because you have surrendered all, I can use you. Not for the sake of using you, but for My delight at seeing you become transformed by My grace and love.

You are a testimony of the saving power of God that will transform a soul and take it to the greatest heights of Heaven; thus, you no longer are of this world. Your sighs of love and desires are of the heavenly kingdom of God. That will be the Kingdom that will reign so very soon. My Word, My signs, My prophets all point to this fact.

But man has cried out for the prince of this world, by his delusion of happiness while immersed in a life of sin. This happiness is not possible. The soul recognizes its alienation from its creator and does not rest in the peace of God. However, if the tugging at man's soul does not bring about the response of returning to God, that soul becomes cold and hardened to God's calls. So the prince of this world has brought this era of darkness, violence, hatred and a lack of respect for human life.

I will leave man to his own folly! I will not hear the cries and lamentations! I will not look upon man with the graces of mercy any longer. Only My own will know My protection, for in the coming days it will be: From the rising of the sun to it's

setting, there will rise the cries, lamentations and travail amidst the chaos and confusion that will exist.

I wanted to give C. and C. the peace of seeing the work of My hand and bring My servants together. This work is the very hand of God, for the salvation of many souls:

For consolation to the unconsoled, for hope to the hopeless, for light in this world of darkness!

The moment of travail is upon mankind! But before this, when all least expect, one of the last acts of mercy will be this: I will allow all to see how they would stand before Me! I will allow this penetration into the darkness of souls by My light of illumination! From one moment to the next all of this will come to be!

These are words of encouragement, consolation; imploring My children to take the hand of My Mother, that We may bring all into the refuge of Her Immaculate Heart!

My daughter you will see great things in the coming days. Keep to your fast. (Yes, I will help 'C.' and 'C.')

And now, My little daughter, bow your head that I may bless you;

I bless you in the Name of My Father, in the Name of the Son, Triumphant (Jesus), and in the name of the Omnipotent Holy Spirit.

Justice Now Cries Out

October 21, 1994 - 11:50 A.M.

(S.J., Because of what I had begun to hear since Tuesday, 10-18-94, I had not been open to the message of the Lord. I had been severely attacked by the enemy, by doubts. The enemy knows well my weakness. Every time I would hear the voice of the Lord, I would command it to go in the name of Jesus if it was not of

206

God. But then I would busy myself and not leave myself open. Friday, October 21, around 11:50 A.M. I heard:)

Jesus: My child, you weary Me so, by your failure to respond.

(S.J., Immediately, I asked the Lord to forgive me and I said, "Speak Lord, your servant listens".)

Jesus: I am the Almighty, one and true, the Alpha and the Omega. With the choirs of Heaven, My name is praised and glorified. This, My Father, Who is One with Me, has bestowed on His only begotten, given as a ransom for many!

(S.J., The following is what I had been hearing since Tuesday, October 18, 1994.)

Jesus. I am going to strike! I am going to strike all of humanity! I Am going to strike this earth from the four corners!

The diabolical plan, spoken of to you before, is and has been in place. But now the forces behind are ready to cast its dark insidious net to entrap the whole of humanity!

Woe to you mankind, who did not heed the warnings of My chosen! Woe to you mankind, for you have not prepared your lamps! Woe to you My shepherds, who have made for yourselves new idols and false teachings to tickle the ears of your flocks!

This moment for all humanity has been spoken of down through the ages. Only those enlightened by the Holy Spirit, and by the consecration to the Immaculate and Sorrowful Heart of My Mother, will experience miracles of protection! These are My promises! This is My word!

All that has been promised will come to pass! All that has been given warning to, will happen! For of the two measures God has for humanity, mercy and justice; justice now must come, for mercy has been refused! Justice now cries out to avenge the injustices committed at every level of humanity.

Do not doubt, little one, the warning will come soon, sooner than you can realize, for this will be a strike to all humanity, their last warning!

Prepare child! Keep vigilant (and open).

(S.J., I'm sorry Lord, forgive me. I only desire not to be deceived nor to deceive.)

Jesus: I reveal these to you, that you may immerse all humanity in the mercy of My heart! Cease not your prayers of the Chaplet of Mercy!

You are much loved, My little one. Do not fear. Do not doubt. All heaven is expectant and ready for the battle about to rage.

My own fear not! I have defeated the enemy! I have won the victory! Trust in My Mercy.

I bless you child.

The Wonders of God

October 31, 1994 - 8:15 A.M.

(S.J., I am praying my Liturgy of the Hours, at the back of which they have non-biblical writings. I am reading a sermon of Blessed Isaac of Stella, entitled, "Mary and the Church." At the end of this writing it says:

"Christ dwelt for nine months in the tabernacle of Mary's womb. He dwells until the end of the ages in the tabernacle of the Church's faith." . . . I then hear, loud and firm:)

God the Father: Look up this word, 'tabernacle'.

(S.J., I recognize this to be the Father, and I first command this spirit to leave in Jesus' name if it is not of God. My (our) Father answers:)

God the Father: I am God, the Creator, I, Who gave this world My only Son, to ransom many from darkness to light everlasting! Jesus is to be worshiped and praised!

(S.J., He then directed me to write the definition of tabernacle. It is as follows:

Latin; tabernaculum, a tent, dim. taberna, a hut.,

1. temporary shelter;
2. human body regarded dwelling place of the soul;
3. portable sanctuary carried by the Jews in their wanderings from Egypt to Palestine;
4. shrine with canopy;
5. a place of worship with a large seating capacity;
6. an ornamental container for the consecrated host to dwell temporarily.

God the Father: He dwells until the end of ages in the tabernacle of the church's faith. When the Son of Man returns, will He find any faith?

Oh, you little of heart and love! If My Son were to return right now, what would He find dwelling in the tabernacles of His Church? In the tabernacles of your bodies? For I can see all and I know!

This dwelling place of God was to be temporary, for I know well what triumphs over man's soul in this age. Is it not evil over good? Is it not self-indulgence over sacrifice? Is it not every kind of perversion over purity? The faith to believe what is consecrated is the totality, human and divine, of My Son, Jesus. But is there any faith?

No, My little daughter, the end of the ages must come, for otherwise man in his pride would destroy all!

Therefore, I am calling My children through My Spirit. Yes, My Spirit goes forth and those who have opened their hearts to My Son are able to receive this all-powerful gift. I reveal the mysteries of God to the little, the humble; those who love much! That is how I know you are Mine! By your love that will go the extra effort.

I am tired of seeing My priests go through the motions! There is no love in their hearts! It is something worse than a duty!

(S.J., How the priests offer Mass, or minister to God's people.)

God the Father: But the true remnant that is persevering, rejoice! I have heard your cries! Heaven has received your prayers! Yes! Through the hands of My Daughter of the Magnificat. I have seen the brightness and flame of your hearts! They are worthy of My Son.

All of you, you know who you are—for I have shown you, I have led you—have **not** to worry or fear! Stay close to your spiritual leader and teacher, My Spirit! My Holy Spirit. The Spirit of God is leading, moving, guiding My Daughter's army.

The finality and totality of the rebellious one's defeat has already been won! It is for you, all My children, to go forth and be **not** afraid!

You will marvel at the wonders of God! The awesome mightiness of My power will be wonderful for you to behold. With the eyes of faith, you must see! With the faith that will once again build up the kingdom of love, which is God; you must remain steadfast.

The time of elections is here again, and again they will elect the godless to pass their evil plots! But this evil age that has chosen to disregard and disbelieve truth, does not change the Truth that I, All-Knowing and Omnipotent, have seen the sacrifice of My Son (it is a sacrifice), go rejected, reviled and refused!

No longer will they say, "Where is your God?"

I say: I Am, so be it!

210

My child continue to lead and guide those I bring to you. I bring them. Soon there will be many more.

From heaven's throne you are blessed.

(S.J., **Note:** Our Father is addressing here the faith, or lack of it, both in the hearts of mankind, and in the whole church. The lack of faith, particularly in the church, by the priests and religious to believe in the presence of Jesus, in the consecrated host, or to say that Mass **is** a sacrifice. To say as Blessed Isaac, "He dwells until the end of the ages in the tabernacle of the Church's faith." In these days, is there any faith?)

The Final Times

November 13, 1994 - 8:00 P.M.

(S.J., After putting the children to bed, I was relaxing, when I began to hear the voice of our Lord. I tested and He answered me.)

Jesus: My little daughter of My heart, know that the prayers and sacrifices received from you and My Mother's children are received with joy and great consolation. Many souls reap the benefits that are My tried and true promise.

Write what was shown today to you at Holy Mass.

(S.J., After receiving Holy Communion, today at Mass, I was meditating, during which time I saw the silhouette of a person standing on top of a globe of the earth. Then there are sudden explosions of bright light, great explosions, and this silhouette of blackness is intensified by the light. I see the person begin to move backwards and cower, as if in fear.)

Jesus: This illumination of men's souls is even now at the point of being. There will come mass confusion, chaos, darkness and despair.

211

(S.J. I am given to understand that is for those in mortal sin. At this point I no longer hear Our Lord, but Our Lady. I tested and She answers.)

Mary: And now My little one, I speak, the Mother of your Lord and Savior Jesus, Mary Immaculate, Mary most pure, Mary most sorrowful.

I come to reveal to you, little sorrowful rose, this day of thunder is upon you. Believe the words we speak are for the preparation of the faithful, for their encouragement. So that the time of stepping out in faith has come.

It will seem to all, the unseen but very real hand of God will reach out and strengthen and guide all who will be open. By the very power of the Holy Spirit, My children will burn in the fire of His love, leading and guidance. These will be times of very great miracles. The days of distress will be lightened by this fact.

Do not worry about your loved ones. They will be brought in by God's Divine Providence and in His time. Have faith in the prayers that **are** touching the very throne of God. These are the final times which will conclude all the fulfillment of prophecy. These will be the days of revealing truth from error, authenticity from falsehood. In all the places where My presence is real, I will make present My signs.

And My Cross, of which the light of its glory will be to greet Christ the King! The glory and the graces that will give light, peace and consolation to many walking in darkness. And to others, be the sign of the gathering of many in My valley, which will shine with its light for the eternity of the Era of Peace!

This will forever give testimony to the Triumph of the Cross! Conversion, salvation and a life in the light of My Son. This light will come to shine on this humanity enveloped in darkness and in this light all darkness is brought into the open. It is then, many will lie in that valley of decision.

So My remnant must prepare to work ceaselessly, tirelessly, and spread the message of today's Gospel. (Saint Mark 13: 24-32)

The sign of your times is here.

With My Son, I bless you.

Do Not Fear

November 30, 1994 - 7:00 P.M.

(S.J., I have been hearing our Lord but was not responding. I then heard our Lady and She told me do not fear. I tested.)

Mary: Do not fear, My little daughter, I am the Immaculate Conception, from whom came forth the Son of Man! Jesus be praised now and forever. Listen to the words of My Son.

(S.J.,I then said, Jesus.)

Jesus: Yes child, I am! Praises are sung now and forever to the Most Blessed Trinity. My child, though mother and father forsake you, I will never forsake you. I am the One who knows the hearts of all. I know your pain. It pleases Me that you no longer dwell inward, but rather upwards to the will of My Father. This is growth that only I can bring one to. Nothing that you have done for love of Me or My Mother has gone unnoticed and will bring its due reward.

But these words you have struggled not to hear. The word of the Lord goes forth and does not come back void. There is no peace until you submit to Me. I love you and have you as My own. The will of the Father has called you to bring much glory to My Father's kingdom. This was your call and you have given your fiat. Child, again I tell you, be not concerned with being fearful over any of the prayers on your heart. All will swiftly come to pass.

213

Do you still not believe this work of Mine, and My Mother who has been able to mitigate much because of the prayers of Her heart? The remnant, the little, the ones who are struggling, and yet are convicted by faith to stay persevering until the end.

But throughout all My works, My Mother, and I with Her, are going to be with all Her little children. At the proper time certain things are revealed. For all things have an appointed time to be. Before the end of this year, I will strike with My warning. Do you believe this is so?

(S.J., Lord, as much as I struggle not to hear, I know what I hear and I believe with all my heart what You say. Forgive me Jesus if I have failed you. Speak and instruct me. I will forever serve You all the days of my life. Jesus, what am I to do with this message?)

Jesus: Alert those (whom you normally do) and pray. This is not to catch you unaware, but in peace and prayer. The days of darkness and distress, blood and trial, are not to catch the faithful unaware, but rather those who have not heeded My words. Peace be unto you and all who pray and persevere. The fulfillment of Calvary draws nigh. I love you child. Graces and blessing descend upon you through the hands of My Mother.

(S.J., **Note:** Because I had begun to hear part of the previous message since the beginning of the week, I had been struggling with what was being said by our Lord. Because of the responsibility that has come with my being a "victim messenger," which is nothing other than to be a "fool for the Lord" and do all that is asked of me in total obedience and love, I have no problem whether this is believed or not believed.

I do know what I have heard, and I know that from the beginning our Lord and our Lady said I was to be a trumpet and sound the warning. That I was to do exactly as Noah did. Thus the previous message has been received. And now it is forwarded so that those who do believe (the remnant) will pray with the intensity that is being asked of Our Lady's heart.)

214

The Spirit and the Bride Say Come

December 13, 1994 - 9:35 A.M.

(S.J., After I tested, Our Lady answered me.)

Mary: My little daughter, I come to you this morning as your Mother, La Virgin De Guadalupe, Mi hijita! Yes, I praise now and forever the glories of God for the gift of His Word, My Son Jesus, the Word Incarnate made flesh by the power of the Holy Spirit. Sing hosannas to your Lord!

My little children, lift up your hearts, raise your hands in praise and steady your drooping knees for the triumph of My Son's and My Immaculate Heart is as of now almost complete.

Believe that I am with you in a very special way this morning. Am I not the same Mother who gave My Son, Juan Dieguito, the message of consolation? Am I not the same Mother who enfolds you with My arms in the midst of your trials?

Yes, My children, through this very special image I have worked signs, wonders and miracles; all to confirm I am the Woman of Revelation! Ponder upon these words, My dear hearts, and rejoice! It is My desire to hold and protect all of you who have been steadfast and yes, I will gather those who come through the door of Divine Mercy that is still open until that final and absolute decision that many will face in the Valley of Decision.

Pray, My precious one, for these souls and if it seems a long time before your prayers and your burdens are lifted, it is only because My Father and yours, knew who He could entrust and trust to carry their own particular cross with faith, love and perseverance, to unite theirs to Calvary and help in this wonderful plan of co-redemption of souls.

But the moment draws near and in the flash of one minute to the next, your prayers will be answered by means of the last great act of Divine mercy.

Rejoice, O little hearts of Mine, our hearts beat together, our voices pray together.

Today let us pray together and see the triumph of your Mother, the Woman of Revelation come!

Come Lord Jesus, come, and the Spirit and the Bride says come Lord Jesus, come!

Hallelujah! Amen!

Blessings from the throne of heaven on all gathered here!

Queen of All Nations

December 17, 1994 - 8:00 A.M.

(S.J., I believe this message to be a reflection on the prayer meeting at the church for Friday night adoration, December 16th. There was a significant increase in the attendance. In my heart I was being thankful for this. Our Lord began to speak to me at this time. Part of this conversation is in this message. Today is December 17th, 1994. I tested, after I heard the Lord, and He answered.)

Jesus: My daughter, I am Jesus, the King of all Nations! Let your songs of praise join those in the heavens!

Because you have submitted your will, because you have persevered, you have shown great love, because you have continued to acknowledge your sinfulness before Me. I say, through your hands I will touch My people, through your lips I shall admonish and instruct My people, through you My Father will do wondrous things for your know all good comes from God. You struggle to hear these things, tell them to My brother 'P.' I will speak through him.

216

Jesus: My Mother has come as Reconciler of All Peoples, Queen of Peace, the Lady of the Way, Queen of All Nations, to precede My coming once again. She has chosen those whose hearts are soft and pliable, that She may mold your children to Our very image.

You saw the results of a holy priest last night. You gazed at the increase in the number of My children. Yes, holy priests make a people holy! Some of those present were totally in communion with Me. They are sponges that absorb every grace I wish to bestow.

And even then, when the sponge is absorbed to its fullest, it can no longer gather and hold My gifts. Other were in My Presence, unaware I am there gazing back at them, saddened that My graces wash over them and they do not absorb.

But I tell you, My little daughter, let the prayers and songs of praise rise! Let them rise and join the songs of praise rising up from every corner of this world! They rise as when the shouts of My people went up and God allowed the walls of Jericho to fall, to come crashing down! So too, will the walls of evil come crashing down!

The word of the Lord has gone forth! It will accomplish all for the glory of the Reign of the Sacred Heart of Jesus, King of All Nations and of the Immaculate Heart of Mary, Queen and Mediatrix of All Graces! Peace child, peace to all of Mine! Once again the gift of the Savior heralds all His children. It is His gift once again. I love you, child.

(S.J., Lord, I love you. Tell my Mother I love Her too, and I entrust all prayers to Her that have been entrusted to me.)

Jesus: The peace and grace of God fall upon you and all My remnant! Shalom!

(S.J., This message came on December 18, 1994, immediately after my talk with Father P.)

217

Jesus: Of all the gifts being prepared to be given, Mine is the greatest. Once again, on the day remembering My birth, My gift will be the greatest.

(S.J., Note: Our Lord has given me to understand that His gift to mankind, once again, is salvation through the warning; of the illumination of one's soul. His gift at His first coming into the world was salvation for all mankind, which has been refused at His first coming, and even now, at this advent of His second coming.)

My Warning is My Gift

December 30, 1994 - 7:15 A.M.

(S.J., During morning prayers and after I hear what I have been hearing all week, I tested and Our Lord answers:)

Jesus: It is good for you to test, but I am the Good Shepherd and My sheep know My voice. I am Jesus, the One who was, who is, and who will come again in glory and splendor, and I will dwell amidst the praises of My people.

My child, I will take you from obscurity and place you in the light and power of My Spirit. You will go where I take you. You will go where I send you. And you will speak the words I will place in your heart and on your lips. All this you will do and in a very short time. The holy wrath of God will come upon those who refuse to listen to you and My other chosen messengers.

My children, those who listened, will be covered and protected. Those called to live in the places of refuge will go and live in community. You will recognize and know each other, and evil will not penetrate there in those places. This time of My warning is My gift to this poor humanity that has chosen to live in disregard of their God and each other. The laws of God are profaned and dissolved by your nation's courts.

Therefore, I will turn your nation over to captivity. This warning, this light into your soul that will penetrate the impenetrable, will be man's last chance and hope for salvation; and for you, daughter and others, the ceaseless work begins.

Teach that God's will **must** reign, God's will must be, God is the Creator and Designer of all things. There is no luck, only God's blessing, God's appointed time. Behold the heavens and angels and saints rejoice and their shouts of gladness and praise mingle with yours.

From a little voice crying the words of God, will come the fulfillment of a very great prophecy. By this they will know you are Mine and a part of My work. Others have done and will continue to do as they are called. Now, I call you.

(S.J., My God, to whom shall I go if not to you? You are life and eternal. I am your servant.)

Jesus: Then recall My Mother's words, ". . . from one minute to the next . . .", and live in that moment. Live it in prayer by what you do. Live it in peace, live it in joy! And watch!

Amen I say to you, it shall be.

My Blessing and peace cover you and yours.

Chapter Six

Warning, Chaos, Ark of Safety

**Messages From January 1, 1995
To June 22, 1995**

Many, Many, Many Souls

January 1, 1995 - 8:00 P.M.

(S.J., I tested and rebuked and commanded the voice to go in the name of Jesus if it was not from God. He then answered me. It was Our Lord.)

Jesus: My daughter of My heart, I would address these matters on your heart. Yes, I am your Jesus, praises be always and forever to the Triune God, Majesty and Omnipotence.

It disturbs you that heaven has been appeased for a moment longer, that you feel like Jonah? For neither did I destroy Nineveh, for they responded to the cries of Jonah. What does it matter to you if it comes before the end of the year, or shortly after. Have I not revealed things to you that can only come from God? Have you not seen signs in the heavens and had the presence of My Mother? How then can you not rejoice with Me?

Because of the faithfulness of My servants these messages have touched many. But what matters to Me, is just one, one soul. Until you understand that, can you trust the acts of heaven's judgment? For those of you who know in your heart and believe all these things will come, and it will soon, then understand God's mercy and love for one soul. How many have converted or caught their awareness because of the words of urgency. I tell you now, little one, **many, many, many** souls. You will never fathom to what degree your faithfulness and perseverance will bring your due reward and vindication.

For now, I thank you that your cry was one of true humility for you continued to say, "Speak Lord, your servant listens". Let those who believe, understand that My delay is love and mercy, and not delay.

For if the difference is hours or days, it will come, of this be assured. The prayers of one righteous avail much. So much more the body of Christ, united under the mantle and banner of My

222

Mother. For She is the Mother who sorrows, who mourns, who perseveres, who leads, who intercedes.

Be at peace, My body.

When you are tempted by the evil one to disbelieve, remember all that I have said, that has come to pass. You say what I tell you to say. I count your obedience above all things. And if you stand an object of ridicule and rejection by all; know this, I came to My own and stood in the same way. No one is greater than the Master!

And this is your call as victim of My love. And I do love you.

Peace child.

Time to Walk in Faith

January 6, 1995 - 1:00 P.M.

(S.J., I tested and Our Lady answered.)

Mary: My little sorrowful rose, I am your Mother and the Mother of Jesus, I join in your praises of My Son!

My daughter, I am being called back to heaven! Thus My apparitions are at an end. The messages for humanity are at an end. What else can I say? How many times and in how many places has the same message been given? The time to walk in faith has come. I must return, for obedience is once again being asked of me.

But to all My little remnant I have offered the secure refuge of My Heart, the consoling arms and heart of a Mother. I am the Mother of All Peoples, All Nations; just as My Son is Sovereign King (1).

I leave you still My love, My hand, My heart, and My consolation to walk now, one and all, in faith. The difficult days of distress! What can I say? They have been told of, described and My children have been prewarned.

223

With the refuge of My heart, I have offered many places of physical refuge. This, too, must be accepted in faith. For those called to be strong, to lead, to teach. I will be with you to inspire and lead the way. You have been called! Always know that We are with you! Trust and walk in faith, the faith of a child.

And I leave you the refuge of My name (2)! Coincidence? No child, there are no coincidences, only Divine fulfillment of time! Those who go must go also in faith; and, for those who don't, it will be most difficult.

The Cross is at hand! The fulfillment of and the completion of(3). Many will feel the rays of grace and love, conversion, consolation, and peace! It will stand for eternity and give light to those who dwell in its midst.

Faith! Faith! Faith!

Believe in what you cannot yet see, soon you will see it! My child in a special way, I bless you and yours and all My children who serve.

(S.J., My understanding is, (1) of All Peoples and All Nations, (2) Santa Maria, (3) The Cross of Peace in Santa Maria, California.

January 16, 1995

(S.J., I will first explain what was shown to me in a vision, at Mass yesterday, January 16, 1995. I see the Holy Father, John Paul II, carrying a cross up a hill. To the righthand side of the vision, I see the Vatican, as if it has been under siege, for I see smoke billowing from the top. I see this in a very far-off distance.

By this I know that the Holy Father is not there in the Vatican. I also see a river, which at first I think is water, but then I see that it is a river of blood. Then all of a sudden, very quickly, I see the Holy Father is turned around, and he is on the cross, dead.)

My Vicar Has Much to Suffer

January 17, 1995 - 10:24 A.M.

(S.J., I am writing this vision in my journal, when I begin to hear Our Lord. I have been praying for discernment of this vision. I also have been hearing this, It is come! It is come! It is come! I tested and He answered me.)

Jesus: Child, I am Savior! Christ who reigns and now claims His kingdom!

It is time for immolation of My Vicar. That he (John Paul II) is away from the Vatican means he will flee, and he will die away from the Chair of Peter!

Woe to you humanity! Woe to you mankind! Woe to you My pastors, head of your flocks! You have left them to be scattered at the moment of God's holy wrath! Rise up oh little children of God, pray and rejoice. Though there is much to suffer, you will see the very hand of God fall over His children and protect them all!

Your children will run to the feet of those whom they have refused to hear. This great time of seeing the fulfillment of Calvary (as I hang there on the Cross as all will see at that moment); those who are in the Valley of Decision will be won by your prayers and sacrifices, by the power and hand of the Woman Clothed with the Sun!

It is come! This moment known from the beginning of creation!

It is come! And I will not be the One to condemn any man! No, by their own rejection of Me will they be condemned!

Pray much, for My Vicar has much to suffer!

Pray child, and do all you have been instructed, and watch. Again, I say watch.

Peace and blessings.

(S.J., Yesterday morning, January 16, 1995, I was asked to fast for three days. To sanctify, to purify, to cleanse myself. That is, Monday, Tuesday and Wednesday, January 16th, 17th and 18th, 1995.)

The Final and Greatest Act of Mercy

January 18, 1995 - 6:55 P.M.

(S.J., I tested and Our Lord answered me.)

Jesus: My little daughter of My heart. I speak, the King of Kings, the Lord of Lords, the One, the True, the Mighty. Praise be to the Father, His Son and Our Spirit.

I your Lord come to tell you, that I cannot contain the love and excitement for Me to reveal these things to you.

Do I tire of hearing your proclamations of love? Oh, little one, you have given to Me, the lover of your soul, and keeper of your spirit, all things, but most importantly your will. I know your pain and suffering, and how in the beginning you asked to have them lifted, and now you embrace your cross. You carry it with knowledge of the many souls that are being won by it.

Know that the enemy cannot touch or harm you. He fears you, for you walk upright, knowing what has been bequeathed to you. You carry Me with you. Greater is He who is in You, than he who is in the world. And the works that you will do in My name, will bring glory to My Father's kingdom.

Describe what I have shown you at Mass, and show you now.

(S.J., I see Jesus resplendent in a white garment with gold. He is beautiful and He is love. He is holding out a robe for me, it is white, long and flowing. He calls me to come upwards. There are angels and Our Lady. Jesus then says:)

Jesus: I take you as My beloved, I espouse Myself to you.

226

(S.J., Lord, I don't understand.)

Jesus: But you will. You have suffered much, you will suffer more, and I will be with you.

(S.J., I am yours Lord, forever.)

Jesus: The people will come, you will go to the people. I call you to be vigilant with Me. Accompany Me through your prayers of praise, through all you do in My name. Because of My name, it has merit. I receive you as you are, full of weakness and defects, and fears and doubts. Assail the enemy with My name, with My Blood, for I have washed you whiter than snow. Continue to prostrate your face to the ground, I warmly accept your acts of love and reverence. I wait for them now.

For My servants whom I will lift up, must have stood the test of perseverance. Endure the passion of your own Calvary, united to Mine at every breath, knowing I, your Savior and God, do not test forever, nor chastise you forever. But now I will lift you up, to continue My work.

I am with you, that is all you need to know. I love you. Be at peace.

For all your children, all that I have spoken to you will be.

Now, exult and praise your God, for the final and greatest act of mercy is come.

I love you and bless you.

January 19, 1995

(S.J., I tested and Our Lord answered.)

Jesus: My child, I have drawn many to Myself, and when I am lifted up again (1), I will draw more unto Myself. I, the Son, glorify My Father, and the Father will glorify the Son, and He will pour Our Spirit on you and all; and the Holy Spirit will empower you to do all that has been told.

227

Praise to God.

(S.J., (1) My understanding is "through the warning".)

The Threads In My Tapestry

January 22, 1995 - 8:35 P.M.

(Message to Sadie Jaramillo, for C. and C. and all Mary's servants of the "Cross of Peace".)

(S.J., I heard the voice of Our Lady, I tested, She answered me.)

Mary: I am Mary Ever Virgin, and humble Servant of God who praises the omnipotence and majesty of the Triune God.

My little one, I would impart the following to all My servants of the Cross.

(S.J., I asked, "Lady is this for the 'Cross of Peace' servants or those who pick up their cross and follow?")

Mary: Are they not one and the same? To and through this work that has been Mine, and Mine alone, I have been able to bring together much that has glorified the Father because of the faith, love and obedience of My children.

C. and C. do not despair, for now the time is come to step out in faith. Faith in God and My intercession and protection of this work will bring it to completion. Do not seek for answers and security before you move in faith. Move first and I will bring all to completion.

I emphasize this for I want to thank you for all that has been sacrificed, and there has been much for this labor of love. Do not forget that is the fruit: love, Jesus' love. I would have all My children come into this awareness and knowledge of the heart, not of the mind.

Be like two little babes, and this anniversary will be as no other. **Do all as required, I will do the rest.** Move in faith, move in obedience, move in love.

Your Father and Mine in heaven has bequeathed to you the riches of His kingdom. He will not fail you. For now, pray and rejoice in the love of your Lord, My Son.

The threads in My tapestry are almost complete. Do not ask questions only heaven can answer, but they will all be answered soon. Be at peace. I have spoken to My little one, and I have given the date for her to be in My "City of Peace."

I give a special blessing through the prayer of My little one for C. & C. and all of My good children who serve in love and obedience.

I hold you all in My mantle.

The Triumphant Prophetess of the Lord

February 10, 1995 - 10:15 A.M.

(S.J., I heard Mary's voice and I tested, and She answered me.)

Mary: I am the Triumphant Prophetess of the Lord, the Woman of Revelation. I come to proclaim the glories of God, to lead all who would respond to sing the praises of My Son, Jesus. The power of His Spirit will burn the hearts of many.

My daughter, I have been the Prophetess of Heaven, revealing many things to many of My chosen. This has been done according to the Divine will of God the Father. Everything of God's is done according to the Divine will. I have told you I would lead you and guide you. This famine will come. Prepare as you are inspired.

(S.J., I understood here that I was not to think preparing, but rather just to do it.)

Mary: These physical sufferings are asked of you for the conversion of My sons.

(S.J., I understood here that She meant Her priest sons.)

Sadie Jaramillo and Fr. Jim Anderson, M.S.A., her spiritual director, at the entrance to "The Father's House of Victory through the Holy Family." Father Jim is a member of the Society of Missionaries of Holy Apostles. He has been a priest for twenty years with assignments teaching high school and seminary courses in ethics, including posts as Academic Dean and Academic Vice President of Holy Apostles Seminary in Cromwell, CT. He is a former attorney with a J.D. in law from U.C. Berkeley and a Ph.D. in philosophy from Georgetown.

The Father's House of Victory through the Holy Family.

Sadie Jaramillo next to picture of Divine Mercy and Blessed Faustina.

Fr. Jim Anderson, Charlie and Carole Nole, Sadie Jaramillo
and two of her children, with Cross of Peace model.

Charlie and Carol Nole, heads of
Cross of Peace Project in Santa Marie.

Picture of planned Cross of Peace project at Santa Maria.

Carole Nole, and friends of the Cross of Peace Project.

233

Jasmine and Chris standing in front of Infant of Prague Statue
at the Father's House of Victory through the Holy Family.

Sadie with daughter, Jasmine, near Altar at the
Father's House of Victory.

Sadie with two of her children, Jasmine and Chris.

Mary: Be not afraid. Share information with your people. This day of illumination is upon you. Live each day prayerfully, watching the heavens and the signs. It has not been too long a delay, only the appointed time of God.

The peace of My Son, God the Father and the power and their Spirit is upon you.

(S.J., During Mass, after Communion, in prayer, I began to hear the Lord and I tested. "I command you to go in the name of Jesus if you are not of God". Jesus answered.)

Jesus: I am your Lord Jesus who is to be praised. I am much consoled by your love. In you I have found a heart soft and yielding to My call. Walk in peace and know that I have said that all systems will be destroyed, and brought to an end. Know that you have given Me your very best.

(S.J., Here, He was referring to 'J.' and 'C.', my two young children.)

Jesus: Trust in Me that even now I am forming a place in their hearts where I will dwell forever. I love your children, all of them.

Heed My Mother's instructions and move as you are inspired by My Spirit and the will of My Father. Go now, child, and prepare. Prepare the way of the Lord. Remember how I called Noah, his response: the completion of the Ark. All these were stages of God's perfect time. But when he was told to enter, to place his provisions and wait, this was the sign of the impending and unleashing of God's wrath and holy justice.

So it is now. And as every man's conscience is revealed to him, he, man himself, will know of My many prophets who were sent to him, and stood in his midst. Among everything else, they will see if they stood as an obstacle to God's holy will, or helped in this awesome work of My Mother.

(S.J., Jesus had me understand the awesome work as the holy work of His Mother.)

236

Jesus: I will still receive all in mercy. But they must ask for forgiveness, repair their obstinate ways, and live out the final days of distress according to My Father's will. Many will rejoice for their soulmates who persevered and brought more preparations for them and their families.

But now, child, go and take care of your final preparations.

My love, grace and blessings.

The Heavens Will Crack with God's Thunder

February 19, 1995 - 3:20 P.M.

(S.J., As I have not been feeling well physically, I have been slow to respond today to Our Lady's request. I began to hear Mary and I rebuked and tested, until She says:)

Mary: My little sorrowful rose, I request you to take down My words. I, your victorious Queen of the World, your Mother and the Mother of all humanity, sing the praises of Jesus, My Son, for I dwell in the midst of the Most Holy Trinity.

I come to implore you to remain united with Me in prayer. The angels of the Lord from on high have been dispatched. They are sent to cover God's holy people with peace, by their protection over them. For the greatest moment of divine mercy will bring many to the foot of My Son's glorious Cross. It will also be a time of chaos and confusion. I clarify to you, to prepare for a shortage of food items upon the arrival of this moment. And then, for the control of famine which will follow.

It is the illumination of man's heart and soul. The heavens will crack with God's thunder. It will be the most awesome, holy fulfillment of Calvary; a moment to choose the path to eternal life, or to be led to eternal damnation.

237

The moment which will lead My remnant to begin harvesting in God's vineyard. You will tire, but you will work ceaselessly. Know that, as our chosen one, every word taken down in dictation has been a prayer for the soul of someone lost. And everything which has been required of you will be brought to fulfillment.

Because My remnant have sacrificed and offered acts of reparation, the Father's holy anger has many, many times over, been appeased. But this time of all times has come. My children have entered into the ark of My Immaculate Heart. With Me are the angles and saints, to bring in the Triumph of the Two Hearts!

So that from pole to pole the cry may resound: **Our Father in heaven, praise to thee for the Triumph of the Immaculate Heart of Mary and the Sacred Heart of Your Son, Jesus. May Your Holy Spirit lead us and fill us with Your holy gifts. Abba, Amen. CHRIST THE KING REIGN! Glorious is the Queen of the Most Holy Rosary's triumph.**

All who have participated in preparing this glorious moment, I bless you from My holy throne on high in the name of My Father and yours, My Son, Jesus, and the Power of My Spouse, the Holy Spirit.

(Personal: My daughter, the time element I speak of in your time is days, to remain focused in your prayer with Me to bring more souls to My Son. Keep your children about you. They will be with an illness that their father will accept and understand your explanations.

Once again, he will be steeped in the sorrow of his own making. You are much loved, oh little one of Mine. My 'P.' (priest) is a gift to lead and console you, through the words My Son speaks through him. The enemy has been thwarted by means of your prayer. Peace, child, peace.

Ark of the New Covenant

March 1, 1995 Ash Wednesday - 9:30 P.M.

(S.J., I hear His voice, I tested and Jesus answered me:)

Jesus: Do not dispute the words you hear are from God! I am Jesus, Second Person of the Godhead, slain for the salvation of mankind! I alone was found worthy to break the seal!

Write My words to you during My Mass: Mourning and sackcloth, fasting and prayer were asked of My children before. Now, mankind will know mourning! By the very hand of God, death and desolation will be everywhere, chaos and confusion for those not sealed with the mark.

(S.J. Our Lord refers me here to the Book of Ezechiel 9:1-11 Douay-Rheims version of which I include a part. Please read the whole chapter as Our Lord requests.)

Ezechiel 9:3-7

(3) And the glory of the Lord of Israel went up from the cherub, upon which He was, to the threshold of the house: and He called to the man that was clothed with the linen, and had a writer's inkhorn at his loins.

(4) And the Lord said to him: Go through the midst of the city, through the midst of Jerusalem: and mark Thau* upon the foreheads of the men that sigh, and mourn for all the abominations that are committed in the midst thereof. (5) And to the others He said in my hearing: Go ye after him through the city, and strike: let not your eyes spare, nor be ye moved with pity. (6) Utterly destroy old and young, maidens, children and women: but upon whomsoever you shall see Thau, kill him not, and begin ye at My Sanctuary. So they began at the ancient men who were before the house.

239

(7) And He said to them: Defile the house and fill the courts with the slain: go ye forth. And they went forth, and slew them that were in the city.

Jesus: Do My ministers believe they serve a God that cannot see? A God that cannot hear? A God that is not omnipotent? Yet, what awaits them! Woe! Woe! Woe! My ministers, you have left your flocks to be scattered! They will be as sheep with no shepherd. (And for this reason) have I raised My chosen and Servants of the Two Hearts!. They will speak, "Thus says the Lord your God . . ." They will point to My signs, they will heed the direction and guidance given by My Mother! All this they will do, for My Mother has been able to obtain from the Father all this, and more will the Father do, for He wills it so!

I will let you know, oh children of Mine; read and understand this Scripture for you have willingly said yes, and you will toil in My vineyard. You will gather into My Mother's Immaculate Heart these new ones of Mine; (into) the Ark of the New Covenant so that My angels will go forth and protect, and guide all who would be sealed with the mark (sign of the Cross).

Trust, oh little ones, trust in the words of My Holy Scripture. Walk in the faith of the ancients (1). When you see the new abominations shake your feet. Let this be a sign unto all, for I will cleanse My House (2)!

My ministers will once again be held as holy and upright teachers and leaders, (and) My Church, established on Rock, will forevermore rise in glory, resplendent with the light that radiates truth, life, holiness, virtues and good works.

But first I must purify, I must cleanse (My Church, the world). I must bring to an end once and for all, all those who set themselves against Me!. They will run, but not be able to hide! They will seek to escape, but they will not! They will be brought to submission by My victory on Calvary, by My Mother's act

of Co-Redemption and promise of victory! Oh enemies of Christ, you will strike at the woman, and She will crush your head with Her heel!

If you, My ministers, did not know (the truth), then there would be no sin in that; but you know and you say you do not. By deception and force, you inflict these teaching of error and heresy. But I, the Alpha, the Omega, the One, True and Brother Priest; I see your deception, I see your dishonesty, I see your willingness to be as Judas to Me and betray Me! And I cry once again, "Father forgive them, they know not what they do."

But now, for the sake of those of you who have suffered humiliation, and despair at seeing My Church plundered, for the sake of those who see the evil that permeates every aspect of life, who moan and bewail this situation; **Now I Come!** And those who were the invited at My Banquet, you have refused My invitation, so I will take all those gathered from the byways, who recognized their time of visitation.

The Bridegroom comes for His Bride, The victorious Queen Triumphant! The Reign of the Two Hearts is come! And the choirs of Heaven sing Alleluia, and the angels rejoice! We bless you child and all who are Ours. Peace, Love is in Our Hearts.

(S.J., (1) My understanding here is to walk in the faith of the traditions and truths of the Holy Roman Catholic Church! (2) And here we will begin to be forced, more and more, to accept the new practices which are not in accordance with teachings of the Church.)

(*Note: Thau is the last letter of the Hebrew alphabet and is signified by the character of a Cross. Our Lady and Our Lord both have said, if we are believers, we have been signed on the forehead with the sign of the Cross.)

I Am Michael, Angel Guardian of God's People

March 7, 1995 - 7:13 A.M.

(S.J. I was awakened by these words from a different voice:)

Voice: "Let the Reign of Christ the King begin! Enthrone Him in your songs of praise! Enthrone Him in the midst of your prayers!"

(S.J., Because I could not recognize the voice, I immediately rebuked and commanded it to go in the name of Jesus, if it was not of God. The voice continued:)

Voice: My child, no enemy of Christ will acknowledge His kingship or give instruction to His reign. I am **Michael**, Angel Guardian of God's people and Church! I, too with you and all the just praise Jesus, Our Lord, King of Kings!

(S.J., I was having difficulty, as I was astounded and asking how could this be? How could I hear the difference? He continued.)

Michael: Child, with God there are no impossibilities, I have been sent to you to warn you that you, in turn, will warn and prepare! Prepare in these next days, extract from your physical being every act of self-denial, and remain united to the hearts of your King and Queen. In your prayer of the heart, imitate in every way Our Lord and Our Lady's unceasing prayer for mercy on those still in darkness!

I tell you, **all** of heaven's saints rejoice, for the time of the banquet has arrived! The angels are rejoicing that the Father has sent forth His decree and instructions regarding the just on earth. Soon, we will be doing hand-to-hand combat with the demons and those who serve them.

But we will also be harvesting from the vineyard. And after this great day (warning), many souls will be taken from the

242

kingdom of death and eternal damnation to the kingdom of light and everlasting life. Do not be surprised. God is doing the same as He did in the yesterdays of time. He is doing the same today and forever.

Angels have preannounced great tidings. So it is today! I bring you tidings of great joy. Joy for heaven and those on earth, and mercy, mercy for those who fear God and mercy for those who don't.

Prepare, oh child of God, and rejoice. Lift your eyes and heart to heaven, your redemption draws nigh! Amen.

Michael, Angel, Guardian of God's people and Church. Amen.

The Way of the Cross

March 8, 1995 - 11:30 A.M. (St. John of God.)

(S.J., I heard these words, "The storms of justice come! Prepare!" After hearing this twice, I rebuked in the name of Jesus if this was not of God. It was Our Lady's voice and She answered.)

Mary: Yes, My daughter, the testing must go forth, for My adversary prowls and devours those who fall prey to his lies.

The sweet voice you hear is that of the Mother of God! The Mother of John, and all humanity! I have been hearing the cries of your heart, your pledges of love and devotion and service to the Two Hearts. God the Father wishes to lift you up higher into His love.

You call yourself less than a slave, a slave of the Cross. But you have been given the gift of being able to be called child of God, brothers and sisters of Jesus the Christ!

My daughter, the sorrowful rose, the Father is angry; for the obstinate and very stony heart of man has not responded to the initial warnings. These messages that cast the warning of heaven are no longer being accepted. Man refuses to acknowl-

243

edge what the signs point to. This is the purpose of My messages; to implore the hearts of My sons and daughters to conversion, repentance, reparation and sacrifice. But the way of the world, the failure of the shepherds, it is as though in reality, the blind are leading the blind.

I have called to everyone. I have wanted to pour the healing balm of Jesus' and My love on the open and grievous wounds of everyone. The way of the Cross is suffering, humility, poverty and charity. Most would accept My messages as long as it cost them nought (nothing). But that is not the way of the Cross.

I am the Lady of the Way. I have often repeated this, for you fail to understand My children. I want to show you how to imitate My love, My love for Christ My beloved; and love to the lost wandering souls, steeped in sin and self-indulgences of all kinds. To win these souls, self-denial must be offered for self-indulgence; sacrifice and penance for those enjoying consolation of the physical senses and all who are lost in enjoying their consolation now.

I have wanted to show the Way of the Cross, for this **is** the only way one becomes hot and not cold, and especially not lukewarm. These cause Me the most grief. I have wanted to point to this time, these times, the fullness of God's time, so that My remnant would make whatever preparations after the spiritual they might be inspired to do.

But over and over I have been refused. Jesus has been refused, for the hearts of mankind are no longer able to respond to unconditional love.

So now, as I mention, the Father's anger will no longer be appeased. For the sake of the just, heaven will move, and earth will be rent with the convulsions of His anger. Holy and just is His justice! Be intimately united as you have been. This is pleasing to the Father, consoling to the Son and makes the Spirit a happy and holy place of dwelling. His gifts will be poured on His faithful.

244

Remain one, with the Two Hearts, cast all your heart into Ours. The graces will be there and all will be given to fulfill the will of the Father. Heed the message of My Archangel Michael. Be open to the leading and guidance We give. You are much loved, as are all our children. Peace.

To the Cross They Will Come

March 9, 1995 - 7:00 A.M.

Vision: (S.J., I see a vision, the Cross, as depicted by the model of the Cross of Peace. It is that Cross. This cross is in the sky. In the middle of this vision and beneath it, is like a doorway threshold. On the left side, people and everything look grimy and dirty, symbolizing sin. Then people are passing through this doorway stepping over the threshold, into what I believe to be hills surrounding the site for the Cross.

All the colors are crisp and illuminated by a light. People are wearing white gowns and I see Jesus in the midst of the people. (The Eucharistic Community?) This understanding is also given that it is not from one day to the next, but a small space of time.)

(S.J., I heard a voice and rebuked it to go, if not of God, in the name of Jesus the Lord.)

Voice: The Cross of Peace will usher mankind through, and over the threshold into the promised era of peace. No one will live in the era of peace as they are now, obstinate and steeped in sin. To the Cross they will come and be thus converted and cross over, into, and through the Peace of God!

That which seems as obstacles are only those things held by God, which allow all to come at the appointed time! [The obstacles] test the perseverance and prayer of the faithful to bring them to be of one mind, one heart and accord, where discord cannot enter.

245

This revelation given to you by the Spirit of God. I am the Holy Spirit. With Me you are able to praise God the Father and the Son Jesus.

You are praying, you are fasting, continue.

Prepare My Little Children

March 24, 1995 - 9:00 A.M.

(S.J., I heard a voice and commanded it to go in the name of Jesus, if not of God.)

Jesus:

I am here!
I am the same Jesus to whom you sing your praise to!
I am the Son of My Father who gave Me as a sign
of His great love for all humanity.
I Am the Son who was by the power of Our Spirit,
placed in the Immaculate Womb of My Mother!
To whom this announcement was made by an angel!
I am the Son who is now coming to establish
My Kingdom on earth!
I Am the Son who is still being refused by My people!
I Am the Son who is suffering at the hands of My priests!
I Am the Son who calls you to holiness!
Be holy as I am holy. Be still and know your Lord.

Now child, little sorrowful rose of My Mother, I have set you as a sentinel in the watchtower. To the few who have believed, I will not leave you abandoned. You will know interiorly of this time.

You will continue to worship truth. You will continue to offer pleasing sacrifice to Me. See on the horizon, see the signs being made manifest daily in your midst.

246

Prepare My little children, I will cover you with My shadow and no harm will come to he that believes. Like a dam that bursts will this come upon mankind and they will scamper here and there, they will seek to hide and be not able to, for the angels of My Father's wrath will seek out **all** those who refused Me and My Mother.

Gone will be the murderer, slanderer, gossiper, the lustful, the perverted of sex, the killers of innocents. The ones who have enjoyed their consolation of wealth up to now.

In the next months your lives will change, forevermore. Be not afraid. I have sent you to My sheep. Feed My lambs and nurture them to adulthood, by teaching and prayers.

Again, I have set you as a sentinel in the watchtower to be a light in the darkness, for those who do believe.

I love you child.

(S.J., Lord how can I ever give back enough of myself for your great love. It seems I am so insignificant.)

Jesus: And you are, but you have been tested and proved. It is not who you are, but who I am, and what I will to do.

I bless you and yours from heaven, and all who believe. Amen!!

The Final Hour of Battle

March 29, 1995

(S.J., I heard a voice and commanded it to go, in the name of Jesus, if not of God.)

Jesus: My child, I am your Jesus, Lord and Savior of all who call upon Me, given by My Father to become the Word Incarnate in the Virginal Womb of My Mother.

(S.J., Jesus then instructs me to write the vision I received in Mass, after receiving Communion at St. Thomas Aquinas.)

Vision: I see the skyline of a city, a very large city. Then an intense flash of light and then what looks to be the destruction that a bomb would do. Blackened areas, buildings left standing are on fire. I see the fire. Chaos, chaos everywhere. I begin to feel a fear and to cry interiorly, "Lord what is this, what are you showing me?

Jesus: I am doing with you what I do to all My chosen vessels, that they might pray and remain constant in their prayer. For if My people do not accept the gift of My warning, and of the miracle, it's not enough. Convert and pray, this annihilation of humanity will come through the hands of mankind.

(S.J., I asked, "War?")

Jesus: Yes. It is enough for you to know and pray. Pray much. So that mitigation might come. For all that has already been foretold is on the point of being. Remain constant, persevere, fast and pray. You have heard My words.

Mankind, you say My prophets bring messages of doom. Tell Me, mankind, which of the world's messages bring less news of doom? Is it not doom and fear that penetrate the hearts of all, nonbeliever and believer alike? The famines? The plagues? The mass murders? The annihilation of the youth? The perverted stories being daily fed to those who sit idly by taking in all this garbage?

(S.J., I questioned the word 'garbage'; however, Jesus wanted it left in.)

Jesus: Which is the message of doom? Is it because I and My Father have seen enough? Is it because We hear the cry of the ones who **do** believe? Is it because the time given to the prince of darkness and his powers is coming to an end?

Tell Me mankind, which is the message of more doom? Because I now come to establish My reign on earth, and through the triumph of My Mother's Immaculate Heart, will bring in the era of peace? Do you think I would coexist with what is in this world? I have up to now, in the tabernacles long ago abandoned. I have waited in sorrow for all to return. I have waited in sorrow, for I can do no more.

My gift was freely given on the hill of Golgotha at Calvary. I suffered and paid the price for mankind's salvation by My passion and death. I can do no more. So I call to the hearts of the children, who would listen, who would believe.

I call you to enter into the final hour of battle. It will be the bloodiest hour. It will be the most intense of the battle. It will be the longest hour. But for mine who have believed, who have accepted the gift of My Virgin Mother, will come the most awesome and mighty triumph!

I wish My priests to more openly profess devotion to Her. They do not take away any of My glory by encouraging devotion to Her. For it is by Her great power of intercession that She brings souls to Me, souls which otherwise would be damned!

Let these be words of comfort for those who believe. I am deeply consoled when I am received into the heart of one who so loves Me and My Mother. I long for words of love and consolation! Be at peace children of God! The angels are given bid over you. The sign is sealed on your foreheads to counter the sign of the antichrist. Do not fear. You will continue to recognize truth. Look to the fruits of the trees. Look to the fruits of the trees.

To the Servants of the Cross:

The hour is late, the battle lines drawn. I have chosen the strong to lift up the weak. All that was done is not without reward, hold your heads up and see the signs in the sky! Only I am aware of the lives that were touched. They will be there

to greet you, for your reward is in heaven. The fulfillment of the Cross is nigh, is at hand! Behold, the door opens, the door opens to the land. Continue to pray, to persevere, to seek My face, and the divine will of My Father.

Jesus: I love you Sadie, My little princess.

(S.J., Lord, I only want to magnify You and let Your love and great saving power be known. Crush me under Your mighty hand if I am not doing as You and My Father Wills.)

Jesus: Be at peace, let no one steal your peace, children. I bless you in the name of My Father, My Name and of Our Holy Spirit. Amen.

I am going to lift you higher into My love.

(S.J., How Lord? I don't know what to do for the love I feel now.)

Jesus: You have been set on this road and I am with you, My Mother is with you. Your physical sufferings are increasing. Be at peace.

(S.J., Thank You, Lord.)

The Triumph of Divine Mercy

April 8, 1995 - 10:07 A.M.

(S.J., I heard a voice and commanded it to go in the name of Jesus, if not of God.)

God the Father: I Am Who Am; the One, the True, the Holy, Omnipotent! The One Who calls you daughter, for I hear your calls to me: Father! (Abba.)

I tell you, My child: Now the moment is come. Every knee will bend, every tongue proclaim the greatness of God.

The gift of My Son, Jesus to you, mankind, you will bend, and proclaim to the triumph of the Cross. You will be rent with grief over your stony hearts and unbelief, but those who

250

would still come will come. Those who remain in their pride and ignorance, you are the ones to choose. You are the ones to condemn yourselves.

I Am Who Am, have allowed more than what was (in) Sodom and Gomorrah. I have given to the fullness of time My mercy, through the perfect sacrifice of My Son Jesus!

Now comes the triumph of Divine mercy, the fulfillment of Calvary! All shall behold, He who comes, who is, who was, and will always be! Once again the sanctuaries will be rent in two.

I Am Who Am, will cleanse and purify My House! I will shake the ministers of God to the depth of their souls and many will turn from the pagan idols they have placed in My sanctuaries.

Behold the days of distress will come upon all mankind as a thief in the night; but for My children of the true faith, again I say: You will walk though the valley of death, and they will fall on your left and to your right, but near you it will not come. The prayers of God's people rise as the shouts of Jericho and the Ark of the New Covenant (Our Lady) leads. These walls will fall for the sake of God's children, but it will also bring down My mighty arm of justice! Prepare to reap from the fields the harvest prepared.

I confirm, renew, and ratify my Covenant. I will be Your God and you will be My people to live in the era of peace, world purified.

The holy of holy days approach and for most not even a trace of truth remains! But when all see My power and My wrath once again, they will beat their breasts and know I Am Who Am is !

My Son is arrayed in splendor and even now prepares to claim the kingdom of God! And She who remains spotless without sin, prepares to reign in Her queenship of triumph!

I Am Who Am say: Woe! Woe! Woe to you Mankind, for the hour of judgment falls!

251

I bid thee My child, to pray still for My faithless ministers, that they may return to the faith. Not one single act of sacrifice and prayer will be without due reward. But if the gift was freely given, and if the gift was freely accepted, you are without charge. Walk in the peace of God! Walk in the holiness of God! Walk in the refuge of God!

I bless you in My Name, and of My Son and of our Holy Spirit! Amen.

April 9, 1995 - Vision

(S.J., I am giving thanksgiving after Communion, when I begin to see men carrying what I believe was the Ark of the Covenant in the Old Testament. They begin to walk in a circle and I can see that they are shouting. And I am given this understanding.

Then I no longer see this, but I see an image of the world, and a rosary encircling the middle. I then see an image of Our Lady being carried on a platform. Being carried on the type of platform I have seen used in processions for Our Lady.

At the top of the world, I see an image of God the Father, (that is in the center), to the left is an image of the Cross with Christ on it. To the right side I see an image of a dove, brilliantly white. Then I see immense bolts of light come from the Holy Spirit, and from the Cross, and all of this seems to fall on the world.

As the Father is at the top, He has His arms extended so that the light seems to come from Him, but at the same time from the other images, separately. But it is all one.

Please forgive me, for it is hard to explain sometimes what I am shown, and the understanding that comes with the vision. Our Father says that the prayers of the people are as the shouts of Jericho. These shouts are the Rosary, being united by this rosary all around the world. The walls of Satan 's kingdom are to fall, and as Our Lady is the Ark of the New Covenant, we are entering into the refuge of God through Her.

Our consecration is the door to Her Heart, and then She takes us to the Heart of Jesus, where we must also take refuge by our consecration. The Cross will be shown at the time of the warning, when we will see our souls as God sees us. This will also be the work of the Holy Spirit.)

World Will Feel the Illuminating Gaze

April 24, 1995 - 9:13 A.M.

(S.J., I tested and Our Lady answered:)

Mary: My little sorrowful rose: I am the Mother of Jesus and your Mother! Rejoice and pray with Me! My little daughter, My Son had need of your suffering.

(S.J., Then Mother, not only my head, take my body as well. (1))

Mary: Do you not know that when the grace is given to you to go and be with more of My instruments; God, My Son looks for those who have already given their fiat to assist in this wonderful plan of redeeming souls?

It is by Me, you are in Me, and through Me, I can work in you.

There were many new souls there yesterday (2), many who will go and the seed of conversion and faith will grow, in good soil. All believers know where God truly is, the enemy lurks. It is the weed among the harvest, and how he raged at My Son and My little daughter, the daughter of unity (3). Because her messages have gone far and wide to tell of God's love and what it is to have true life in God.

As with all of Mine (4), the message does not divide. It is the hearts of the prideful that divide, for they cannot comprehend

253

how God has chosen that person and not them. The pride, which God knows well is in their hearts, keeps them always looking for the gifts and not the gift giver, the miracles and not the worker of miracles. Only in the little and the poor and the ones childlike in their faith, will they move in obedience to the request and will of God.

You know the message to your heart, I hold you bound to My Heart because in every moment you give Me permission to do this. I am truly Your Mother and the Mother of all who will let Me be. I can only say now, and it is now, the whole world will feel the illuminating gaze of Him whom they reject. All things said and done in the darkness will be held in this light.

I implore and beg you do not concern yourself over those daily cares that I Myself will see to for you. You do My work at My request, and I bless you in every moment. Soon there will be joy for you where there has been sorrow. Do not ask where or how, just wait joyfully and expectantly. I have said it and it is given from the heart of My Son.

From heaven on high, I bless you from the midst of the Trinity, for the Father calls you daughter, and the Son rejoices with you, and the Holy Spirit empowers you.

You are blessed in the name of the Father, My Son, and My Holy Spouse, the Spirit! Amen.

(1) Our Lady addressed the terrible headache I had experienced the previous day.

(2) At the Divine Mercy Congress to hear Vassula Ryden.

(3) Vassula.

(4) Messengers.

Harvest Will Be of Multitudes

May 5, 1995 - 5:07 P.M.

Jesus: Dearest daughter, grave events are now on the point of being.

(S.J., I then tested, commanding the voice to go if it was not of God, in Jesus' name.)

Jesus: I am Jesus, the One who saves, I am Jesus, the One, true, and holy Son of God! Saints and angels praise and glorify Me, Who am!

My daughter, grave events are even now on the point of being. I tell you this to implore you to sacrifice and pray according to your state. (1)

I stood with My Mother to receive your prayers, praise and petitions last night. (2)

Oh the prayers of the children, how they rise as a pleasing fragrance to My Father in heaven. How much mankind owes to the prayers of the children, it is by their prayers that so very much has been mitigated.

But that which is come, that which is here, is come to mankind for he no longer calls out to his God for blessing or protection, in praise or thanksgiving. No, the deity of mankind is himself, thus, he (mankind) has only himself to blame. Can he (mankind) change the course of God's anger?

Oh mankind, all that I have done to call you to My heart! I have given My Mother to announce the time of mercy through extraordinary means and measures of Her presence. She is rejected and ridiculed. My instruments are persecuted, My prophets disbelieved. Mankind, mankind, why do you not run to Our hearts? So full of love, mercy and forgiveness? Why do you reject **truth** and embrace and fondle error?

255

The darkness of sin continues to fall on humanity. To what depths of perversion has mankind sunk? I tell you it is lower than Sodom and Gomorrah! Children of Our Hearts, pray for those who will be lost in the many grave and horrifying events yet to befall mankind. Children lost now is an act of My love and mercy. For in the hands of unbelieving and godless parents, what is worse? To bring them before the age of reason, pure and sinless to My kingdom? Or leave them with no chance of learning the true way?

The man of iniquity and all his evil plots are laid bare before My eyes. Thus this diabolical plan **will not** devour the children of the Two Hearts! I say this with emphasis child. Those truly living the way, the remnant, stand in My shadow!

Continue child, pray, pray, pray. There is no time for frivolous pastimes. For to continue in that life style is folly, like those spoken of in scripture, they will be laughing and making merry, just as in the days of Noah. None knows the moment nor the instant the hand and the wrath of God will fall! But I Am tells you this! It is soon to be a reality in your midst.

Rejoice, for the time to purify is come. Prepare those who will come to you. Teach of the Two Hearts. Consecrate to the Two Hearts.

(S.J., Lord do you want me to follow a certain format?)

Jesus: The format is given to you (3).

Many events will happen simultaneously, so as to continue to keep fear an element that will dictate a person's judgment or decision. Many (events) will happen as part of the one who opposes Me. His plan is to entrap all of humanity, to ensnare all those not grounded in the Rock!.

Remember child, soon My Vicar will be taken, and all will need to know the truth of the way. You will need to teach the true way. I am He who gives life by My Body and Blood! I am He who strengthens, for greater are you if I am in you than he who is in the world. My Body and Blood are real food to strengthen and nourish you for the time ahead. You will be strong for I am strong and I will support you in all you do.

The days of silence and preparation are coming to an end. No more the exile. No more the banishing of My faithful ministers. Soon the harvest will be of multitudes. For this harvest, My remnant has toiled in suffering, pain, poverty, and dejection. But come now and reap what has been sown!

I will renew your strength, and you will be a laborer. Day will blend into day, for the work will not cease, but I will nourish you. I will seek and I will find! And all who do not embrace Me now, will embrace Me from that moment, that I bring into the light what lies hidden and bound by darkness!

Sing alleluia to your King! And praises to Him, for He has bought this hour of salvation by the price of His Blood and death! He rose and lives to receive His Bride! Sing of the triumph of the Two Hearts! Be vigilant and watchful of the signs.

I bless you in My Father's Name, My Name and the Name of Our Spirit!

(S.J., Note: Our Lord in this message refers to many things important to the remnant. He refers to His sacrifice, His presence in the Eucharist. As more and more are abandoning this truth, and call the Mass a banquet, he addresses very strongly this error. The true way He refers to is the teaching of the Holy Catholic Church, united with the Holy Father!

For the Holy Father is with us now, but soon he will not be. Once this happens, forces will try to abolish and deny the True Way, the true teaching of the Catholic Church. Those who do not even have memory to help them remember, or they were never taught, will be hard pressed to follow the new error.

257

And a sure way to avoid getting into error is consecrating one-self to the Sacred Heart of Jesus and the Immaculate Heart of Mary, remain in the state of grace, daily Mass, adoration, frequent confession. It is becoming increasingly difficult to find the sacraments readily available. This too, is a sign.

Our priests need prayer, more and more prayer. Don't criticize them, pray for them. Offer sacrifices for them. When the time comes that God will show us the state of our souls; they too, the priests, will have their opportunity to repent and come back to the true way, the truth of the Gospels and teaching of the Catholic Church.)

(1) According to my ability, considering my duties as mother of four children still at home. (2) Thursday night prayer group. (3) Already dictated for us during the Thursday night prayer meeting.

Carry the Banner of the Two Hearts

May 21, 1995 - 9:45 A.M.

(S.J., I tested and commanded in the name of Jesus to go if this was not of God.)

Jesus: My child, little sorrowful rose of My Mother's Sorrowful and Immaculate Heart, I Jesus, Who am, I Jesus, Who is revealing the glory of the Father where I am wills, receive the praises and proclamations of love from you and all of mine.

For with you, all of creation on the earth, above in heaven and yes, even in the bowels of the earth, **all** proclaim to the glory of the Father, that I, His Son Incarnate, comes again from the Father's right hand to establish the kingdom of peace and God's love, by our Spirit Who is being sent to the hearts of the small. The Kingdom of God's Love is being prepared.

You believe the silence to you is an end of your call, but I tell you now, little one, the silence has been for you to be still and know I am God, your God and the God of all those who follow My law of love that must be written on their hearts.

This kingdom of love and peace is being revealed to those who are meek and humble and not puffed up in their own pride, who carry the banner of the Two Hearts on their own (heart), to console, and appease, to plead, and to ask for the favor of God.

Indeed there are many works to glorify My Father, but not all. With discernment from the Holy Ghost, He it is will quicken truth to truth and error to error. My children must pray and indeed I ask you to make a continuous plea to Him, that you, all My children, will be protected. Always pray, My children, that only the will of My Father be done every instant of your day, from the greeting of the day, to the dismissal.

There are those in My Body who (would) manipulate and take away what I have given. By deceit, lies and error they seek to gain their own end and will. Oh, to their own folly and condemnation! All is laid bare for their God to see.

So the Spirit now is revealing God's glory to prepare for this kingdom of God's love. My messengers, My prophets have been refused by the vast majority. My Mother is all but rejected and ignored, for almost all seek signs and miracles to believe. They do not accept that the miracle must begin with them, in their hearts, by conversion and repentance.

The signs that go forth (now) will be more intense and indisputable as My own. Yet they will still be ignored, as mankind is shown how he stands before the Just Judge. Many will rage against Me. They will run to, and embrace him who opposes Me. But this they will do in their own obstinancy and hardheartedness.

Gird yourself, My people, with the truth. Hold up your shield of faith, prepare for the battle, for it intensifies quickly!

259

Jesus: The Ark of the Covenant goes before you, and Michael Angel Guardian and his angels are given bid about you. The fulfillment of all comes quickly. They will no longer say, "Oh another prophecy of justice unfulfilled." No longer will the division in My House by My ministers go unpunished. He who is not with Me, is against Me!!

With the agony I saw and shed blood over these, and now the promise of the Ascension comes!

I bid you, My little daughter of My Heart, rejoice, fear not. I am with you, as is My Mother. In peace I leave you and all, My blessings.

(S.J., On the same day, at Mass, at the consecration, I hear Our Lord. I tested and then He, Our Lord, gave me the following message:)

Jesus: The land of the red sun, will bring the dawn of the red sun; for it will join the white bear, and through them they will bring the scourge of the sword and persecution, and they will continue to spread their error. The threat they bring will bring the one who opposes Me on the scene. Thereafter he will reign.

(S.J., In a vision, I see the flag of China with the red sun, and the white polar bear, hammer and sickle. It then begins to turn red, from the top running down. Our Lord then refers me to the following scripture for the unfulfilled prophecies and protection of the remnant.)

Ezechiel 12:21-28
Douay-Rheims: (Regarding unfulfilled prophecy.)

"And the word of the Lord came to me, saying: Son of man, what is this proverb that you have in the land of Israel, saying: The days shall be prolonged, and every vision shall fail?

Say to them therefore: Thus saith the Lord God: I will make this proverb to cease, neither shall it be any more a common saying in

Israel; and tell them that the days are at hand, and the effect of every vision.

For there shall be no more any vain vision, nor doubtful divination in the midst of the children of Israel. For I the Lord will speak; and what word so ever I shall speak, it shall come to pass, and shall not be prolonged any more: But in your days, ye provoking house, I will speak the word and will do it, saith the Lord God.

And the word of the Lord came to me saying: Son of man, behold the house of Israel, they that say: The vision that this man seeth is for many days to come: and this man prophesieth of time afar off. Therefore say to them: Thus saith the Lord God: Not one word of mine shall be prolonged any more: the word that I shall speak shall be accomplished, saith the Lord God."

Ezechiel 14:21-23
Douay-Rheims:

(Regarding the promises of protection over the remnant, the ones who are living the message of Our Lord and Our Lady from their hearts:)

"For thus saith the Lord: Although I shall send in upon Jerusalem My four grievous judgments, the sword, and the famine, and the mischievous beasts, and the pestilence, to destroy out of it man and beast, yet there shall be left in it some that shall be saved, who shall bring away their sons and daughters: behold they shall come among you, and you shall see their way and their doings: and you shall be comforted concerning the evil that I have brought upon Jerusalem, in all things that I have brought upon it. And they shall comfort you, when you see their ways and their doings: and you shall know that I have not done without cause all that I have done in it, saith the Lord God."

No Life In God Without Suffering

May 26, 1995 - 5:00 A.M.

(S.J., I heard a voice and I commanded it to go in the name of Jesus, if not of God.)

Mary: Little sorrowful rose of My Sorrowful and Immaculate Heart, I am your Mother and the Mother of this poor humanity. I am the Mother of Jesus, God Incarnate, born of My flesh and received back to the glory of heaven by the Father.

He is now preparing to receive, to the glory of the Triune God, His body and the elect remnant. Let us together extol and praise His Name: Jesus! Come, My child, let us pray together.

(S.J., We prayed a Glory Be, an Our Father, and a Glory Be. At the end Our Lady said Amen, Amen, Amen.)

Mary: I want to tell you, that the days of thunder, and days of distress, are here. Just as in the last act of sabotage and hate, the explosive power caused that building to come crashing down in Oklahoma. The explosive charge of the Holy Spirit will cause this wounded and bruised daughter of Mine, the Church, to come crashing down.

It is by the power of the Spirit, that the glory of God is being revealed. Let him who has eyes see, and him who has ears hear, and deny no longer the times of tribulation. Deny no longer the great apostasy spoken of in Holy Scripture. Deny no longer that God is still God Omnipotent, all knowing, mighty and powerful! Deny no longer that My Son's Vicar, John Paul II is son of My Heart, for he carries in his heart, agony for this state of the Church. Deny no longer the evil force of Ecclesiastical Masonry, that has set itself to destroy the truth and tradition of the way.

From the beginning of the Church, I was there to oversee, lead and guide this beautiful gift of God's plan to its estab-

lishment and formation. **Deny no longer, dear hearts, that I would oversee, lead, and guide through the worst attack on the Church from the beginning of its creation until now.**

That God would permit Me this work done in the simplest of ways, for the Spirit cannot be restrained, contained, or restricted. The Spirit falls on whoever has the simplicity to believe as a child. Deny no longer My children for the Spirit will perform the most wondrous acts of glory to God that have not been seen since Pentecost!

As you gather in cenacle to await this return and mighty outpouring of grace and love, you will be empowered by Him, The Holy Spirit, to go forth and prepare the hearts of those open to be received back into the fold (1).

I have been preparing you and others to be the strong for the weak, for in your total surrender your strength is the very strength of God.

None of what the enemy has deviously planned as attack on you, to destroy or deter you, has landed on his mark. It has been deflected by Mine, and your childlike trust in My Son. You will see the most momentous victories and rejoice as I rejoice.

I will give you the most obvious sign you desire, and have abandoned, to the will of God. Because My Son gives to Me dispensation of these graces, as I suffered most intimately with Jesus, I know these graces were dearly bought and paid for.

But you serve a tender, loving and compassionate God who allows only what is most necessary for one's purification and spiritual growth and edification. Through the cross in your life, you come to the truth of the Gospels, which recount for you the magnanimous suffering of My Son. I tell you, daughter of My Son's Heart, there is no life in God without suffering, for the value to that soul, and to other souls, if united to Our Hearts, is priceless.

Glorify My Son, children. Carry your crosses with love, humility, obedience, tenderness and more love.

God will, to His glory and tribute to Me, allow this church to rise, more resplendent, purified and glorious, more precious than gold or any treasure and it will be totally united to Him and free from error!

I love you, little one, I know your pain. Trust. With God all things are possible.

Be vigilant and watchful.

I bless you in the name of The Father, My Son Jesus and the Holy Spirit. Amen!

(1). **Our Lady refers to those who through the illumination (Warning) will be ready to receive instruction on the faith.**

The Beloved Remnant

June 8, 1995 - 10:35 A.M.

(S.J., I heard a voice and commanded it to go, in the name of Jesus, if not of God.)

Jesus: Daughter of My heart, come rest in the silence of your heart where I have made My abode. I Jesus, Who Am, prepare My children and apostles of the last days. I dwell in the midst of your praises and love.

The Father will glorify the Son, and I, the Son, the light, the truth and the way will glorify the Father. Our Spirit has come to light a fire, a fire of love in the hearts of mankind.

To all those who have entered into the protection of My mercy, who have worked towards the coming of the Father's kingdom, who have entered into the heart of My Mother; you have reserved for yourselves a special place in heaven, for you are the beloved remnant.

264

In this image (1), I am. From this image I will pour torrents of grace and mercy. For now torrents of sorrow will be poured forth from the hand of My Father's justice. You have refused Me mankind. You have rejected My instruments. You have persecuted the brothers of My Heart for the truth they proclaim!

You will now reach for the one who opposes Me. But, you will find, too late, you were held bound by the deceiver. Too late, you will acknowledge the truth.

I speak and those who walk in My love, My Father's will, under the influence and power of the Spirit, are the beloved remnant. They hear, they see, they believe. They have taken the hand of My Beloved Mother and have allowed Her to lead and guide.

Come, My children, rejoice with Me, your Savior and Christ, for soon We will dwell together in the midst of peace and love, God's love, and His divine will.

I pour torrents of graces on those who believe, on those who trust.

Torrents of sorrows! Torrents of sorrows! Torrents of sorrows! For you, mankind would not believe. For the plot of the evil one has cast the net ready to draw all into his reign of deceit. Now is the time appointed and known to the Father, revealed to the saints, and the children of Mary.

I love thee child, hurry with that I have given to your (2) and My Mother blesses you, embraces you and kisses you in return for yours.

From the Eternal Father's throne, He blesses you. I Jesus bless you and the Holy Spirit blesses you. Amen! Amen! Amen!.

(1) Divine Mercy Image acquired through Pawel. (A like the image, blessed by Fr. W. in the Cross of Peace Information Center.
(2) To finishing the Divine Mercy Image Banner.

Time of Intense Prayer and Rejoicing

June 12, 1995 - 9:30 P.M.

(S.J., I heard a voice and commanded it to go, in the name of Jesus, if not of God.)

Mary: My little sorrowful rose, it is I, your Mother, and the Mother of Jesus, the Mother given for all humanity. Praises are sung to the Triune God now and forever.

My child, at what urgency I speak to you tonight. There are so many incidents about to unfold and be revealed.

(S.J., **El terremoto Ya Viene.** (1) I have been hearing this phase, spoken in Spanish, since Sunday at Mass.)

Mary: The earthquake given as a sign comes (2)! There has been much that has been mitigated. There was to have been one other quake of devastation that was mitigated by the prayers of the children and My remnant. But the one given as a sign approaches and from the one moment to the next there will be very intense times. Intense for those walking by faith in My messages of love and fearful for those walking in ignorance to the truth.

The feelings you felt in the depth of your soul are Mine too (3)! Yes, the masses of people gathered as the hawkers of their wares are the same today as those My Son chased from the temple in His righteous and holy anger! The profaned temple of God is, as it was then, led by hypocrites and those who are too prideful in their positions to see the souls entrusted to them.

The graces that were showered upon you and 'S.' were as that sudden downpour that burst forth. They are the graces that will carry you through all the times of trial ahead. I tell you child, it was the very wrath of god that was shown to you; and yes, it is also the measure in proportion of the evil one's rage at your fulfilling the mission sent to you.

266

Do not allow yourself to be led astray by all that is shared to you. There is the prayer of discernment that must be prayed at every moment. Pray first, test and then wait, for the answer will come.

You must be ready at every moment, in every instance, for this is a time of intense prayer and rejoicing; rejoicing that the kingdom of the Father is being prepared to be revealed.

Your walk has been a walk of faith and will be to the very end. All My children walk in faith, not by sight. Trust in your Lord and Savior Jesus and in the Mother given you at the foot of His Cross.

(S.J., I then ask Mary, regarding the sign. Is it the earthquake, followed by a cross in the sky, or the warning?)

Mary: Both! Do not fear! Pray, wait expectantly with a prayer on your lips and in your heart.

(S.J., Lady, will you please tell me which will come first?)

Mary: It is as you have been given interiorly. The warning must come first, but it will come amid great upheavals.

(S.J., Mother, when will I be invested in the Trinitarian Scapular?)

Mary: You will be invested tomorrow, on the 13th. I, your Mother give you to the Trinity; God, My Father and yours, God, My Son and your brother, God, My Spouse the Holy Spirit; all three distinct persons, all three in one God.

You are much loved.

Pray Children.

Peace and blessing descend from God on all of you.

And I thank you for the response of your prayers to My requests.

I love you all.

(S.J., When I received this message I went outside and looked up into the sky, towards the west, and there was a cross in the sky.)

267

(1) (**El terremoto Ya viene.** In Spanish, a very large and powerful earthquake.)

(2) (5.5 earthquake in Victorville, California, followed by Jesus Crucified in the Sky.)

(3) (The disrespect, irreligious and irreverent attitude displayed by persons at Our Lady's shrine in Mexico City.)

Consecrations to the Two Hearts

June 22, 1995 - 11:00 A.M.

(Vigil of the Feast of the Sacred Heart of Jesus.)

(S.J., I tested and commanded the voice to go, in the name of Jesus, if not of God.)

Jesus: My Child, daughter of My Sacred Heart, I Jesus, Am! I Jesus, come! I Jesus am praised and acknowledged in the cosmos of the universe, in My divinity and humanity.

This Sacred Heart bursts open at the angry thrust of a Roman soldiers lance. From this Heart, Divine yet human, the world is given the graces of mercy and love, forgiveness and refuge and in these, the Last Days, I repeat, torrents of graces and mercy, which will lead to repentance, conversion, and salvation!

You recall My words to you? Soon you will be working ceaselessly and tirelessly in My harvest of souls. I tell you your work begins, as of now, the dawn of the warning. As the souls of some are feeling the conviction of the Holy Ghost, go forth and bring them, who would accept, into the consolation of My Most Sacred Heart, and into the refuge of the Ark of the New Covenant, the Immaculate Heart of Mary, My Mother most sorrowful, through the door of safety, by their consecration.

Take My image where you go. I open doors. Prepare, oh My children, for this great work comes as promised.

To you, who would not heed the invitation, messages, messengers and prophecy, neither I nor My Mother can do any more. You remain as stone. You gaze at the destruction of My House and complacently accept and yes, you clap and welcome it.

You remove the King of Kings and Lord of Lords, and prefer instead the temple and worship of yourself. You are once again causing grievously open wounds in My Sacred Body! You are walking in union to the flames of hell. You reject truth, who I am, and embrace and fondle the error that leaves the stench of your mortal sin in your souls. One and all, you follow those who will stand in judgment before Me.

Brother priests, I consecrated you for the glory of God! I set you apart to beg My Father's mercy on the sins of My people and your flock, to perpetuate those seeds of truth and faith with prayer, sacrifice and incense, teaching, preaching, and faith. When the Son of Man comes, what little faith will be found!

Read My sacred scriptures, recognize these signs of your times. But for the sacrifices and prayers of the remnant, much more would have come to you already. Recognize this great apostasy, for truth is no longer being allowed to be told, but told it must be.

To My soldiers of My Mother's army, take up your weapon, the rosary! Cry out your battle cry: Ave Maria! Wear your battle fatigues: the scapular and the sacramentals! Hold up your shield: faith.

Put on your battle shoes, zeal to take My messages of love to those who will hear, all under the banner of the Two Hearts: Oh Sacred Heart of Jesus, have mercy on me, a sinner. Oh Immaculate Heart of Mary, pray for me now, and at the hour of my death.

You do not know, do you mankind, when you will be called to stand in judgment? Soon you all will be. Then you must choose. Choose life eternal, or eternal damnation.

Now, My little ones, let everything about you spread the light of God's love! Do not judge. Judgment is mine. Do not cast away. I refuse no one yet.

Keep vigilant as to the hours of your day and nights (1). The work begins to increase on this vigil of the Feast of the Sacred Heart of Jesus. Call a fast in your assembly (2): a nine days novena to the Sacred Heart of Jesus and fast to your measure and call.

This blood shed for you covers you with protection. This Heart which beats with love for you, has taken you deep into the interior of My Heart. This Sacred Face, so wounded and bruised, is imprinted on your soul to make you mindful of My mercy, and mercy I give to all who will come to me. Come soon!

Your Savior and Lord Jesus, I give you blessing on your undertaking.

Peace to you.

(1) For Prayer (2) Prayer group.

(S.J. Note: Our Lord gives me the understanding with this message, that it is very important to have everyone consecrate themselves to Our Lord and Our Lady. That we all have attended cenacles, large ones, but now we must go into wherever they will accept us, and help them begin, and lead them in the recitation of the consecration. That if we go, in faith, He is the One Who will open the doors, and then the grace for conversion and to believe will be given.

This is preceding the day of warning. For too many that awareness is being given through many different means. Many nonbelievers are feeling stirrings of conviction in their souls as to the state of their soul.

270

This is the mighty outpouring of the Holy Ghost, a fulfillment of the prophet Joel. Father Gobbi's consecration in the Marian Movement of Priests, and the consecration to the Two Hearts, are the consecrations Our Lord refers to.)

Chapter Seven

The Defeat of Evil and The Era of Peace

**Messages From July 7, 1995
To December 25, 1995**

The End of This Era Is Come

July 7, 1995 - 9:40 A.M.

(S.J., I tested and the Lord answered.)

Jesus: I am Jesus, in whose Heart lies mercy and love for all those who would still come to Me! All of the Saints in heaven and on earth praise Me Who Am, the Second Person of the Trinity, and the Godhead, Three in One is praised, adored and glorified!

Meditate well on My Holy Scripture (1). It bears the message for humanity today. From the four corners of the earth, I have dispatched My instruments to proclaim the Word of the Lord.

And the Word of the Lord is this:

Thus says the Lord your God: Now the end of this era is come. Now is the end of Satan's stranglehold on mankind. Now is the defeat of evil. Now is the cleansing of My House. Now have come the days of distress and upheaval!

For you have made your own choices, mankind. I desire pardon and mercy, but your sins call for justice, punishment and Cleansing! Can one letter of the law be wiped away? No!

Mankind, you deceive yourself and others, the blind and the proud lead the blind. You have no freedom mankind; it has already been taken away. It only remains to be openly stated. Your nation, My nation, was founded on God's laws and principles. But now you are led by those you chose to bring prosperity, peace and security. But gaze all around you and what is it you see? What is it you hear? The cries of despair and sorrows, for none can restore but God alone!

This month (2) will not end before you know the terror of upheaval in all that happens. Those who believe will lift their hearts to the One who saves and protects, and know that redemption and justification are here! You who believe not, now will, through the prayers of supplication and intercession of others, come to your King of Mercy!

My Mother's beloved remnant: For many it will be the time to walk by faith, in all you have learned, in all you have been given through My chosen instruments. By your life of prayer, daily sacrifice of the Mass, and your time before My Sacred Presence in adoration! Now the graces are given to persevere until the end!

For My revelation to you at Mass is not new, it is truth (3). It is I, Jesus, who is there consecrating the species of bread and wine into My Body, My Blood, My Divinity, and My Soul! Through the hands of My Beloved Priests, with great joy I present Myself to you and all who would accept.

Woe to My shepherds who do not recognize, nor believe, the sanctification of their vocation. I called you! I set you apart to be Mine! I call My holy priests to drink of the cup of My chalice, to suffer for the sake of souls. This should be your business, priests of Mine: (the) business of saving souls, at all costs, at all inconvenience. You are not here to be served, but to serve!

Pray much My daughter of My Heart, for My Vicar ascends to his Calvary! Child be at peace and know all this is given to you through the graces you receive by your great love for Me. How your love gives Me consolation and I find refuge from great indifferences and cold hearts with you.

Sound the trumpet, give heed children of My Mother!

The Queen is victorious!!

The Queen is triumphant!!

Do not doubt but believe!!

I receive you into My Heart!

Peace and blessing to all My Mother's remnant.

(1) Our Lord gave me Ezechiel, Chapter 7, in my prayer time yesterday.

(2) July, 1995.

(3) Here Our Lord refers to the daily Mass that I attend, where a certain priest celebrates. He (Our Lord) showed me that it is Jesus who pronounces the consecration, and who elevates the Sacred Species. Not even the priests, at times, are aware of the sacredness of offering the Holy Sacrifice of the Mass.

The Final Hour Arrives

July 26, 1995 - 11:11 A.M.
Feast of Saints Joachim & Ann.

(S.J., I heard a voice and commanded it to go in the name of Jesus, if not of God.)

Jesus: I am Jesus, your Lord and Savior, the Savior through whom redemption came to mankind; Savior of many, but not all, for they refuse me. To the glory of God the Father, the Trinity is praised, adored and glorified.

The time is Now! The time is Now! The time is Now!

I will crumble mountains and convulse the sea. The civil strife will light like a flame and burn from one coast to another. For those who revel in their world of materialism, from one moment to the next, they will have nothing. My children, the children of God, prepare; for thus speaks the Lord your God!

Lift up your eyes to the heavens, the sign is there! Lift up your hearts and sing praise to God! For now the people of God are moved into action! To those who have persevered, come, reap the rewards of your sowing for the field is ready for the harvest.

To those who have doubted, fall on your knees and beat your breast. Repent and do not persist in your unbelief. Gather in your communities of believers, for woe to the world, you now fall into the vomit of your sins and perversion, for your lord (Satan), is the deceiver from the beginning.

Daughter of My Heart, do not let any of the attacks of the enemy, let you lose your peace! He knows those who are raised to be the mouth of God! I send you as I sent Jonah and Moses! Though many have disbelieved, they will know it is true! Remain steadfastly ready and vigilant.

Prepare children of God, the trumpet sounds, the final hour arrives. But look beyond and see in your hearts the new era of peace, the new era where, I your King of Kings and Lord of Lords, will gather you to My breast and your tears and sorrows will be no more.

Come, shepherds of My flock! Come to the One who calls you to lead, to prepare, to guide through the final bloody hour. I offer you the chalice of My suffering to bring the souls I thirst for, to bring the souls I cry for, to bring the souls I died for. To stabilize once and for all the Church founded on Rock and all its truths! My peace will see you through.

My hand, with the mantle of the Queen of Heaven, My Mother, will cover you with protection. My holy angels will fight along your side and protect what I bid forth. (What I give instructions to.)

Peace, graces and love to all My children and daughter of My heart. I love you and ask you to be not afraid, My little victim of love. I receive all you do with gratitude and love. I am consoled by your love and many others like you. The blessing of heaven upon you.

(S.J., I asked Our Lord about the communities. He gave me the following:)

277

Jesus: Some communities already exist, others will be, by the very course of events that are coming. (This has been told of Santa Maria, California!)

Prepare Remnant for Great Tribulation

July 28, 1995 - 2:30 P.M.

(Sadie: I had just finished praying the three mysteries of the Rosary, when I heard a voice and tested: In the name of Jesus, I command it to go if not of God.)

Mary: My daughter, little sorrowful rose, I, Your Mother and the Great Queen of Heaven speak: With you and the remnant, the Body of Christ, I praise My Son Jesus, and the Father in heaven, who for the glory of the Trinity, and by the power of the Holy Ghost are receiving the praises of all Our children, and this moment known to the Father and revealed by the mysteries of God, is to be the most merciful act upon the whole human race. "Praise the Father and the Son, Holy Ghost, three in One".

You wonder My child at the message received by you from My most Holy Son. But I come as your Mother and Mother to all. Do not, for one moment doubt that all will come to pass. My little sorrowful rose, could you, or any have known the role for which you were being prepared? (1)

The division in many of the prayer groups has been foretold, "even the elect, if possible, will be deceived" (2). What makes it possible for deception? Pride, the evil one's tool from the beginning.

My children will have to walk by faith and know all that has been given was to prepare the remnant for the great tribulation, through which you are going to go, the final bloody hour. Pray now, child, for the souls that will be lost in many devastating events.

278

My messages to you have become less frequent. For all has been said that could possibly be said. The action now rests with the souls who will see what God in judgment would see (of that soul).

There will be messages of direction and instruction to benefit those called to be leaders, (to) be strong for the weak. The silence ends. Now the cries of as Ramah will be heard (3), all for the obstinacy of hearts who have **not** responded to heaven call.

It is a Holy and Awesome act that will occur. And know that in the twinkle of an eye, from one moment to the next, all things will change. Believe and be at peace, for your family will be a holy family soon.

I bless you and keep you always in My Heart and with Me. The Father, Son and Holy Ghost smile upon you with favor. Amen.

(1) Messenger or visionary and their mission.

(2) Scripture is being quoted. Saint Matthew 24:24.

(3) Here Our Lady compares the wailing of the mothers at the slaughter of the Holy Innocents to the cries of sorrows that will be for many people. [Jeremiah 31:15.]

Violent Changes In Weather—My Signs

August 1, 1995 - 11:11 A.M.

(S.J., I heard a voice and commanded it to go in the name of Jesus, if not of God.)

Jesus: My child, daughter of My heart, and My Mother's little sorrowful rose; I, Your Lord and King, bearer of mercy and love, come this morning with words of love and consolation. My Mother is here with Me.

(S.J., I then heard our Lady's voice and I tested.)

Mary: My little sorrowful rose, I too, your King's humble Mother, given to all of humanity, stand at My Son's side, to praise, with you the King of Endless Glory, Who in the beginning was the holy Word of God with Him and given to mankind by the Infinite Father's love. Given by the power of the Holy Ghost, the word of God becomes Incarnate in My Womb. Praise and bow before the Infinite omnipotence and glory of God!

(S.J., It was then, as if Our Lady stepped aside, and Our Lord continued.)

Jesus: My child, do you not see the warnings and fulfillment of My words come to pass? For all My children would have the fulfillment of all yesterday (1).

But I have given My reasons for mercy, not delay: one soul. That soul could be the one who stands to read My words to you, or someone of your family.

There are many, many souls who perish every moment for lack of someone to pray for them. Did not even you bow before Me, prostrate before Me, for I placed this grace in you heart; and did not even you cry out to Me for pardon and mercy? Prayers of many are heard, (but) for the "terror of upheaval" signs are given.

(S.J., Jesus then instructed me to look up the word "upheaval". The second meaning is "a sudden violent change". I am given to understand this is the meaning intended.)

Jesus: All is being fulfilled even as I give My words to you. Yes, violent changes in the climate, these are My signs! And sooner than most believe or realize, All, All, All will be fulfilled. I emphasize, for in that way, you understand.

My chosen to persevere must be able to stand even more . . . persecution, for this, too, will come. Do not worry, you cannot change one thing by worrying. Prayer and oblivious reaction to persecution, this brings you graces needed for perseverance.

280

Perseverance to the end!

Many, many have fallen by the wayside for they do not ground themselves in Me. The reality of Me in the Eucharist! The reality of Me in the Word of God! The reality of Me in the Sacraments! The reality of Me in all that is given by My Mother!

We are One! Our Hearts beat in unison, My desire is Hers, My will is Hers, My power is Hers!

This day you are sorrowful and remember My Mother's first words to you. All of our children's tears are falling and have fallen in our laps, as tears of gold!

The purpose of your suffering, beyond your own purification, is of so much value, you will not fully comprehend in this world, as it is now. Only in the coming Kingdom of My Father, will you, and all, understand!

My children have been running too far ahead of Me up to now! But the pace of My faithful remnant has slowed, and must fully understand it can only be the divine will of God that is fulfilled!

In all things comes the appointed time. My words to you speak of the time as now, for it is; but things and events will happen according to the will of God.

I give this message to console your sorrow, to receive your love and prayers, to encourage you to do all that I say. You have been formed and molded, as many of the true remnant have been. Who is the true remnant? Those who cast their wills and desires aside and desire only holiness and God; who acknowledge My Mother as leader and Triumphant Queen, and respond to Her simple, yet powerful, requests.

Now I bid you with My Mother, God's peace and grace to reign in your heart and go where God's will is for you today.

(S.J., Our Lady now begins to speak to me.)

281

Mary: My little sorrowful rose, I too, the Queen Triumphant, encourage you to persevere as My Son directs you. You are much loved and your obedience is always tested, your love too, and then your humility, as a servant of God. Your heart is beautifully radiant with God's love, and your reward will be great in heaven.

The testing of perseverance increases for My children must be strong, and only the strong, in God, will pass.

Your Mother enfolds you this day of Our anniversary.

With My Son, I ask God, Our Father, to strengthens you by the power of the Holy Ghost, with gifts to serve!

Amen!

(1) The fulfillment of all the prophesy, of the prophets.

They Compromise Truth for Error

August 21, 1995 - 12:00 Noon

(S.J., I heard a voice, and tested, and He answered me.)

Jesus: My daughter, I desire to speak to you. I am Jesus, King and Lord. I came in the flesh, a gift of salvation to mankind from the Father, by the power of the Holy Spirit. Praises are sung in heaven and on earth, to the glory of My Father.

Daughter of My Heart, the words from heaven come down to prepare, lead and guide the faithful remnant of God's people. Through many instruments, by the submission of their wills and their preparation, they have been chosen to speak in My name and the name of My Mother. You recognize some (locutionists and seers) as false and they are just that! The deceiver from the beginning does not rest, child. He knows, not only that his time is short, but that his defeat is definite.

My words speak of his abilities to perform wonders and prodigies of all kinds. He can and will appear as an angel of light. But to those, who do not take their salvation for granted, and are striving to fulfill the will of the Father, to them will the Holy Spirit quicken, error to error, or truth to truth.

Many have been shaken and have fallen away, and the shaking continues for the time of testing for all comes.

We come, My Mother and I, to encourage, console, comfort, lead and guide those faithful shepherds and flock, through these most difficult times of distress. The strong will stand! Have I not said, you will not be left alone, that hell and all it's forces **will not** prevail?

It will for a time seem that his victory (Satan's) is assured, and this is because My shepherds who should be taking a stand for God's truth, have abandoned Me once again.

By their own hands they defile what is holy. By their own hearts they abandon My call on their lives. By their words and actions they abandon My Holy Vicar on earth.

Listen, oh you people, if you have ears to hear! Do you not recognize truth any longer? No! Because it (error) leaves you comfortable and languishing in your vile sins. You commit abominations, on abominations for you believe you receive Me. In your sins and hard heart, you commit folly, for your lives bear no resemblance to the light!

And My priests! They walk a road comfortable for them and they compromise truth for error! My priests, look and see if you are walking the road wide and easy, filled with many, or straight and narrow with few to accompany you? You disbelieve divine revelation and scorn personal revelation, given to the childlike, for they will speak, and speak obediently and truthfully, where I lead them.

Oh yes, the deceiver places many false (locutionists and seers), but for the true remnant, the great Queen of Heaven protects and the Spirit of God leads! For they recognize truth and they see and recognize holiness, and holiness for many of My priests has become lost and forgotten.

Rejoice, oh shepherds of Mine, for the voice of God did not fall on deaf ears or hard hearts, when My instruments were chosen, and because the words come down from Heaven, many are praying for you, and your conversion will be due to their heroic acts of sacrifice.

My words go forth, I call you to pray unceasingly for My Holy Vicar, for My true Church, for God's people, for those conversions still to come! As My holy Vicar prepares to take the steps for ascending to his Calvary, know that the interior of the Church will go very dark, but the light will burn in the interior of other places, and the many gathered there will praise God for the cleansing that is come!

The enemy of My Church will take his seat and for a time victory will seem absolute. But, My faithful have been told that they will recognize the fulfillment of prophesy, and in actuality, their sign of deliverance. Mayhem, chaos and confusion! This will seem to all those not grounded in Me. Mine will know! Mine will recognize and Mine will be saved, for the truths of the Church in all her glory and splendor will rise from the ashes! And these saved will go forth into the era of peace and a time that cannot be comprehended now.

The flash point will begin in the East and move towards the West.

Again I say, follow not any person, but follow truth, and truth in its entirety. Look, My signs are already becoming manifest.

Be vigilant and grow not lax. You know not the hour, but know it is come. I solemnly assure you, all will come to pass.

284

Now rejoice, as I bless you in the name of My Father, in My Name, and of Our Holy Spirit, and through the hands and heart of My Mother's intercession!

Amen!

(S.J., As a confirmation, Jesus told me to read Jeremiah 12, of the Douay Rheims Bible.)

The Cup Is Full and Running Over

September 1, 1995 - 8:00 A.M. First Friday

(S.J., after Holy Communion I had this vision. In my backyard there is a grape vine. It doesn't look very healthy, unlike the healthy ones seen in vineyards. It looks withered and sprawls all over. Jesus asks me to write what I am shown in this vision.)

Vision: I saw an image of our Lord Jesus, He goes over to this vine, reaches in and pulls out a perfectly formed bunch of grapes, big and healthy, unlike what this vine would produce. He then says:

Jesus: These will be pressed into the cup of My wrath. (Then He motions me to look and I see angels with sickles.)

(S.J., I don't understand this vision, but I'm told to come home and go to the book of Apocalypse, Chapter 14: 6-20 (Douay Rheims). After reading, I still don't have a very clear or complete understanding.

(S.J., The next morning, first Saturday, September 2, while preparing to go to Mass, I begin to hear a voice and I test. He answered me.)

Holy Spirit: I am the Spirit of God, Third Person of the Trinity! Praise the Father, Praise the Son, Praise the Holy Ghost! I am to reveal the meaning of your vision. This vision has a twofold meaning:

First, the grapes to be pressed into the cup of the wrath of God. God has decreed that the sins of men have reached their

fullness. **The cup is full and running over. No longer will mankind be left without the retribution of God. God, the Father is very much offended. Man has refused the laws of God! Man has refused the Son of God! Man has refused the prophets of God! But now it is the Church who refuses all of the above!**

From the Scriptures you recognize all that is happening **must** happen. Those who have left the faith, the Roman Catholic Church, have no faith to return to! For if it would not be that God will strike, with all His power and might, all would be lost!

The second meaning to your vision: Though the vine is very sick and unhealthy, Jesus has made provisions for those on the vine (the healthy grapes). He has seen that though most of the vine is sick, there have been able to remain a few grounded in the truth, in its entirety. The vine is the Church and its sickness is real. The angels with sickles are dispatched to fulfill the decrees of God according to His word!

I, The Holy Spirit, reveal this to you that you would continue to pray for the ministers of God who no longer do the Will of God! For man, that he opens his heart and soul to the revelations God will allow him to see. At all times, little one, be prepared, be vigilant!

I now bless you in the name of God the Father, who called you, God the Son, who redeemed you and My name, Holy Ghost of God, who empowers you! Amen.

September 18, 1995 - Early Monday Morning

(S.J., during a dream, I heard Jewish songs, singing and chanting, and I see this lady with other people scurrying about, and she says, "You better go now and get ready!" I asked, "Why?" "Because there is a storm, the likes of which humanity has never seen, and it's coming soon". The lady was short and rather stout. She had black hair, but I didn't recognize her. I woke up and felt very moved by what I had seen and heard.)

Warning Comes Amidst Great Confusion and Turmoil

September 21, 1995 - 1:41 A.M.
Feast of St. Matthew

(S.J., I heard a voice and commanded it to go in the name of Jesus, if not of God.)

Mary: My little sorrowful rose, I am the Virgin who keeps vigil with My Son. I, who bore the Incarnate Word in My womb, give praise to the endless omnipotence of God the Trinity in whose midst I dwell.

I ask you to keep vigil with Me, as great events are now upon this nation of yours. I ask you to console My Jesus once again, abandoned, left alone and betrayed.

Know that the greatest prodigy of the Holy Spirit is upon mankind. It will be the unveiling of one's soul, before the omnipotent light of Christ in whose light, perfect and true, all darkness of sin and guilt will be revealed! Many now are in that valley where the decision for or against God will be made!

I ask you to keep a continuous vigil with me, praying for souls. Souls that will receive grace to repent, to convert and to believe. Do not fear what man can do to you. Trust in the Divine Providence that you have surrendered to. He it is who will keep you. He it is who will sustain you. He it is who will defend you.

A storm of enormous portion, death and destruction, will strike. The storm revealed in your dreams. There will follow, as a continuous scourge, one disaster after another. Amid Great Confusion And Turmoil, Will The Great Warning Come.

Many of the faithful now will lose faith! The interior of the Church will go very dark. The enemies will rage and persecute truth and

287

those who follow it. My guidance and instruction for you come, that you, little child of mine, will persevere, that you will be consoled.

Be at peace, for Father P. goes forth at the direction and will of the Father, but you will not lose contact. I have said that another will be given to you. A priest whose heart is like the Mother's, for the Mother's heart is like the Son's. Keep vigil in the approaching hour, for the hearts of the little, My faithful remnants, although few in numbers are great in the power of prayer before the throne of God.

The final darkness approaches and woe unto woe for those who have not believed, for those who have not prepared. Be at peace in your heart, for there it is that your King of Kings dwells, (and who can harm you)!

At the prompting and leading of My Beloved Spouse, you will continued to be led, and I too am at your side. I do not abandon those who have entrusted themselves to Me. I shed many tears for the sorrows of Mary, are in these days, renewed and many.

However, My vigil at the foot of the Cross and at the tomb of My Son, was constant and unceasing, as it is in this new Calvary, to which the Church, holy and true, ascents. For as Christ was betrayed by His own, so too is the Church betrayed, by those ministers ordained.

I now repeat, do not fear Divine Providence in your life, allow yourself, as a small babe in the arms of its Mother, to be carried and led. Keep vigil with Me for My Son's most holy Vicar. Soon all revealed in reference to him will be fulfilled.

From the Heart of God the Father, and God My Son, and God the Holy Ghost, I obtain blessings of grace and peace. For I am the Daughter, the Mother and the Spouse. Amen.

Call to Conversion, Repentance and Preparation

October 13, 1995 - 5:50 P.M.

(S.J., While driving into Santa Maria, California, I begin to hear Our Lord and then Our Lady. I tested, and as I had planned to go directly to the hill (Cross of Peace), I receive this understanding to do so. At the hill, I am given the entire message. It follows:)

Jesus: Little daughter of My Heart, I am Jesus, your Lord and Savior, come in the flesh! I have called you forth to be a great courier of Mine. It is not by any earthly physician you are lifted up, but by the very finger of your Heavenly Physician. You carry what I lay upon you, for you are well disposed to My intentions and desires. This is given to you so that you will proclaim the words that now My Mother gives you.

Mary: Little sorrowful rose of My Son's Heart, come, sit at My Hill and allow yourself to be given the graces and blessings I wish to bestow upon you.

You tell one and all: On this anniversary of the great miracle of Fatima, I knew even then what was to come, and I have come in these waning years of the fullness of time, that My voice would be heard as the voices from the Churches became stilled (voices of the priests). That My voice would direct all to the saving power and love of My Son Jesus. That My voice would call all to conversion, repentance and reparation.

Many have not believed, many have grown tired, many have grown indifferent amid the cares of the world. Many refuse to recognize the times which have arrived. But as My voice called forth a few, very few responded. Responded by their total commitment to My desires, instructions and implorings.

And these are the mouths that give voice to My words. That all would recognize these as the times spoken of to many, many of My visionaries at My apparition sites. Now comes the fullness of this time and many of My children will believe and return to the truth. For I come now to lead many of My remnant through this final bloody hour.

Through this final hour many will be forced to go underground as the enemy rages against all that is of Christ. For he is the antichrist in the world and ready to unleash the fullness of his fury against humanity and in particular the Church. These are the signs to which I point, and these are the times of which you will speak.

To all of My servants in this valley, prepare, for you will soon be in action, the fruits of this labor of love will soon be called forth. To My C. and My C., soon, very soon, all will be made manifest. And I say with My Son, "Well done, good and faithful servants" (Matthew 25: 2l, 23). I will confirm in a very special way this message of love.

I am the voice that calls all to be anchored in the sea of faith to My Eucharistic Son. I am the voice given power and authority to form the heel that will destroy Satan and all his works.

To the glory of God the Father and My Son who is living and dwells within you, and by the gifts bestowed upon you to serve by the power of the Holy Ghost, I bless you all and say, peace of My Son Christ, Amen!

I Am Coming Soon!

October 23, 1995 - 7:16 P.M.

(S.J., I heard a voice and commanded it to go in the name of Jesus, if not of God.)

Jesus: Daughter of My heart, I am Who am calls you. Come! Allow Me to draw you deeper, ever deeper, into My Sacred Heart!

Torrents of mercy are there (in My Heart), and soon this mercy will be poured out on all humanity. I speak clearly to all who would listen, to all who would hear.

Your wonderment at how I can use you is that you recognize your nothingness. Your proclamations of love, your total abandonment, allow the grace and the will of God to move through you. My message of this mercy went forth long ago, and as you read, you dared to believe them to be true, and so they are, for I am true to My word, and My word testifies to Me Who Am! For the Word has always been.

I have told you I set you as a sentinel in the watch tower and it is true. For I am coming soon and all who have not by then believed, will by the breath of My Mouth, be annihilated. Not one, hear what I say, not one enemy of God will exist. Many do not believe I am coming. So be it. It does not change the truth! Many choose to ridicule and disbelieve, but I tell you, after my warning, they will return to My Father's House.

I am coming soon! For My enemy and the enemies of all who believe, will for a short time, play out his reign of terror. But for your sake, and all My chosen, I will come and seek out My enemies and they will be no more. But We have not left you abandoned. You are there for the weak, for those who fear to approach Me! In you I have one who came and has known My love. Nothing will harm you. As you seek My Face, the graces needed will be provided.

Is this not the truth to My Blessed Faustina's messages of Divine Mercy? Trust is the means which determines how many graces you receive. If your trust in Me is little, then what you receive will be not, what I desire to bestow.

This Cross (of Peace) will be a sign for all of eternity as to the great price by which humanity's salvation was bought. My sorrow is that not all accept.

291

The rays that flow through the holes, where the nails were, will be graces, the same graces that burst forth from My Heart, opened on The Cross. Then they, the graces, will freely flow and be lovingly received, as those who truly believe become smaller in number. This is a fact in itself, that bears to the truth. For does not My Word say, "When the Son of Man returns, will He find any faith"? (Saint Luke, 18:8.)

As you continue to persevere, know that your time of silence is come to an end. I give this word as to call you to attention. I am pleased at your fast, continue and pray.

See My signs in the heavens. They are there.

Peace of My Heart descends upon you and all who would believe.

Amen.

The Lives of All Will Change

November 13, 1995 - 1:00 P.M.

(S.J., I heard a voice and rebuked it to go in the name of Jesus, if not of God.)

Jesus: My Mother's sorrowful rose and daughter of My Heart: I, Jesus who is coming in glory! I, who became the Word Incarnate! I who am give praise to the Father for the moment of triumph arrives!

And I speak these words to you:

My people perish for lack of knowledge. It is not because the knowledge and the truth is not among them, but because they refuse to hear and to see the call I have given through many of My instruments.

Now knowledge will be given to all. Knowledge of My triumph on Calvary. Knowledge of who I am. Knowledge of how I bore the sins of each and all. Knowledge of the Father's great love to send Me to mankind, that salvation might be made available to all. Each will know, to the tiniest speck, all that stains their souls!

I am King, and I will return to take up My Scepter and rule with all who have enthroned Me in their hearts. I will give My mercy, which is limitless and boundless, to all who will receive it! For this you and many others have been praying. For this you, and many others, implore the Father to make His will known in the lives of all His children. For this, the petition to send forth the Holy Spirit, unceasingly ascends to My Father. For this, My Mother and yours, has been granted Her requests to make the hearts of Her smallest children the place where Her triumph begins.

Those who have taken refuge within Her Immaculate Heart, those who have allowed Her to mold, those who have embraced and followed Her way of humility, Her way of holiness, Her way of love, know then, how to embrace the crosses of suffering, that through God's will, have come to them. The triumph is in the Cross!

What I speak is not new but, it is truth, and the truth cannot be changed! All that has been spoken of will come to pass. In the next moment your life and the lives of all will change. I will come to all as the King of Mercy! To Jew and to Gentile. To all I will come. All will be able to see and hear and know the truth. Then, as their will is free and a gift from God, they must choose. Then I will take My seat as the just Judge and none will stand before Me and be able to say "I knew not."

Through the impending events, My hand is on you and all who are Mine and My Mother's. This triumph of Her Heart is the peace that will see you through and lead you into the Era of Peace! Now know that clearer direction will be given to you. Remain at peace and persevere, child. You and others like you are strong for the weak.

Jesus: Describe, child, what was shown to you.

(S.J., Here Jesus is talking about the vision shown to me last Sunday, November 12, after receiving Holy Communion. This vision was not clear nor did I understand it until now. It became clear as He asked me to describe it. After the description of the vision, which is written below, Our Lord then continues:)

Jesus: Now, child, I, Jesus bestow upon you and all who hear, My peace and blessing of the Trinity! Amen.

(S.J., Following is the description of the November 12, 1995 vision, and then the understanding of this vision.)

Vision: I see a church, a Catholic Church, that could be anywhere and a large number of people sitting in the pews. I am shown this from a vantage point of looking out at the people from where the Gospel is read. Everyone has a starving look, hollow-eyed and gaunt, very sick and unhealthy.

And then I see a small number of people, who seem as though they have a light within them and around them, as though they are illuminated, go under a floor.

Understanding of this Vision.

Most parishes have a large number of organizations and activities, but it is the state of their soul that is starving for the truth. For most priests do not speak of things that the church should teach from the pulpit, so, it is as though people are starving for knowledge.

I believe that is why I was shown this view from the pulpit. Such people receiving Communion in a state of mortal sin, confession not being given to penitents according to the Roman rite, loss of teaching of the Church's standing on birth control and abortion, hell or purgatory, or devil's existence. Most do not believe there is a devil.

All of these issues are no longer preached about. Consequently, many people are practicing birth control and have liberal views on abortion. In other words, they are living contrary to the truth.

As to the smaller group, it is the remnant, for the illumination is the light from within our souls, Jesus within us. Going under a floor represents that soon we will go underground, due to the increase of persecution from the new church and forces of the antichrist.)

I Am Co-Redemptrix, Mediatrix of All Graces

December 2, 1995 - 1:15 A.M.

Vision: I see a transparent pitcher of water, very clear, crystal clear, like liquid diamonds, catching light, brilliant and sparkling. Then suddenly this water is released and the lighted water begins to flow, in the form of a river.

December 2, 1995 - 5:30 A.M.

(Sadie: I heard a voice and commanded it to go, in the name of Jesus, if not of God.)

Mary: Child, I am your Mother. My little sorrowful rose, from My womb came forth the Son of God, Jesus, who is praised, adored and glorified, and will be until forever!

Write these words to you:

From the throne of God flows this river of everlasting life (1). It is the water that fills the thirst for holiness. Through the love and plan for Me, the Father deemed that I, humble handmaid of the Lord, be born Immaculate and Pure, without stain of original sin, for in this first tabernacle of our Lord (2), it should be as all tabernacles for Him, brilliant, surrounded in holiness, for My adoration of Him was constant and up to now unceasing. My love and de-

295

sire to fill the Holy will of the Father became My **all.** Jesus is the Water of everlasting life! And He says to all: "Come all you who are thirsty and I will give you life!"

Many are the sorrows of your present age and this invitation and call to holiness is given that the sorrows and burdens can be replaced with His gift of this season: **Peace!**

His peace cannot be imitated or replaced by any other acts of peace. And now while they are saying "peace and security for all",(3) the plot for otherwise becomes increasingly open and obvious for all to see.

Peace will not come to this nation of many gods and idols, to this nation that has turned its back on God! Christ must reign in the hearts and in the governments.

God's laws cannot conform to the world, the world must conform to God's laws. But it chooses instead, greed for power and wealth, and eternal damnation (4). In this choice it brings down also the fulfillment of time, the living out the days of distress, the final and most painful and bloody of these days!

Once again, as at Calvary, I see the crucifixion of My Son, the crucifixion of His Body, the Church. At Calvary I was comforted by few. Again, I am consoled and comforted by few, in proportion to the many. At Calvary I stood by in silence and prayed for the forgiveness of those who had inflicted the most torturous and painful blows of My Son's passion. Retribution was reserved for the Father alone.

At My command, My faithful remnant, again prays for mercy. And again, it will be the holy and just anger of God that begins the cleansing of profanation of His Temple, His Body, His Church!

The schism, split, has been foretold to you and many others. The world wallows in mire and sin, exalts and revels in every kind of base perversion. Truly, as has been said, it is many

times worse than Sodom and Gomorrah. I lead, I console, I guide, I am Co-Redemptrix, I am Mediatrix of all Graces. This is given to Me by the Triune God.

The warning will come in the midst of upheaval.

The chastisements continue and will increase, the blood will flow deep. For this United States, its downfall will begin in the West (5). But My faithful are given peace. Live every moment in this peace, for the Holy Spirit, the Spirit of the Living God, is being poured out in abundance, preceding the Second Pentecost, on those who have willingly surrendered, prepared and remained watchful.

The Bridegroom comes for His Church!

I, Your Mother and Mother of God, embrace you with My Heart and cover you with My Mantle.

And the signs continue in the Heavens! Continue your vigil and fast!

The peace and blessings of God upon you and all My remnant.

(1) Refers to vision.
(2) My womb.
(3) Government leaders
(4) By the sin in the individual lives and laws to allow sin.
(5) Coincide with turmoil and devastation.

My Justice Is Mercy

December 24, 1995 - 3:00 P.M. Christmas Eve.

(S.J., Holidays are hard. The children go with their father. I talked and cried to Our Lord and He began to speak to Me. I tested and rebuked and He continued.)

Jesus: Come My Mother's little sorrowful rose, and enter with Me, Jesus, King of Kings, into My Heart. Come with Me to Bethlehem on this eve of Christ's day. For to you this day is given, in a town called Bethlehem, the Savior of the world. I am called forth, as the fruit of My Mother's womb, the most pure and holy of all. For in that, Her womb, I am constantly united with Her in Her prayers of intercession, receiving of Her adoration, and Our Hearts beat in unison. I am called forth according to the fulfillment of My Father's holy will.

You feel the chill of this cold day, and it is as the night I was born. Born into a home, hastily made, poverty for the King, but filled with holiness and love. And that cold cave is transformed by My Light, My Being, and the love that was shown by My Mother, and tender and compassionate foster father, Joseph. That cave was filled with wonder and awe at the mighty wonder-working power of the Almighty God.

A night filled with reverence, love, joy and peace. A holiness that was even acknowledged in the stars and in the heavens, whereby three kings with wealth and all the things of the world came and knelt and adored the Child Jesus.

I, who am Jesus, come with tender love and compassion for My children who mourn and cry in this world, where peace is only an action of signing paper, for peace does not exist. I come with tender love to gather from you, and all who suffer for My Name's sake. But, I have a firm glance, as I gaze at the majority of this humanity which has sunk to depths that call down and justify God's holy wrath.

The bitterness of this cold is only a foretaste of what awaits those who live in total rejection of Me. With one hand I will cover My children, the children of My Mother, and protect them and lead them through the inspiration of My Holy Spirit. With the other hand, I let fall and signal to the Angel of My Wrath, to commence the cleansing.

Mercy to justice, I now tell you, that the choice of where the souls will go, which side they choose, has come to be made.

298

Choose My mercy, love and protection or My justice, wrath and punishment. Be assured that in My justice, even that is mercy, for the souls you and others pray and sacrifice for.

I take from you all that is of this world, that you may decide for Me, and you have. But as your crosses of suffering have increased, as foretold to you, you have remained strong in Me, persevering until the end. For this, pray constantly.

Your pleas of My Heart for My priests, I have heard and received. There are many priests now, who will have the grace to convert. If you had not sacrificed for them, they would have suffered eternally.

Jesus: On this night I have come to console you in your solitude. To pour My healing balm on your wounds and to prepare you for what swiftly comes.

I am the Christ, whom you adore, Jesus, Son of the Father and with My Spirit, We dwell in your heart. Rejoice, oh little one, redemption is nigh.

Peace, child, and blessings of the Trinity.

December 25, 1995 - 12:45 A.M.

(Vision at Midnight Mass.)

(S.J., I see seven letters with seven seals, all broken. Then I see a large bridge being knocked down by a very large wall of mud or lava-looking substance.)

Chapter Eight

Church and Pope Attacked

Messages From January 2, 1996
To June 17, 1996

The Warning—Beginning of the Harvest

January 2, 1996 - 2:27 P.M.

(S.J., I began to hear Our Lady and then Our Lord. I tested and began to pray Saint Michael's prayer and prayed the Precious Blood of Jesus and rebuked what I was hearing in the name of Jesus to go if not of God. Mary's voice continued.)

Mary: My little sorrowful rose, I come today with My Son Jesus, who, with you, I praise God the Father for this gift of His Divine Son made flesh in My Womb, by the Spirit of God. Power and dominion are given to Him.

(S.J., I immediately heard our Lord.)

Jesus: Do not fear child, I Am Jesus, King of Mercy, with My Mother. **We Come To Announce To You A Message Of Grave Importance.**

(S.J., Our Lady then continued.)

Mary: Child, at My behest, I have repeatedly implored the Eternal Father and My Divine Son for mitigation, Mercy, and postponement of many devastating events that would have brought the days of distress to the world much sooner than now. It has been able to be lessened and mitigated by the prayers and response of My children.

It saddens Me that now many of those who originally embraced My messages of love have cast themselves again into the most terrible of all states of awareness, that of complacency. That of having lost their first love and fervor towards making My Messages known and praying with total abandonment, as I have repeatedly requested.

As My triumph begins to take on a most obvious form, the enemy who has known he will be defeated, but not how it would come, has assailed and assaulted within the Church

My beloved priest sons. From the most esteemed to the littlest priests, all have come under his ferocious attacks. Many, many have succumbed to his lies, to the things of the world he has given them if they would but forsake the truth.

But My Son, Who is Truth, My Son, Who is Light, and My Son, Who is the Way, has given life to you and all the little, most insignificant victim souls of love, so that as the darkness that exists and will come still; you and others will take courage and be the light for many who will come scrambling like little lost children, running towards the light that calms the fears and the terror that will assault them.

Now child listen closely as this year will bring the revealing of many things told in times past and kept hidden until all is fulfilled. For many of these secrets will have actually set the stage for the revealing of the one who opposes My Son. All is known to God. Remember this. Go about your work, knowing that in any moment My children will be cast into the final phase of the time . of chastisement.

Much blood will flow and the loss of life be great, many grave events will threaten the whole of humanity. For those prepared, for those vigilant, you know, as it is spoken of over and over in the messages and in the Word, you will be protected, and led by Me, the Queen of Mercy and Peace.

At the moment of the great outpouring of God's Spirit on all, so none will deny being given the chance to choose, you will see the beginning of the harvest. You will see new hearts replace cold stony ones, you will rejoice with Me, for the fruits of the labor will become visible and apparent.

My Son who loves you and all, smiles with favor on your mission, and upon that of many who labor and trust in My words given to the little and most insignificant of this world. The Spirit of God will speak to the hearts of those who are open and who surrender their wills to the Eternal Father.

The threat of another nuclear incident looms on the horizon. The financial floor will crash. Rome will be besieged and the Holy Father will meet with His greatest agony. As the enemy prepares to proclaim his greatest triumph, the true Church will survive by means of those who have prepared now. The persecution will be great, but the prayers and sacrifice will rise, as a fragrant offering, and thus obtain the final Triumph of the Two Hearts. Many miracles will be.

As you were in adoration to bring in this year of 1996, many graces were poured upon you and your children. I urge you to sacrifice, prayer and fasting. Be as continuous as you are able. Much depends on the response of My children. As this will be the year of the great tribulation of all tribulations.

As we gaze upon you, My Son Jesus blesses you in the name of The Trinity and I embrace you with My Motherly heart.

(S.J., I was waiting for Our Lord to see if He had any words. He then spoke.)

Jesus: My child, I, Jesus tell you, there will be a great breakthrough for the Cross of Peace. As My enemies will scatter and We will gather. He who does not gather with Me is against Me. Amen.

(S.J., Amen.)

Outpouring of Mercy Before Final Justice
January 25, 1996 - 8:57 A.M.

Feast of St. Paul's Conversion

(S.J., I tested and rebuked in the name of God and Jesus answered.)

Jesus: It is I, Jesus, King of Endless Glory and Second Person of the Godhead! I am consoled by your praises for I am to be praised. Your suffering is necessary!

(S.J., I have been suffering intense head and neck pain for three days.)

Jesus: As was told to you and by your yes, by your acceptance it has been increased, in these critical last moments before the whole of humanity falls under the hand of God's mighty justice! I have told you I set you as a sentinel in the watch tower and so, I announce to you that which you will pass through is now upon you.

The conversion of My Apostle Paul was a precedent set in My word. It was his experience of private revelation! As he was blinded by My light, he knew he could no longer deny the One whom he persecuted.

And now all will be caught in this moment of Mercy as My light reveals once again my persecution! For what is sin, no matter what kind, if not my persecution.

I am consoled in the hearts who have surrendered their all to the will of My Father. In these hearts, as in yours, I have revealed the mysteries of faith and My grace has given you a love of the cross, a love for suffering to assist in the mystery of co-redemption. In every moment of pain, I am united to you. I sustain you. I hold you near to Me!

Tell My people: Gird your loins, strengthen your weak knees, lift up your hearts and prepare to be moved by the power of My Spirit into this great exodus of God's people.

As you are illuminated in My light and this moment (that) will be just you and Me, you will see your persecution of Me, but even more you will see My great mercy and love. And this day, which will be to many as a night of terror, will pass and then many, for whom you and others have suffered, will be brought into the harvest.

I, Myself, am coming for you, and for all who will pass from tribulation to peace. My Spirit will sweep over mankind and there will be many then who will know truth and renounce the error they now embrace. My Spirit will speak in the hearts of those who will listen. My Spirit will lead and guide as Spouse of My Mother and My Mother will gather together those whom She has prepared for these times.

Among those will be the brother priests of Mine, for whom you suffer. The princes of the church now stand at odds, one against another, cardinal against cardinal, bishop against bishop and I behold all. I see all. The living fulfillment of prophecy becomes clearer and clearer with each passing moment.

As My people drink of the lies told as truth, they become as though drunk on wine and one blindly follows the other.

As prophecy in this regard becomes fulfilled, there yet remains the outpouring of Mercy before the final justice.

And this I announce to you has arrived!

Do not think or measure by time standards that have gone past, but as I speak it is fulfilled. My peace and blessing are upon you and all those who follow Me.

(S.J., Jesus, I love you. Thank you. I am your humble servant.)

It Will Be The Greatest Harvest

February 21, 1996 - 9:00 A.M. Ash Wednesday

(S.J., I heard the voice of Our Lord and I tested, again and again, till Our Lady said "My child, hearken to the words of My Son.")

Jesus: "Thus says the Lord your God," I, Jesus, given as ransom for mankind, shedding My blood, crucifying My body, opening My Heart, My Heart of mercy and love for humanity, begin the

306

New Covenant for which God the Trinity is praised, worshiped and adored.

As this season of reflection begins, few are they who truly meditate on this preparation time given. As this season of Lent begins, I tell you truly, My herald of truth, it will be as no other. In this season of Lent, the fulfillment of many prophecies told to you and many others will come to pass.

I ask My remnant flock, scattered, at times fearful, rejected and ridiculed: The Master says, Come, follow Me! With the slivers of My cross laid upon your shoulders, Come, follow Me. I, your Master and Lord, am leading those who have allowed themselves to be molded by My Mother's great intercession before the throne of the Trinity. Ascend with Me the hill of Calvary, bearing the sins of the world.

Stay at the foot of My cross, as My one true Church forsakes Her Master once again. Share in the sorrows of Mary as She silently, yet most intimately in the Spirit, felt My great passion and as She once again shares My pain at seeing the state of the Church.

To the shepherds of My flock: Woe! I say woe to you! You have walked in the flesh, not the Spirit. You have fallen into the temptations of the evil one, the ones he tempted your Lord in the desert with.

You have set yourself in luxury and riches and have abandoned the souls I entrusted you with the day of your ordination. You flaunt and desecrate the greatest miracle of all miracles, My priests, you and no other can change bread and wine into I AM.

Thus, less and less have graces been given, less and less truth is preached, more and more souls perish eternally in the flames of hell for your neglect. Now the cleansing of My House, My humanity, My world! No more! No more! No more!

Little victim souls, the flowers of My Mother's garden have spoken where My priests have not! Know that many who pray for you, My priests, will be the graces of conversion to your soul so that you can come to Me, repentant and ready to work in the harvest. The alarm was set long ago and now it has rung.

There will only be few precious moments left of preparation, but it will be the greatest harvest as they who have crucified Me will see Me! My angels surround you, My people. Near you it will not come. My justice is holy, My justice is exact, My enemy is defeated. Heaven's army is on the move. More miracles will confirm My Word.

From the throne of Heaven, I bless you in My Father's name, The name of Me, Your Jesus, and the name of Our Spirit, with blessings of peace. Amen.

Nineveh Heard, Received and Repented

March 14, 1996 - 3:00 P.M.

(S.J. I heard the voice of Our Lady, I tested, and She answered.)

Mary: I, My daughter, who dwell in the midst of the Trinity, praise God the Father, God My Son and God My Holy Spouse, The Spirit of the Everlasting God. Hearken to the words of My Son.

(S.J. I then heard the words of Jesus and I tested.)

Jesus: And I who am The Second Person of the Trinity, praise the Father and proclaim that I, who came in the flesh, to do the will of The Father and with the Spirit, have received the praises of God's children.

I come that you would hearken to My voice and the will of the Father, for "Thus says the Lord Your God"!

As I once spoke to Jonah to go forth and proclaim the number of days left to Nineveh, to call to their ears and hearts the sins that would draw down the anger of God's justice, so too in these days I have sent many as Jonah to proclaim the same message.

But, the difference between the people of Nineveh and humanity, is that they, the people of Nineveh, heard, received and repented. They prayed as one and fasted as one and put on sackcloth. They wailed and lamented for their sins and I, in compassion and response to prayer, did not do what I had proclaimed.

But oh mankind you are so dull of heart. My many Jonahs have gone forth to proclaim the same, and, as I, The Master was once rejected, ridiculed and persecuted, you have done the same to these I send you.

In these 20 and 2 days the sins of Nineveh will come to light as the soul of every man, woman, child of reason, sit in the seat of judgment. What you have done in darkness will be shown in the light. What you have plotted as evil will be revealed to the minutest detail.

And I will be the King of compassion, embracing you with My mercy. You will come and I will wash you whiter than snow. And, as at Calvary, I will give you My Mother to be your Mother and through the ministering of the remnant flock you will be brought into the one true fold.

But prepare, oh children of Mine, for then the enemies of Christ, and the antichrist, will rage even more. Through the confusion and mayhem, you will walk. Many will be gathered in pockets of peoples with the protection of God upon you.

My Vicar will be martyred and the abomination of Daniel's prophecy will come to pass. What you now see in the churches is the prelude.

Jesus: But I have called many who will rise to the occasion of these last days and they will proclaim My Words. Some will give their blood to water the seeds of faith that will flower in the era of peace.

Do you still fear, My children? I am who am - living holy and true. You must remain in Me and in My shadow, therein is protection. With the mantle of My Mother, We will hover over you as a hen with her chicks.

Be concerned only with prayer, united as the one true Mystical Body. Remember that prayer is what will open the hearts of many to convert at this great act of mercy, the gift of My life, for your salvation.

For I am ready to take My seat as just judge!

Pray for My shepherds. Pray for My Vicar.

The Spirit is moving and soon will light the world with His fire of light.

My signs are in the heavens, for as the star of Bethlehem was an announcement to many and the sun at Fatima a sign to many, so too will this day be with signs and wonders. You are united under the banner of Mary to the Two Hearts! Rejoice, children of Mine, for no more will they say; "Where is your sign?"

I bless you in the name of the Father and My name and of Our Holy Spirit!

Peace and blessing.

(S.J., I then said, Ave Maria! Jesus Be Praised!)

(S.J., Upon returning home from Mass I prayed about this message. I asked Jesus, why have you given me this message? Our Lord responded.)

Jesus: Because of the great work that will be required by the whole body. The "generals and commanders" have had their time of preparation before the soldiers are given their orders.

So it is with the remnant, I have set the strong to prepare the weak and because of the tremendous work load, it will give the body time to prepare to "reap the harvest."

(S.J., At Mass, in a vision, I saw the Holy Father at prayer. Then an image of the devil, trying to devour him, but two angels were protecting the Holy Father.)

This Is My Plea

April 9, 1996 - 5:00 P.M.

(S.J., I heard a voice and tested, retested and rebuked and pleaded the Blood Of Jesus and it was our Lady. She responded.)

Mary: I am the Mother of the Christ Crucified, the Christ Resurrected, the Christ Glorified. All praise, honor, glory and thanksgiving to the Blessed Trinity.

I come to bind up your wounds, I come to console, I come to lead you ever stronger forward, to accomplish that which God the Father has bestowed upon you as His will.

Do you not know what has come to you, comes to all, called by God? That God allows all that comes to you for your growth, spiritually, that My adversary and God's is constant to accuse and cause pride to be your downfall.

So that what God allows is answer for your prayer to remain ever humble. These are tests. For the testing that comes to all soon, will cause all that you have undergone up to now, to pale in comparison. I tell you this now for those who have disbelieved over unfulfilled prophecy today, will not stand in the trial that comes.

Those who know, as you know, this event and great prodigy will happen soon. Those who go forward unshaken in the face of abuse and ridicule, will be, and are, the strong who are anchored firmly in the will of God and the Two Hearts.

311

Look and recall that which has been fulfilled and hold in your heart all that has been spoken of. To believe, without any doubts, of what is being accomplished by means of you and many others in heaven's tapestry.

For this is My work and My triumph will be brought about through this humble work of mine. To be ever ready, as if you knew the day, for it will come when least expect. This is My plea, My call for the body of believers. Let the unbelievers be covered by your prayers.

You will suffer increased physical pain for the glory of God. (1) God heals, God touches, but you have been asked to share in this cup.

With you tonight, I will bless and touch My children. (2)

I leave you in God's peace and wrap you in My mantle.

(1) I took a severe fall a few days ago and have been in much pain.

(2) Tuesday night weekly meeting of Marian Movement of Priests in my home. This message was played, via audio tape, at the Cross of Peace Tuesday night prayer meeting in Santa Maria, California.

Marian Dogma Will Be Proclaimed
May 3, 1996 - 9:20 A.M.

(S.J., I began to hear a voice, so I rebuked it and pleaded the precious Blood of Jesus, if not of God, then be gone. The voice continued.)

Jesus: I am, asks you to pick up your pen and write!

I am, the Second Person of the Holy Trinity. I am, receives your praises and I am, find solace and comfort to the wounds being inflicted upon My Body (the Church). I am, with you and I am, praise the Father and the Spirit and they give testimony to who I am.

Describe, My sorrowful rose of My Mother's Heart, your vision.

(S.J., For the last three weeks at different times in prayer, I have seen the Holy Father standing on a balcony high above a crowd. He is throwing rose petals to the crowd below. Most of the crowd, as they have their faces raised upward to see the Holy Father, have a look of furious hate and they are cursing and gnashing their teeth.

The vision ends, but I am given an understanding (with no words), that this refers to the Marian Dogma to be proclaimed and that it will be met with furious anger and opposition.)

Jesus: Now I AM tells you and all, your time of silence is over. You have wondered at the length of time since your last message. I have never left you. I have been ever near to hear your proclamations of love. I told you once, this virtue of perseverance does not come easily. God wills that all adversity and opposition be the trial through which you find yourself overcomers!

I am overcame!

I am victorious!

I am returning the glory and splendor to My Church!

I am coming as just judge!

I am King of Mercy!

This dogma, which My Vicar will proclaim, will be to the sheep, who know their shepherd's voice, a time of great joy. Joy at hearing prophecy fulfilled. Joy at knowing it is My Mother through whom I wish all to come. Joy that this part of Her triumph is complete.

But the enemy will rage at the faithful flock and the sheep will scatter for a time. But also, as part of My Mother's role, She will continue to lead and guide all who hear with faith the word of the Lord! Is it not said, "When the Son of Man returns, will He find any faith at all?"

Review all the words spoken by My latter day saints and apostles. Words which to many are lying in drawers unread and unlived! Those who recognized the voice of the Shepherd, for I am He, will know the path to follow.

My faithful ask, "When Lord? When? Your soon (heavens time), or our soon (time as we know it)"? I tell you, your soon!

I have used you and others to prepare the flock, to reach the pastors, My brother priests who now stand ready, many of them, to form another church where I am not! Woe to you My brother! Woe to you when you stand accountable to your King and Lord!

My faithful: Your Shepherd will never abandon you, heed My voice and the will of My Father. I tell you Our Spirit will be poured upon you and My signs, wonders and miracles will seal these words as My Own.

They will strike the staff and the sheep will be scattered, but they will gather where they hear the Shepherd's voice.

The culmination of this most painful time for humanity is come. Take heart My flock, I am with you! Heed My Mother, gentle and pure. Heed Her requests while there is yet but a moment of time. The time of extreme chaos and confusion will fall.

But to those prepared, you will walk within the hand of God and only those called to be the new martyrs, will shed their blood for the era of peace, souls of many, and triumph of My Church, visible and true.

My Love, peace and blessings upon you and all My faithful!

(S.J., Ave Maria.)

Suffering Will Fall On Humanity

May 21, 1996 - 4:00 P.M.

(S.J., I began to hear a voice and commanded it to go in the name of Jesus if not of God, and I pleaded His precious blood to cover me and ask all the Holy Angels for their protection.)

Mary: But you know the voice of your Mother. I am Mary ever humble Virgin - Mother of Christ who came in the flesh. I am the "Woman Clothed with the Sun" and I praise the Most Holy Trinity for there is where I dwell.

Jesus: And I Am Jesus, Son of Mary, blessed and pure. I came through Her the first time and now, again, I desire to come through Her. For through Her I came in the flesh, lived, died, was resurrected and ascended back to the Eternal Father, though Whom I am glorified and to Whom I give glory! The Spirit of the Father and the Son, Holy and One!

Mary: My child, little sorrowful rose, how pleased I am at those, who along with you, continue to persevere in response to My requests to join the army of the Mother, who came to show you and all, the way and the life! I walked with Him on the Way of Calvary and I remained to establish the New Way after His Ascension.

The way for His Mystical Body is today the exact footsteps of His way. His way of love. His way of obedience even to a death. His way of humility, King of Kings, to live a life of simplicity and humbleness, a life of poverty. His way of suffering of showing mercy and forgiveness. He embraced a suffering so great and death on a cross, a cross where He gave even His Heart. That is the life of the Christ, a life so contrary to the lives of many, if not most, of My children.

But in the acceptance of His Mercy, divine and complete, comes the peace of My children. Yet peace is what eludes them for they reject the very heart of the Cross, that of suffering.

315

I have come in these latter days to call all to embrace His way. To call all back to their Father's house, to call all to enter into My Heart, immaculate, yet pierced with new sorrows.

For the time left to this humanity is now so little and in these days the suffering, whether embraced or not, will fall without exception on this humanity.

To many who say "this is fearful", do you not see in the lives around you of those who even now are passing though this door of suffering, yet with no consolation; for they live without God's love, knowledge or protection. My new sorrows are so great.

My Son's Holy Vicar, and the Pope of My heart, suffering on the way to his immolation. My priest sons, from the highest to the littlest, betraying their Lord with the kiss of Judas. The life of the family so destroyed and degraded in the cesspools of inequity which include every kind of perversion.

The lives of the innocent as the little ones were once slaughtered outside the protection of their mother's womb are now slaughtered with the mother's permission from within that womb of protection!

The desecration of the temples of God, which once caused My Son to erupt with His holy anger for thieves and irreverence there. Now many of His houses of worship do not even resemble holiness.

My sorrows are great, but they are relieved as you and many of My little remnant come and offer Me the fragrance of love from your hearts, from your prayers, from your sufferings and sacrifices. I weep at those, who are many, who have rejected My plea for they do not know what quickly awaits them. But keep your eyes on your Lord and your Mother as we draw to the conclusion of this bloody time of suffering. The punishment of Sodom and Gomorrah awaits all those of like beliefs and lives. They, too, will have been given a chance to repent.

316

The winds of change will blow quickly upon all My children, and from one moment to the next. The fire of the Holy Spirit will penetrate the most hardened of hearts and all will be given the opportunity to repent and shake loose the chains that held them bound.

And what My Son did not do the first time, judge His betrayers and persecutors, He will soon come, and judgment will be pronounced on each and every one; for His time of Divine Mercy will end and His time and moment of judgment will be fulfilled. My children, your judgment will be brought upon you by your very lives and rejection of His mercy, love and forgiveness. You will condemn yourselves if you persist in your lives unchanged.

With great love and Motherly concern, I bless you in the Name of the Father and of the Son and of the Holy Ghost.

Jesus: Now I Jesus tell you and all, Beloved of the Two Hearts, the time of all times will see you protected and as you open your hearts to the graces poured upon you in prayer. You will be inspired by The Spirit to the will of the Divine Father. I am a jealous God and I desire to keep all the Father has given over to Me. Our Spirit will be poured out and the very elements of nature will convulse at this miraculous event.

Thus changes will sweep the four corners of the earth and after a time, which has been appointed by God, the fire of purification will fall in the darkness and those who chose their perversion and false gods, to their dismay, will too late discover the truth of the One True God!

Jesus: Behold I say, the final days of tribulation will pass, they will come to many by surprise. Only those of the Two Hearts will recognize the signs and follow the promptings of the Holy Spirit which will be given for their protection and sustenance.

317

Hold on to your faith, which will be shaken, and the days of the coming era of peace. For I come quickly to establish My reign and restore My Body.

Amen, Amen, I say to you, It shall be.

From the throne of heaven, I bestow blessings and My peace!

(Note - My understanding: Jesus is coming this second time through Our Lady as He did the first. It is His expressed desire that all should venerate and love Her, consecrated to Her. They will be protected and led and sustained through the period of antichrist's reign. That our faith will be shaken as the Holy Father, and the Mass, are taken away. That we will then walk by faith and what we have been given through the messages. We will have to remind ourselves that this period is short and the era of peace is close.)

Every Life Will Change

May 23, 1996 - 12:55 P.M.

(S.J., I heard a voice and I commanded to go if not of God in Jesus' name and pleaded the Precious Blood of Jesus to cover me.)

God The Father: I am the Great I Am, Who was, Who is, Who will always be, omnipotent and powerful.

I gave My only begotten Son to redeem mankind from his sins.

I created mankind in My image, that in all I created I would share My goodness and My love. (That) In My creation all would praise and honor My Son, Jesus Who took upon himself the human nature of man.

Recall now, little one, as this nation that was founded under the laws of God, has been so blessed by Me; I revealed to you upon election of this man (Clinton) that I would turn My back

on this nation as those here have turned their backs to Me. But I have given time because of the prayers of My children held in the Two Hearts. With your prayer children you have appeased My anger (which) is holy and just.

But now I am openly mocked, I am openly renounced, I am openly ridiculed.

My child, I am now telling you to prepare, prepare. By My very hand, I am giving protection to those who have surrendered their will. They have given over to Me their wills, that I might supersede over theirs.

I am a loving Father, waiting for the return of My prodigal children. But they reject all I have given through My Son and His Mother.

On the Feast of Pentecost immeasurable graces will be poured out, the graces will transform the lives of many, but not all. The gifts will be so as they will feel the transformation within themselves. I solemnly reveal to your heart that I will not be put off and mocked any longer.

Those who have prepared are prepared and those who have not will find great and numerable the difficulties.

My children will find themselves with nothing that they lived for, (those who have lived for only material possessions).

My children, I have given this time of grace, for always I desire to be merciful and loving. But I cannot, I will not be mocked any longer! The time of My just retribution is come! Every life will change, In which way depends on their free will.

Free, because in no way will I veto a person's choice to inflict My own. Not one person, no not one, will be able to stay in ignorance.

I, the Father, holy and powerful, bring warning and notice as I once did to Moses, that the time of exodus has begun!

319

You will find yourselves being always led and guided by My Spirit. By My very hand I protect. To the Lily of Heaven is given triumph and victory!

And the fulfillment of the victory of Calvary will soon be.

Do not fear for you are never alone. Recall at the end of these words to you the vision and message, for the time to pray and intercede for the lost has been given.

I am your Father who dwells in your heart.

(S.J., My Father I am your nothing, but always I will serve you.)

God the Father: I bless you from heaven's throne.

(S.J., Amen, Praise be to Jesus!)

(S.J., I am reminded of the vision over three years ago, in the February 3, 1993 message. I did see darkness cover the world and I understood in this message it will come.)

June 2, 1996

Vision: I see a pair of scales. On one side is Jesus sacrificed on Calvary with a multitude of people around the Cross. On the other side is a cup with blood overflowing, which represents the sins and choices of abomination on top of abomination. Sins of lust, homosexuality, abortion, impurity, sins against children, sins of every deception and sins of His priests. This side of the scale showed the most weight.

Signs and Warnings of Grave Times

June 5, 1996 - 8:00 A.M.

(S.J., I began to hear a voice and I tested and it was our Lord.)

Jesus: I am the Bread of Life, I am He Who has given you everlasting Life, for My Flesh is real flesh and My Blood real blood. I am Jesus, Son of God, given as a ransom for mankind!

Many are they who reject Me! But in the hearts of My little victim souls I have found solace and consolation from the wounds of My Body (the Church).

I have sent many to go forth with words of comfort, hope and appeal for a change of men's hearts. Many have refused My messages, My messengers, My prophets and priests. My priests, true to My words of everlasting life and My teachings, have been held in ridicule, rejection, scandal and every kind of persecution.

But I, Who have promised to be with My Church, even to the end of time, I see all and it will be I Who fights your battle and defeats your enemies. Yes, I will do what no other can do, for I, Your Lord and Master, Teacher, and your all, I too, received this same treatment.

God is Infinite and you are finite. You are not able to comprehend all that the Infinite One has prepared. You seek to understand with your minds, when you need to accept with your hearts, what cannot be understood with your human wisdom. The wisdom of God has been revealed to those little of God and you, My Mother's little sorrowful rose, are one (of those little).

To you, who are the most unlikely, I have whispered truths of faith, teaching and love. I have given warning, for many are they who do not want warning. They cannot believe what I, the Lord, would give as signs and warnings of these grave times through which you are living.

My children, your lives will change, whether you are ready or not. They will change soon. For God has appointed to these days the culmination of many prophetic messages announced long ago. You, who are nothing, are amazed that what is given

to one true instrument is also given to another, unknown to you, or you, as an unknown to them. (Our Lord refers to the confirmation in the messages of one to another.)

So to those who choose, for it is your choice not to heed heaven's call, again I tell you: I, the Lord, have spoken to give time of preparation, to call all to a change of heart, to move in this great time of grace and serious events that threaten the whole of humanity. Much time of grace has been given, still many of My children, who say they love Me, do not detach themselves from the world.

Yes children, your life will change and all those who form the remnant will recognize the truth of what I say: prayer and sacrifice, fasting and reparation, an appeal from heaven for souls to be won. It is necessary to achieve this triumph.

My priests, for whom you have prayed, will be moved by the very power of God to do all that will confront them very soon. They will know, by the very events through which they will live, that these are the times for which humanity has been prepared.

The essence of their vocation will be what they recognize and embrace, what they will, yes, even give their lives for. Up to now many have chosen not to believe, but by the revelation of God, they will choose, and live and die for their Christ, Who once died for all. These events are even now ready to be revealed and many will be caught unprepared, though they were given great time of preparation.

You see in the spirit (vision of June 2, below), the scales of God's justice and wrath, for the times of Mercy will end, and the cup has been overflowing for a great long time.

Do not fear the path I put before you, I am with you and you will be directed in all that you do. I am the God Who has prepared you and many others for these days.

With this, child, I bless you and all My children who believe, and give you My peace.

(Note: The events our Lord refers to, in regard to living through the actual events themselves, which will bring many priests to believe are:

1. Great calamities of nature.

2. The exile and martyrdom of Pope John Paul II.

3. The revelation of the antichrist.

4. The warning.

5. Extreme unrest coast-to-coast (racially and economically).

6. The crash of the stock market. (I don't know in what order, but many will happen almost simultaneously. I was clearly given these as I saw the vision.)

Fast and Pray

June 16, 1996

(S.J., During Mass this morning, after Communion, as I was giving my thanksgiving, I saw something very strange. There was this man, dressed in black, in black pontifical robes, with a black miter, the type the Pope wears. I felt nothing but evil looking at this man who will be the next Pope, the false Pope.)

June 16, 1996 - 7:00 P.M.

(S.J., I heard a voice, tested and rebuked, in the name of Jesus, if not of God.)

Mary: I am Mary, Virgin Mother of God! Jesus, My Son, came in the flesh, to live and die, for the redemption of man. What mercy from the opened Heart of My Son awaits those who call upon Him, and in the refuge of My Immaculate Heart, My chil-

dren find answers to the woes of this world. And though all are
My children, those who give their all to Me are those I will protect and lead through the storm soon to break on this humanity.

**This man exists and awaits his moment to take the seat of
Vicar of Christ (1), though he, along with many, are the wolves
in sheep clothing. This day is near. This storm will break, not
only in the Body of Christ, but then onto the world.**

There have been many courses that have been changed due to the
prayer that has risen. But it has also sifted ever more those who
would persevere, this virtue so hard for many to continue.

Allow Me children, to lead you as blind children holding the hand
of their Mother. The winds of change that will buffet every side
of your world, that for the moment still exists, will see those who
have gone through their trials and testing vindicated.

Through your consecration you have given Me permission to mold
and form you into that which conforms to the holy will of God
the Father. Do not, My little sorrowful rose, fear the road through
which I and My Son lead you.

The time of travail is come! There will, to the North of you, come
again intense shaking (2). After that, there will be a short time until
the sign given for Santa Maria will be.

**The day of warning!
The day of warning!
The day of warning!**

**I ask you, My little sorrowful rose, to fast. Fast and pray as
was given to you. You will fast for the many souls who will die
through the continuance of many accidents (3), the priests of
My Heart to work for the harvest, and the souls of those to
live through the warning.**

Without the many, responding to My pleas, this day will not reap
the harvest of souls that God would save. God wills life, not death,

but cooperation of the field of victim souls is necessary. For the enemies of God it appears they have the victory but, oh child, the triumph of God, the triumph of My Immaculate Heart will, in the end, be swift and powerful.

Punishment through these means is not God's will, but is necessary because of the stench of sins rising continually to God. The plans of the enemy to ensnare humanity will be implemented, thus the diabolical forces will be countered by means of My remnant.

There is hope if you trust, trust in the mercy of God. Only heaven's intervention can defeat and cleanse the stain of men's sins in the body, in the world. Then you will see heaven and earth meet and transformed into that which was taken away through the fall of man, the paradise of the era of peace.

Do not fear, children, do not fear. Count as nothing that which you suffer, for God's grace is sufficient for you to overcome. With the love of your Mother and the peace of My Son, I bless you in the name of the Father, the Name of the Son and the name of the Holy Spirit.

Amen!

(1) Referring to vision earlier in the day.

(2) The following two messages were given three weeks before the Northridge California earthquake on January 17, 1994.

A. December 28, 1993 "Feast of Holy Innocents".

   Mary: Shortly after the first of the year, there will be an intense shaking.

B. December 29, 1993

   Jesus: This shaking will be the hand of God. . . It will be shortly after the New Year.

(3) Planes, autos, trains, the increase of death.

325

Chapter Nine

Final Combat

Messages From July 5, 1996
To February 24, 1997

All of Heaven Fights With You

July 5, 1996 - 5:00 P.M.

(S.J., I heard a voice and tested in the name of Jesus, if not of God, for the voice to go.)

Jesus: I am Jesus, God Man, brought into world by the will of the Father through the womb, Immaculate and Virgin, of My Mother.

Daughter of My Heart and sorrowful rose of My Mother, you have seen many things revealed by the will of God, My Father and yours. Do not fear the circumstances and the road ahead of you.

It is by My design that those raised to assist you, through My Father's holy will, have been put here for you. Your acceptance and joy in all that you surrender daily is the joy of My Heart, sweet and consoling, to counter the many acts of sacrilege committed with every passing moment of time.

I have called all to respond, not only I, but My Mother, gently imploring, always requesting Her children to respond to Her pleas of repentance, conversion and sacrifice. Daily, multitudes of souls are snatched from the enemy because of the remnant who prays in The will of God, the Father.

"Why do We repeat the same message"? Many wonder. I tell you, because the urgency of these days fails to be recognized by many. The seriousness of these days passes unnoticed by most of humanity. Though My signs are constant, they are not recognized. I can do nothing if faith and prayer are not there in the world, and for most this is so.

I have sent the world My prophets, I have sent the world warning after warning, and still the hardness of man's heart dictates his eternity, for man chooses where he will spend eternity.

Though My peace abounds in the hearts of Mine, the world has been lit aflame by a spirit of hate. This hate will rise quickly and dramatically around you, because this nation, once rich with God's grace, has rejected God and His kingship. I tell you, many will be taken into captivity by those who would oppress and conquer a people, a nation, the world.

An international incident is on the point of happening.

For the purpose of this message, I reveal to you that it will come by an assault of the Islamic forces and be supported and assisted by the Red Dragon of Communism. This will signal to you the beginning of the end. All that will follow daily will be uprising and one faction against another. Already you see the fulfillment of My Words in regards to the racial incidents (1). In the midst of this My remnant will feel My peace and protection, and the preparations will be ready.

My Vicar will go into exile until his martyrdom. My final act of mercy, that which My Faustina prepared the world for, through that image, will be fulfilled (2).

The time of oppression, by he who would oppose Me, is ready to be cast like a net on the whole world.

I do not give you these words to place fear in the hearts of My Children, but rather to give you the signs of impending incidents that you and all would persevere in prayer, for therein is your peace, and that My Children would be not caught unawares. You do not fight this battle alone. All of heaven fights with you and for you.

There is great hope, for you know, I would not abandon the world, the creation of My Father. But I would seek the souls willing by their yes to stand strong; who would speak words that many are uncomfortable hearing and want to reject to their own folly.

And I Who am, the cornerstone on which My Church is built, all you who will accept My teachings and words of everlasting life, who still look towards the Chair of Peter, My Vicar, as my true representative, you are anchored safely in My heart and the heart of My Mother, two yet one; and the storm that comes; will not prevail.

But in the end, for My enemies, fire will rain down from heaven and the mighty hand of God will seek you out and destroy you, every last one, and you will be no more.

I have never left My Church, though in many churches I have been put out. I will see you through the storm, and you will increase in courage and strength, for it will be by the very power of God those destined to be My remnant will go through these final dark moments. Just as I opened the way, in many other times of persecution, so it will be again.

I leave you and bless you, in My peace.

(1) Here our Lord refers to the riot of July 4, 1996, in Los Angeles, California.

(2) Here Jesus refers to the fulfillment of the messages and image of Divine Mercy.

Be Not Afraid—We Are With You

August 1, 1996 - 5:45 P.M.

(Anniversary of first visit of Our Lady to Sadie.)

Vision: (S.J., Today at Mass, after Communion, I saw an interior vision of Jesus on the Cross, looking at Him from the side as the Good Thief: a profile side view. As He looked back at me, I saw a brother of mine at the foot of the cross. Our Lady explains this vision in the following message. I began to feel Our Lady's presence and heard Her voice. I tested and here is how She answered me.)

Mary: I am the august Queen of Heaven, Mother of Jesus, The Christ. I dwell in the midst of the Blessed Trinity and I praise My Son, Jesus for His coming in the flesh.

330

I praise God the Father's great love of His gift to humanity, His only true beloved Son, and I praise the Holy Spirit, being poured out in abundance in these the latter days, by whose power He will change the hearts of mankind. Indeed He will change the very face of the earth.

Your reflections of this day (1) have warmed My Heart, now so intimately united to yours. You could not have known, four years ago this day, that which I had come to call you to and prepare you for.

If that day I spoke of how little time was left, imagine child now, that the time of times is come. You have learned, you have grown. Yes, you have failed in some things, and this was all allowed as part of your ascent up the spiritual ladder. What is this ladder, you ask? It is the ladder that takes you to heaven.

Sometimes you progress upwards and sometimes you slip and fall back, but your goal in your heart is upward. By your imitation of Me, your Mother, you have grown in the virtues of My heart. I have helped you overcome those areas of weakness that alone, your efforts were futile.

If four years ago many of My children did not know of the urgency and shortness of time, many have now elected to ignore the warnings, and the warnings daily have been given, are increasing and will increase.

The conspiracy grows and will be played to the hilt to open the way for the captivity by the evil one's plan. Remember, My child, all that has been given in advance. With the fulfillment of each, the victory becomes closer and closer a reality. The victory is assured. The victory is!

All that is happening to you now has been planned by the Father, for in His Divine will there are no coincidences.

(S.J., Here Our Lady makes a personal reference to the vision regarding my brother, representing all my family including the father of my children, that She told me four years ago.)

Mary: All that has been told to you will come to pass, if you wait for the Lord and trust. Within moments great atrocities will become a daily occurrence.

The tumult and turmoil of the earth and all natural elements will convulse under God's mighty hand of justice. But the darkness that surrounds the Chair of Peter prepares to play out to the fulfillment of Scripture (2).

Heed My words to you and those of My Son. God has prepared many others like you to stand vigilant, yet at peace. Your daily surrender assures you of that peace. For the enlightenment of the soul to reap as many souls as possible, God, My Father and yours, requires prayer and sacrifice.

Be not afraid, We are with you and all who will allow Us to lead them. On this day so etched in your heart and Mine, I bestow upon you great graces in answer to prayer.

The blessing of God, His Son and the Spirit are upon you. Amen.

(1) Four years ago today was my first message from Our Lady.

(2) Daniel, chapter 12:11: "From the time that the daily sacrifice is abolished and the horrible abomination is set up, there shall be one thousand two hundred and ninety days".

Much Has Been Mitigated—So Great Is God's Love

August 10, 1996 - 10:00 A.M.

(S.J., before going to the hill (1) in Santa Maria, California, I stopped by to pray at the Jesus of Mercy statue and heard a voice that I rebuked to leave if not of God.)

332

Jesus: I am Jesus and I ask you to go to the hill of My Mother, who awaits you to bestow great graces and blessing upon you.

(S.J., Arriving at the hill, I was singing and praising my God. I heard Our Lord and rebuked in the name of Jesus, if not of God.)

Jesus: I am Jesus your Lord and Savior. Praises are sung continually to the Blessed Trinity and received to the glory and praise of God, My Father.

I am the King of Mercy and mercy I desire to bestow. For the last moment before justice I call you and all to be apostles of divine mercy. The will of God the Father has called many, and few have responded. Yet for the sake of those few, their prayers of the heart have been heard and much has been mitigated, so great is God's love.

Pockets of My people will preserve the true faith. Many will die to defend this faith. This deposit of faith in the souls of My brother priests and faithful has come about through surrendering themselves as My instruments to My Mother's Heart.

The truth as once proclaimed, is no longer proclaimed, and to those who do, much persecution comes. For if the world does **not** recognize truth, the demons who fight against it do, and thus seek to slaughter and steal and destroy.

But My Word, which is truth, cannot lie. It lives in the heart of the very humble and the very little. Even now, many are teaching to pass it on to those whom I have called.

Be not afraid as you enter still deeper into the time of tribulation. You cannot see the angels that defend you according to My instructions. As you step out in faith, I will move mountains and open doors no others can open. I will confirm the message with signs and miracles and wonders.

Prepare for the days of intense harvest. We are always with you. Pray, pray, pray for My brother priests that they turn their hearts once again to their Teacher, Lord and Master.

From this holy hill, My Mother and I, bless you and your work this day.

Go in peace.

(S.J., I then said, Amen.)

(1) Cross of Peace project hill in Santa Maria, California.

Visions - August 11, 12:00 Noon:

(Vision 1.) I saw the world as a sponge, soaked and dripping with blood that became a dark scarlet color. I then saw Our Lady kneeling before the Father and with one hand offering prayers and sacrifices and with the other hand She covered the world with Her mantle. During this time Jesus was standing at Her side. Seeing this vision, I pulled the car off the road and began to weep.

(Vision 2.) The vision then switched to the "Cross of Peace" Center where yesterday I gave a talk. Jesus was standing at the back of the room, where He raised His hand and blessed everyone.

Jesus then started to walk among the people, resting His hand on some people and gazing at others as He walked towards the front of the room where He stood by me for a moment and then is gone.

There Is A New Dawn Coming

August 11, 1996 - 12:15 P.M.

(S.J., I heard Our Lord speak, which I tested and He says:)

Jesus: Thus says The Lord your God: The world cannot contain the weight of the innocent blood that flows and thus I will bring judgment upon all those who have allowed this to be. (Vision 1)

334

As in the early days of the church, My gift to humanity, the miracles and outpouring of The Spirit touched and converted many hearts to God. It strengthened those who believed to go out to the highways and byways, despite danger of persecution, and proclaim to all who would listen that truth passed over to the Apostles by Me. And so that deposit of faith preserved whole and complete in the hearts of the remnant few will be proclaimed again.

My presence and Spirit will convict those who are now stiff-necked and hardened of heart. I will increase in the heart of those who believe, and My promptings will strengthen those to move and do extraordinary works in My name.

There is a new dawn coming and there is an era and a new time of peace ahead. Hold this steadfast in your hearts.

(S.J., Vision 2 is repeated.)

Jesus: My servants of this work (1) will also be guided in this important work of My Mother's. I leave the graces of My blessing upon them, that they grow in strength, unity and prayer of their heart. Very, very soon, the inundation of people will begin. Go now child, and we will continue later.

(1) Cross of Peace Project.

Prepare For The Priests Who Will Flee

August 12, 1996 - 7:15 A.M.

(S.J., I heard Our Lord's voice and I tested. This is how He answered me:)

Jesus: I praise the Blessed Trinity, One yet Three. Peace, My child, I your Jesus, Lord and Savior, continue.

Very soon now, 'J.' and His family will seek you out.

(S.J., I have been hearing this for the last week.)

Jesus: God the Father has heard the cries of His people: the cry of lamentation, sorrow, the cry of despair and loss of hope. All this crowned by the sorrow of loss of respect for life.

The blood of innocents, you see, has drenched the whole entire world (1). For the loss of life through abortion brings about a loss of respect for anyone's life be they small, young, old, big it matters not. The perverse spirits of murder, lust, hate and perversion have inundated this world even though the call has gone out to repent. Convert your heart to the Lord your God; who swiftly will come to establish His reign of peace, triumphant with victory of the Immaculate Heart of Mary, My Mother.

I have much to reveal to you still yet to come. Do not fear! Those who are signed with the Cross will know My power and protection.

There will be intense changes in the weather soon. Prepare! The wolves who hide in sheep's clothing are known to Me as they prepare to remove My true Vicar from the Chair of Peter.

Prepare for the priests who will flee.

My Spirit will quicken to all who persevere and pray their way through these days. Rest in the peace of My Spirit, and the power of My love.

In My Father's name and Mine and Our Spirit, I bless you this day.

(1) Refers to Vision 1 of August 11, 1996.

The Blood of The Innocents Cries Out to God

September 7, 1996 - 11:45 A.M.

(S.J., I heard the voice of Our Lady, I tested and rebuked in the name of Jesus if this was not of God, and this is how She answered:)

Mary: My child, I am the Mother of God and I praise Him for His wonders, His majesty and His might; and because Jesus, the Incarnate Son of God, assumed flesh from My virginal flesh, thus salvation has been bought by the price of His Blood for mankind.

Little sorrowful rose, I ask you to offer your pain for a time longer. I know, as does your Lord, your pain and sorrow. But you see all around you the multitudes of those who continue oblivious of the signs of God. My remnant must pray, little one, for daily, multitudes of souls fall into the abyss of darkness for eternity.

(S.J., at this point Mary asks me to go to Her Son's Holy Scripture, Book of Apocalypse (Revelation) chapters 8-12. Chapter 8 speaks of the silence in heaven for about half an hour and the earth trembling with the angels being dispatched and Chapter 12, speaks of Our Lady "Clothed with the Sun." Our Lady continues:)

Mary: Now I, as the "Woman Clothed with the Sun," the River of Light, do announce that the silence of heaven is over! Many and many times over have I tried to work, and the evil one and those subject to him thwart My plan. Division, discord, false imitators of true instruments, closed hearts of My Son's priests everywhere. As the enemy never sleeps, he has sown these things.

I, as the River of Light, because I obtain from the Heart of My Son, Jesus, graces and blessings, always within the will of God, the Father, and Jesus is the Light. He is the way. He is the truth. My will is surrendered to the will of God the Father to lead all who will sweetly surrender their lives and hearts to Jesus. To this River of Light and life I take them! He brings new life to those dead in sin! He brings new freedom to those held captive! He brings new meaning to life to those now merely existing.

The blood of the innocents cries out to God, the Father for justice. Of this, the horror knows no bounds. You cannot com-

prehend this great suffering of God's littlest creatures or of those used and abused for Satanic purposes.

Thus all that has been revealed to you and many, many others will be fulfilled. Woe to you mankind, you who have scoffed and laughed or impeded My work. My beloved priest sons, for you many now pray. For you, many now suffer, for the time of God's retribution is upon you.

I, as the River of Light, will magnify My presence as this darkness pervades even more this humanity, to you and others to encourage and console and comfort you. It will seem for a time that hell and all its forces have triumphed, but it will not be able to stop or conquer My work.

My image that has been sustained down through the centuries is an ongoing miracle (Lady of Guadalupe). From that image a great triumph will come. Is it not through that image I touched your heart? Everywhere I have truly brought My presence, will have My sign and through this sign great healings, conversions and wonders will be wrought!

As your Mother of mercy, I tell you your King of mercy will touch every heart and soul, every sinner, every pagan, every priest and religious, and the hearts and souls of the chosen race will acknowledge this Jewish Mother and their Messiah!

The pinnacle of this great tribulation has yet to be reached, but it will come swiftly, and then woe to those who have fallen prey to the lies of the antichrist!

But you, little hearts of mine, your seal is seen by the angels who protect you, by those sent to pour the justice of God and will pass over you. (Sign of The Cross.) Do not fear, Our Light gives you light in the time of darkness. The threshold of hope is upon you. Many, but not all, will cross over. Glory to God in the highest!

(S.J., At this time Our Lady instructs me to write a vision I have been having all week.)

338

Vision: I see President Clinton riding a train, standing in the rear car giving a victory sign. At the same time directly underneath this vision I see the Holy Father surrounded by two or three Cardinals. He is hurriedly being rushed off to the left and the Cardinals seem to be gathering a few articles. I am given an understanding that at this time something of a very grave nature will happen to the Holy Father. Our Lady continues.)

Mary: This man (Clinton) who speaks nothing but propaganda, will be reelected and you have been shown how he is an abomination to the Lord, for he does nothing to protect life and everything to enslave it. My triumph comes and mercy is fulfilled. The Cross's triumph is that over all hearts. God has shown His mercy, even on those who will rage even more and thus condemn themselves to the abyss; the abyss shown to your littlest son.

(S.J., My nine year old son, 'C.', a week ago, was shown hell by Our Lady in a dream. He heard screams, cursing, and smelled horrible odors. He saw flames and demons in them. He also saw Our Lord and Our Lady standing at his side. Our Lord was blessing him.)

Mary: I am your Queen of Peace, your victorious Queen of the Light. From My heart flows a River of Light! In His Light and Grace, I bless you and all who persevere. Amen!

(S.J., Our Lord begins to speak and as I always do, I tested. I rebuked what I was hearing in the name of Jesus if it was not of God. Our Lord answered as follows:)

Jesus: My daughter of My Heart and sorrowful rose of My Mother, I am Jesus, King and Messiah! I receive your praises and with you I praise God, My Father for His kingdom and the divine will that reigns in the hearts of some of His children.

As your passage of time continues, this will of the Father will be done. It is His will that gave Me to humanity; it is His will that gave humanity the gift of My Mother from whose womb I came. And it is His will that calls to the hearts of His children, so that they come to Me Who will wash them whiter than snow by the forgiveness of their sins, through My sacrament.

I Who am the Bread of Life, so that I can enter into the hearts of all and abide with them. It is the will of God the Father that all know the power of His Spirit to strengthen and empower those who accept, to become sons and daughters of the living God.

The miracles that will be wrought in the coming days through many of My instruments will amaze many, that the trial that comes and intensifies is overshadowed by My power and presence, protection and love. Though evil will abound in every direction, near My own it will not come. You will seem as though you are traveling on a road with much chaos and turmoil around you, but you shall walk through it. I will give you courage and peace to guide and sustain you.

This great moment of time that will shine in the darkness of the hearts of mankind, that no power or force on earth or of the evil one can stop from triumphing over the hearts of all.

I say to you: "They shall all come to you for truth and consolation, comfort and counsel and I shall speak through you and many, many others." Be not afraid, the fulfillment of all things comes.

For the Cross of Peace, the breakthrough is complete!

Pray and fast as much as possible for My priests and for My Vicar. His time of exile swiftly comes!

Keep truth in your hearts, for soon that is the only place you will find it (truth). But underground it will flourish (truth). It will grow bright as a fiery furnace and it (truth) shall overcome.

Pray and remain at peace!

From heaven's throne, the blessings of the Trinity descend upon you. Amen.

340

September 9, 1996 - Early Morning.

(S.J., Early this morning, Monday, I am awakened by a very intense dream. I see a missile hit the east coast. I hear the word Manhattan, and then, "Many of My people will hide in the mountains and the hills. My people will flee to take refuge." Later in the day, before the Blessed Sacrament, I hear Jesus' voice again. I tested.)

Jesus: This day is upon you (missile attack). Many of My children will come before the sign (warning). Many more will come after. They will experience extreme fear, for My peace is not with them.

"I will bring some who will assist you now in this time, it is part of My will for you, to accomplish that which has been given to you."

(S.J., I ask the question, "Why me?" Jesus responded:)

Jesus: Again I tell you, you are the most wretched of all My children, so that in all that is accomplished through you, there can remain no doubt that God has accomplished it all by means of your surrender. Therefore, you acknowledge God's triumph, power and glory.

(S.J., Amen.)

I Am the Woman of Revelation

October 1, 1996 - 3:30 P.M.

(S.J., I began to hear Our Lady's voice and after testing She continued. I felt the presence of Jesus.)

Mary: My child, My little sorrowful rose, I am the Woman of Revelation. I am the Lady of the Way and I have come to show, to lead many back to God their Creator, Jesus, My Son, and to be filled with gifts abundant by My Spouse the Holy Spirit. And I

341

was the first to bow and prostrate Myself to the Blessed Trinity with songs of praise!

(S.J., Jesus then began to speak, I tested and rebuked in His name.)

Jesus: And **I AM** the Way, My Mother leads those who respond back to. I too praise God, Eternal Father for the wonders of His creation and for His gift of redemption to which I submitted. It is in My human nature, I suffered a death violently, surrendering My Divine Nature to God's will.

We have come to announce this: "Let him who has eyes, see and prepare! Let him who has ears, hear and prepare, for to many, grave warnings have been given, for God is the same yesterday, today and forever."

God has always saved those who had the faith to believe, to believe that God is ready to let His hand fall in judgment, that the Divine King of mercy prepares to show His mercy in the heavens and in the hearts of His creatures. Truly Our mercy and love which is limitless and boundless is what God always desires to show. But as My Word states, "If God would not shorten this time, all would be lost."

We are consoled by your love, by the home We have entered and been made King and Queen of. Truly though, there are few who have responded to our messages, but those who have, the degree of heroics they have risen to, is enough to guarantee the most souls in this final harvest. For God's anger has been greatly appeased by your and many, many other victim souls' prayers and sacrifices. And God has heard the lamentations of His children and so He wills We prepare those open to Our leading.

We are inspiring you and others to storm heaven for graces: for the condition prerequisite to grace is prayer. My Mother speaks.

Mary: Little sorrowful rose, the way to Christ is through humility, great love and charity. This will bring all the other virtues. As The Lady of the Way, I have come to show first you, then others, the way back to My Son, to teach you the way of love, the way of forgiveness, the way of charity. Many of My children distance themselves from God's healing because of unforgiveness. Now My sadness is that many who are used in different ways, all desire to be the leader.

(S.J., Our Lady refers to the division in the different types of prayer groups.)

Mary: There is no leader but Me, child. I am the one leading and inspiring, obtaining the graces that are innumerable from My Son.

How I urge all to unite as never before, for as the Woman of Revelation, I am revealing these days, final and terrible. Pray as you are and storm heaven for those graces to be granted for the final stage.

On the 13th of October, many of My children will gather to commemorate the Miracle of the Sun at Fatima. This pales to the miracle for which all humanity awaits. Fatima was one location. This will be worldwide. There will be signs and wonders and God's power and presence will prevail.

Pray for My priest sons who, by virtue of the power granted them as priests, call down upon themselves untold torment if they do not turn from the heretical road they follow. By that same virtue, gross abominations are committed against Jesus and it is as if He is being recrucified. But His will is for souls and He embraced His throne of the Cross for this.

So too, My children, embrace and unite to Him for souls. His love for souls overpowered His enemies. Your love will do the same.

I commend you to the Father for His blessings upon you, and Jesus and I together bless you, encourage you, and love you. May His Spirit, holy and mighty rest on you.

(S.J., Note: Our Lady is not saying the 13th of October will bring the worldwide warning or the illumination of the souls. But we do know, it is close and that on the 13th there will be signs in the heavens.

Our Lord also told me that there would be continuous gas explosions with unexplained reasons. He showed me a swelling deep beneath the surface of the earth.

I was also shown a dragon, huge and terrible, coming at me, however, I felt no fear. A large number of people were falling prey to his discourse and taking the sign and following him and then suddenly, extreme chaos and pandemonium prevailed.

In this extreme darkness I saw many small lights, like campfires, which were the remnant of Mary's followers and believers gathered together in places of refuge.)

The Miracles Through The Rosary

October 7, 1996

Feast of Our Lady of the Rosary

(S.J., Our Lady began to speak, I tested and rebuked in the name of Jesus.)

Mary: Come deep within the recesses of your heart little sorrowful rose. I, the Queen of the Holy Rosary, do acknowledge My Son, The Christ, who came once in the flesh, walked among men and now still walks with His people, for in the heart is where His kingdom triumphs! Hand in hand our triumphs will come, for God, your Father and mine, wills it so.

You cannot comprehend to what extent the cohorts of Mine extend themselves to the promptings of heaven, for indeed this is an urgent time.

Your effort today gives Me great joy and this I say to all who come: they will receive a grace for which they pray, if it be not contrary to God's will.

(S.J., I was inspired by the Holy Spirit to start a nine-hour novena in honor of the feast of Our Lady of the Holy Rosary and storm heaven for graces.)

Mary: And the intentions today must be for the Pope of My Heart. How he suffers. I will receive him soon to be clothed in his heavenly garments and martyr's crown.

For the priests of every movement of mine, for the priests who lack courage, for the priests who have grown cold, for the priests who no longer believe, for the priests who deceive, for the priests who are inclined to their own wills and not God's, for the priests who are heretics: for these pray today. Pray for those ministries who will be sustained through the chastisement. This in itself is a very great miracle and answer to prayer.

Pray for all nonbelievers, for all cold in heart, for all lukewarm; for all atheists. Pray for the conversion of Russia. Pray for the peace of Jerusalem. Pray for all who have died today and will die in the coming days.

Pray for those who promote, condone and practice abortion. Pray for all My true apparition sites; for today I bless, all instruments to go forth humble and with love. The success of their missions will be swift with prayers. Pray for those who today place themselves as obstacles, for tomorrow they will be removed.

Pray for those now suffering in illness, homelessness, abuse, and perversion, for they will receive the light of grace. Ask My Archangels Michael, Gabriel and Raphael and the heavenly host to assist you, for the saints of heaven to join you; for they stand in awe of God's majesty, might, and power. Know that nothing will harm you, that I have heard and received every cry, tear and sorrow, every agony, every pain. Lovingly and tenderly I embrace those who cry out to Me for assistance, for I am afforded great power and I will answer each call.

I desire no one to be left out. I desire all to come to the Heart of Jesus and receive that which He desires to pour upon them.

In these seven days, October 7th to 13th, the power of the Rosary will defeat many, convert many and prepare many for the coming days. Write your vision. *(Editor's Note: This was also the International National Week of Prayer and Fasting for the conversion of nations and to end abortion.)*

(S.J., I received this vision on October 6, 1996, at Mass, after holy communion.)

Vision: I see the sun brilliant and golden and from within this globe of great light, Our Lady of Grace appears. Then I see an explosion of light and then I see roses, like it is raining roses. There are so many that they cannot be counted. Then I see Our Lady embracing the Holy Father, like the picture that is promoted by Gospa Missions. Mary then continues.

Mary: Now as you are a very small link in My chain, My gathering in the valley of My name will bring much fruit, success, and I will make present in the heavens, indisputable signs. I will let fall a shower of roses on My children, and those who have worked tirelessly will toil more and be joined by more, and love will bring about My project.

The priest of your and other's prayers will be touched in a very special way. This will be so for all whose hearts are single-hearted for God; whose efforts are pure and intentions My own. But I will step, as on the serpent, on many whose are not.

(S.J., Note: Many people hide behind a mission of ministry, saying that they are working for Our Lady, but really promoting their own intentions and purposes.)

Mary: Look child, how many now wander with no life and no purpose. Soon many will find the reason for their existence and the victory of the rosary will once again be remembered.

The miracles through the Rosary will be as numerous as the roses you saw falling in your vision.

Go, My little one, with your preparations and pray and storm heaven for all this I ask, and heaven will grant it!

I bless you, little sorrowful rose, in the name of Our Father, and the name of My Son, and in the name of the Holy Spirit!

(S.J., Amen.)

October 19, 1996

(S.J., While attending a beautiful traditional church, I heard Our Lord say, "Weep bitter tears, child". I don't understand and continue to pray. Interiorly I see a vacant chair. Again our Lord says, "Weep bitter tears, child, for they will soon come and pillage My sanctuaries and the Chair of Peter will soon be vacant of My chosen Vicar.")

The Great Illumination of Man's Soul

October 22, 1996 - 5:45 P.M.

Jesus: My child, I, Jesus, your Lord and Master, call you to take up your pen and write.

(S.J., I heard our Lord's voice, rebuked and tested it. He responded.)

Jesus: Yes, I praise God, the Father with you for I who am, came in the flesh into the world to do His will.

The gathering that took place in Santa Maria was very important, for there and everywhere My Mother's children who are truly open to these times, gather in prayer and celebra-

tion, great graces are poured out, for these are the final moments before the height of the tribulation is upon you.

To be able to recognize these times does not come by your willing it, but by grace. Thus to those children this same grace is being poured out. For many start to believe and then the enemy sows seeds of division and discord to steal this grace.

The fruits of those who received healings and were touched will be too numerous to count.

(S.J., For me, but not for Our Lord.)

Jesus: By faith you pray and by faith it comes into being. The self-disposal of yourself to My spiritually hungry, by you, C. & C. and C. A., and all those who consider the job(s) they do insignificant are great in My eyes, for with My eyes of love I see the intention and the heart. Too often people go about their jobs with cold hearts and thus what they do bears no merit.

It is your voice I speak through and your arms I hug with and your efforts I am glorified with, for you acknowledge, and so do I, your nothingness, but you unlocked the secrets of God by the love in your he···.

Oh yes, I will try you, I will chastise you, I will probe every thought and heartbeat. And to those who persevere, great love and secrets are revealed.

As you prayed over the people, and would gaze up and see the long line, child this does not compare to the coming days. There will be no sleep, so I ask you to rest in these final days before the great illumination of man's soul. Prepare yourself well and I will do the rest. I have brought you to fulfillment of going forth as My herald of truth. This is what My people hunger for, truth.

To the group (prayer) I took you for a specific reason. I do not reveal this to you now. As you were enraptured of Me in adoration, I, too, gazed back longingly to you, for too many do not love Me. And your great invocations of petition, praise and thanksgiving show tremendous growth.

(S.J., I remember here the days of praying and only asking for something.)

Jesus: Indeed the beauty of the interior of that church holds all that is treasured and helps people. My people feel the mystery of faith. Mystery because they do not yet see Me, but I am resides there. And yet I ask you to weep bitter tears for all that will be plundered and pillaged. The Chair of Peter will be vacant, and by great power and majesty will the one who opposes Me come into the world, dominant and powerful. And many will fall away with him.

That was a spiritual battle, against Satan, Saturday night, but My angels were there to protect you and Saint Michael, defenders of God's people, to fight away the demons who sabotaged your car. Do not fear, for always your angels behold My face and I am quick to respond.

(S.J., My tire blew out on the expressway. It was a very bad situation, but help was there.)

Jesus: I receive your efforts and prayers and all that you intend to offer Me. The intention with love is great. There will come final changes in your life, but as you go through, you will see My hand in it all.

Now go in My peace and know that I am with you.

(S.J., Jesus, I love you. I do not deserve this grace. Help me to love you a thousand times more than I ever offended you. Amen.)

Great Marvels and Wonders of Mercy

October 23, 1996 - 11:30 A.M.

(S.J., I heard our Lord's voice and commanded it to go if not of God.)

Jesus: Yes, I, your Lord and Master, Son of the Father, Word made flesh, ask you to let go of all you think you know and allow Me to reveal the truth.

Behold the heavens proclaim the glory of the Lord, but My priests and people in the blindness of their hearts do not recognize this time of great marvels and wonders of mercy. Weep bitterly with Me, children, for the choice has been made.

You once again have refused the prophets of God sent to awaken your dead spirits and reconcile you to The Lord your God.

The glory of God will move in a mighty way and will lead the remnant through the darkness. Already many have seen this and have not known what they have seen, as the enemy heightens his attacks on God's people. If My people will hearken to their God, they will see My omnipotence and power, majesty and might.

Expect miracles! They will be spoken forth by faith and prayer. Weep bitterly, My child, for many have chosen and will choose to remain stiff-necked and blind in their spirits.

Where you go make provisions so none are left out.

(S.J., The understanding was that none of His children of different ethnicity be left out.)

Jesus: I want all to hear the sound of warning so they will recognize the gift of My mercy. This is your message and you will proclaim it from the rooftops. I will confirm with My signs this message, and My Mother's presence will also be heightened and manifested (made present).

The time of great travail is upon mankind and yet, rejoice and hold your heads high. Your Lord comes! Do not seek to understand, only move in faith, for you will see great wonders! Those who remain close-hearted will suffer much and many will lose their lives. Pray now and continue to sacrifice for they will be snatched from the enemy by this. Heed, My children, the cry of your Lord!

Peace be to you child!

(S.J., Amen!)

(S.J., This is a personal message.)

Jesus: Prepare your belongings, swift to move, and your case will be settled soon. Make your move (to Santa Maria) and worry not for time left will be swift, then all will follow. Prepare your papers (visa for travel to Garabandal). I desire you be present for the great miracle. The money will come. Do not ask for signs, first move in faith, the signs will follow. You will speak to large groups so that they will be awakened.

Severe Financial Crisis Will Be Worldwide

November 8, 1996 - 8:10 A.M.

(S.J., I was awakened and after testing the spirit, Our Lord answered and said:)

Jesus: Please write in your book these things I revealed to you.

(S.J., Approximately three or four weeks ago I was awakened by these words. "Soon this entire country will be under martial law.")

Jesus: Sorrowful rose of My Mother's heart, I **who am** receive your songs of praise and, because of your surrender, you have become a dwelling place of Our love. The Trinity dwells in you and in the center, the Daughter of My Father, Who gave the Word to dwell in Her Immaculate Womb. Espoused to the Spirit, He moves in the heart and soul of all the children of God who listen and move to His voice and inspirations.

I allow all you are persevering through, I am nearest to you now that you do not ask to follow your own inclinations, but the holy will of God. The prayers of God's children reach the heavens and God's very throne.

The hold of the enemy is such that this world cannot be touched but by a supernatural act of God. The world closes its eyes and ears of their seared-by-sin consciences, so that they elect a man to rule who has continued to ignore the very basis for which this nation, once under God, became a beacon of light and hope. For God's very hand used good men, holy men, to implement His laws of love and justice. That was long ago and the insatiable hunger for power, money and man's own self-indulging vices have corrupted this society.

What happens now is prophecy fulfilled. The pockets of many now full will become empty. The floor of the financial market will crash and the repercussions will resound worldwide. The despair of many will cause their own self-destruction. The world has not seen anything like this to be. Why, My people, do you have eyes, but yet are blind to the truth? Why do you have ears and fail to hear the truth?

(S.J., Tuesday, November 4th, 1996, election day. Here I am instructed to write the message given on this day at Mass after I received Holy Communion. I heard Our Lord, I tested and He responded.)

Jesus: Once again this nation has looked to a man (Clinton) for the answers to their financial woes. Now I tell you to pray, child, for the financial crisis that comes quickly to man will surpass that of anything seen up to now. Pray for the children of God.

(S.J., The infused understanding; there will come a crash of the stock market so severe many people will despair to the point of

352

*suicide. I am given the understanding that this crash will far sur-
pass anything that has ever happened. Our Lord asks me to pray
that His justice pass swiftly over the children of God, the believers.)*

Jesus: For justice will swiftly come! And for My Church once.

(S.J.,We are interrupted by my children. Our Lord dismisses me
and says we will continue later.)

The Thunder of God's Justice

November 9, 1996 - 4:30 A.M.

(Continuation of previous message).

(S.J., I am awakened hearing: "Daughter of My Heart, will you
take the dictation of My Heart"? I test and Our Lord responds.)

Jesus: Praise and glory to the Three in One, Father, Spirit and I,
The Son!

And for My church once resplendent, (it) is now stained and spot-
ted and full of wrinkles. This is not the Church I am coming back
for! The Church of My Heart will be cleansed and purified. It
will be holy and one, brilliant like the sun!

**Now the thunder of God's justice will resound. Nature will
mirror the fury of God's anger and many will be brought to
their knees. Great confusion and chaos will abound. This nation will soon be under martial law and many even now see
the signs.**

The persecution of ethnic groups will increase, but I will have
My own in the eye of the storm and it will not overtake you!

The stage is set for the fulfillment of great and wondrous things. The
light that will break through the hardness of man's heart and conscience will suddenly break through, but their woes are yet to begin!

353

But you, My Mother's faithful, who have persevered through a great humiliation, great persecution, who have allowed the prayers of power to storm the gates of heaven; you are My own and these I will protect as My own. You will bring in a great harvest of souls for My Father's kingdom. Even now the kingdom of God's reign begins to show fruit in the wills that have surrendered to the Father and so His will is being lived in preparation for His triumph!

My children do not fear! I am with you. My Mother protects you with Her mantle. You are anchored safely in the harbor of the Two Hearts! If you have responded to great grace, you have nothing to fear!

But you, oh enemies of God!, tremble, for God will seek you out and destroy you! Repent before it is too late! Great mercy have I shown you for justice to be postponed so many times, but no longer will this be. Mercy will be fulfilled and justice will reign!

In the peace of My Heart, I bestow upon you and all who are Mine, peace and blessings!

(S.J., Amen!)

November 19, 1996 - 9:30 P.M.

(S.J., Tonight, during the prayer meeting, this following vision was shown to me.)

Vision: I saw an image of Our Lord, like the Sacred Heart. He appeared gazing around the whole world, knowing all that was happening. There seemed to be people entering into His Heart. Multitudes of people were on the outside, completely oblivious to what Jesus' presence means or stands for. Then a flash of light and flames raised in His Heart. After the flames, people began to leave His Heart, all wearing white gowns, very brilliant.)

The Cross In the Heavens

November 20, 1996 - 9:50 A.M.

(S.J., I heard a voice and I tested.)

Jesus: My child, tell My children, I am Jesus who dwelt as the living Word with the Father, and I, the Word, came to redeemed mankind. And so I gave My fiat to the Father so I could dwell among mankind, and I could begin to prepare mankind to live in the reign of God.

Praise be to God the Father and I, Jesus, His Son and the Holy Spirit, three, yet one.

Soon you will behold the greatest prodigy in the heavens. You will behold this with your eyes and feel it in your soul. You will see Me on the Cross in the heavens and the weight of your sins will be revealed in your soul. By means of your consecration to My Most Sacred Heart, I have truly placed you there in My Heart.

You will behold this great manifestation of mercy from within My Heart, and the flames of My purifying love will raise and will consume all that is left, that keeps you from totally loving Me.

The world that exists all around Me, but separated by their choice, will experience this, not by being protected in My Heart, but as they are, separated from their Creator. It will be a most painful thing. It is in this time you will not only be refined and purified as gold in My Heart, but you will emerge from this, empowered by the Holy Spirit. You will then work as My laborers in the great harvest, as we prepare to fulfill prophecy (1). The whole church will read the very prophecy, about to be brought to fulfillment, and they will not believe, and they will not hear, and they will not see (2).

The darkness of evil continues to descend and thicken so that if it could, it would eclipse My Body, but that will not be, for I am the way, the truth and the life. And He who is held in the sanctuary of My Heart will be taken by Me through the darkness.

I give you these words of love, truth and consolation, to show you how this will come to be for the faithful remnant.

The ones I hold in My Sacred Heart are the same ones held in the Sorrowful and Immaculate Heart, of My Mother. There are great and wondrous miracles you will behold, and in the coming days, great answers to prayer.

Be at peace in My Heart, My children. (S.J., Amen.)

(1). All of Heaven. (2). Daily readings at Mass from the book of Revelations.

The Great Light of Revelation

December 9, 1996 - 10:00 A.M.

Feast of Immaculate Conception of the Blessed Virgin Mary. Anniversary of first apparition to Juan Diego from the Virgin De Guadalupe.

(S.J., Following a phone call from Father P. and immediately after prayer with him, I began to hear a voice, which I tested in the name of Jesus to go if not of God. Our Lady responded.)

Mary: My little sorrowful rose, I wish to address you on some very urgent matters. I who am the River of Light, have and will always prostrate Myself to praise the Most Holy and Blessed Trinity. I who am immaculately conceived, that My pure and Virginal womb would become the first tabernacle for the Holy Son Of God, the Word made flesh of My flesh, God's gift for the redemption of humanity.

356

He, Jesus, came to give peace to the world, and yes, how the angels of peace weep bitterly, for the peace of My Son reigns in too few hearts of men. The world foolishly says peace is here, peace will be accomplished, and yet they ready themselves with arms (weapons), to bring the contrary.

First of all, in this weekend of prayer, many, many graces were showered by Me on My children: those who have been sent as heralds of truth to go forth and prepare the souls to receive a great outpouring by the Holy Spirit, to give warning to the grave threats of danger ready to be cast on mankind, to comfort and console the faithful, and to the Magisterium of the church who see the darkness of the coming days.

For the souls of My priests lie perilously in danger. Some have not the courage to fight and stand against the errors of disobedience. The darkness that comes will reveal the true light. It will separate My faithful from those who will gleefully embrace the great apostasy of the Church. Up to now changes have been through rebellious acts of disobedience, but very soon the cry will resound from East to West - No to Rome! (No to the Holy Father!)

My priest sons, if it was not for your Mother, who I am, you would be eternally tormented and left to your actions of your free will and their consequences. Graces will be poured upon you and you will find yourselves in that valley of decision.

When you have decided for your God, you will encounter great trials. But I will then be able to intercede on your behalf. I will then be able to afford you the protection of God. Do not worry "where you will live" or "how you will eat." Your God will not abandon you. Though you are unfaithful, He will not be unfaithful to you. Become holy as God is holy.

You are set apart from people to intercede for them by your offering of the Holy Sacrifice of the Mass, the Unbloody Sacrifice of Calvary. **Take a stand for your God, and He will stand for you.**

For the peace of God, the Prince of Peace, continues to be rejected. And in the fullness of God's time, you find yourselves in these final days. The material comfort, that now keeps you from surrendering to your God, will be torn from you by the fury of God's wrath. And it is the very fearful wrath of God that will purify and re-establish the reign of Christ the King, and the triumph of My Immaculate Heart.

Children of God, prepare yourselves well. Take up your weapon, the Rosary, and pray and I will lead you through. Am I not here? Am I not your Mother? Which of you mothers would abandon the hope and prayers for your children? Nor will I abandon you.

The sickles will be laid to the harvest and the Angels of Death are sent to do the word of God. (Book of Revelation.)

The Cross of Peace (1) will rise before the Spring and it will bring the signs of God. Many will be brought to My valley of peace (2), and because the time of trial is here, the signs will increase.

Those who spend their days opposing God's plan (3) will have little time left to repent. But in that great light of revelation (4), they will be shown mercy, if they choose mercy.

My army is ready, the battle cry will go forth and the victory is already assured (5), on this great day of honor to My name.

I extend to you and to all who read, My Special blessing for the days ahead.

Glory to the Trinity. Freedom for the captives.

(S.J., Amen.)

(1) Cross of Peace Project - Santa Maria, California.
(2) Santa Maria, California.
(3) Cross of Peace and other's.
(4) The Great Warning.
(5) Victory over Satan.

This Nation Will Know Captivity and Economic Collapse

December 24, 1996 - 6:00 P.M. Christmas Eve.

(S.J., In Mass today, I was shown this vision.)

Vision: I saw the Holy Father praying on a kneeler and he was facing towards the Tabernacle. He was dressed in a white coat and the little white hat he usually wears was red. Then all of a sudden, I began to see blood trickle down from this forehead.

(S.J., I heard Our Lady's voice and I tested in the name of Jesus to go if not of God.)

Mary: Peace to you My little sorrowful rose. I, the Mother of God, bring the Prince of Peace into this world. His name is Jesus, the name to be worshiped and praised. All creation, gives acknowledgment to His domain.

I Myself am the first to worship the Son of God. What a great privilege. Receive Him, the Prince of Peace, as a child, to praise Him without reservation, to abandon yourself totally to Him. For a child has great capability of loving, of following with trust. This is how He desires all to come to Him.

With great joy I come to give these words of love to all My children. It is known by the omnipotent God how few in number the children who truly rejoice on this day. Too many revel in their sins, concerned only with the pleasures of this world, with the true meaning of Christmas far from their hearts.

If they would listen to the many instruments raised to make way the path of the Lord, instruments that have received, as you have, implorations of love from heaven to return to their Father's house before they die of cold and hunger. (Spiritual death.)

359

Few have listened, believed or lived the messages. For many, the evil one quickly steals the words they hear that move in their hearts the truth of what is being spoken.

You share My tears for the Vicar of Christ, chosen and prepared by Me, for this his great sacrifice. He is in his agony and soon he will flee to his ultimate immobilization.

(S.J., I was crying during the Papal Mass on T.V., as I saw how frail the Pope looked.)

Mary: Catastrophic events await this United States, events that will bring many to their knees in fear. Your time of preparation is coming to an end. And soon all that you have done will bear fruit. It is the will of God that you have remained up to now hidden. You will be sent forth for a time longer and, as you know, your suffering (physical) will increase.

Many more will come to you. But as many along with you, victim souls, have helped cooperate in this battle of all battles for the infernal enemy. Many souls will be snatched from the enemy, and priests will be brought back from the edge of the abyss.

The horsemen of the Apocalypse are sent forth in this time of plagues, famine, war and strife, and will bear the justice of God. For this sinful nation will be brought to its knees. This nation will know captivity and economic collapse. Only those who have entered into the ark of My Immaculate Heart, will know peace, protection and guidance.

The last grain of sand has gone through the hourglass, and the time of all times to accomplish the triumph of My Immaculate Heart and The Eucharistic Reign of Christ is here

As the Holy Family found refuge in a cave, away from the world, enveloped totally in the presence of His Divine love, so will it be for My children.

Pray for the princes of the Church and My priest sons, that I may intercede on their behalf. I can do nothing if prayer is not given. Prayer can do all things. Let us together pay homage to the Prince of Peace.

(S.J., together we prayed the Our Father.)

Mary: Now My child, in the coming days you will see chaos, confusion and fear. But you will feel peace, the gift of the Prince of Peace. Alleluia, Alleluia.

(S.J., Amen.)

The Ball of Light

January 5, 1997 - 7:00 P.M. (Feast of the Epiphany.)

(S.J., This is a two part message. Jesus said that an interruption would happen between the first and second message. Also included are visions and a dream given by Our Lord.

The first part of the message points to the warning by reminding and showing me a series of three visions Our Lord gave me three-and-a-half years ago. (August 18, '94.) (Vision # I) I saw a large ball of light with a tail. This ball of light is located far out in the blackness of the galaxy. (Vision #2) It, the ball of light, is still far from earth but now the earth is visible. (Vision #3) This ball of light is now about to hit the earth.

During another vision, shown to me at different times since the first of the year, I see a bright flash of light and a man who is running in terror and then falls on his knees.

During yet another vision, again shown to me several times recently, I see a seismic cam, an instrument that is used to measure earthquakes. The needle on this cam was shaking very violently. In my opinion, it was shaking more than during the Northridge earthquake of January 17, 1994.

In today's message (January 5th), Our Lord refers to a dream of a week ago where I am kneeling in prayer at my chapel where I attend daily Mass. I fall into a deep sleep and when I awake I see babies crawling all over the altar. Several women carry on a loud conversation as if they were in a hall or public place. I rebuke them for their actions for this has always been such a holy place. They turn to me and say; "What concern is this to you? Anyway, you don't belong here."

Again today, not able to attend Holy Mass at my regular church, due to a dead battery in my car, I attended Mass at my hometown church. During this Mass a new priest, who now is the pastor, mentioned that the tabernacle would be returned to the center of the altar. He explained that his chair was moved from in front of the tabernacle because he didn't want to give his back to the Blessed Sacrament.

These messages, visions and dream are mentioned in the following message.)

(S.J., I heard a voice and commanded it to go if not of God.)

Jesus: Child, I invite you to enter the recesses of your heart that you might commune with Me. Behold your King of Kings and Lord of Lords, ever close to you. Praised be the Holy Trinity, Omnipotent and One.

There is nothing that will not be turned around to be used for My Glory for those who believe. Though the enemy sought to keep you from attending My Holy Sacrifice, I allowed that so you could see the priest who ministers in My name. He has been brought, for he will minister to multitudes who will seek out in their fear, the reconciling of their souls to their Creator.

Behold, I am able to bring all this about, for I know Mine who have persevered and sacrificed and now, I your Lord, will rebuke the devourer for your sake. You know those things that have been shown to you as the events that will be signs. These elements of nature mirror My fury, do they not? I tell you your suspicions are correct, because you are in My hand, you are protected. Not one hair of your head will be touched.

The time of great change is here. Your dream was an announcement of things soon to come so that you understand the change will bring about My victory in the hearts of many. For you will soon, very soon, experience your move. (1)

My Father's will for your life will be brought about because of your fidelity and perseverance. For what you consider your treasure, is what all should feel.

But contrary is true, and many now face the trial of seeing their prizes and possessions disappear in an instant. They will not stand as their idols any longer, not their homes, nor their jobs, nor their money, nor their pleasure idols, nor their perverted ideas.

None of it will stand in the fury of My justice nor in the fury of the control from the one who opposes Me, that he will show to those who will live through his reign. (2)

I am asking you to prepare by fasting and prayer, for My divine intervention will prevail over My vineyard, My harvest, My shepherd, My flock.

I am sending those who will assist you at the appointed time. Remember this is cause for great rejoicing, for no other time has seen the great work of God's might in the signs (3) and heavenly signs (4). This ball of light will explode in the conscience of man and he will see the dread of his soul. He will fall to his knees and My enemies will curse Me to their perdition.

I do not exist in your measure of time, but I do say, your time is now. Prepare, for nothing will be the same. What exists today will cease to exist and control, total and final will be in force. (5)

(S.J., Here we are interrupted by a phone call.)

Be Still and Know I Am Lord

January 6, 1997 - 7:15 A.M.

(S.J., I heard a voice, which I tested. Jesus answered.)

Jesus: I am Jesus, whose name has been exalted and lifted above all others by the Father which brings glory and praise.

Tell C. (6) I am his Divine Intervention, to understand with his heart and not his mind. I do not operate in the confinement of your time but rather provide all that is necessary to bring about the completion of a project which is of a divine nature.

Human nature and heart have participated, but it is a project given by heaven for the uplifting and consolation of the human misery. It will be a great sign of hope, and graces will flow profusely. But you must always see with the eyes of faith.

When you have done all you can do, be still and know I am Lord, and I will do the rest. All the people who work on this project have been chosen by Me. Some have done their part, others yet will be called. Proceed as usual until you know otherwise, then the miraculous will prevail.

Peace to you and all the children of God.

(S.J., Amen.

(1) To Santa Maria, California.

(2) Antichrist reign.

(3) Weather, floods, famine, earthquakes, etc.

(4) Signs in the sky, crosses, images etc.

(5) Antichrist reign.

(6) 'C.', Cross of Peace Project.

364

Man of Perdition—The Antichrist

January 31, 1997 - 2:00 P.M.

(S.J., I heard a voice and I tested.)

Jesus: Little sorrowful rose of My Mother and daughter of My Heart. Praise, glory and honor to the Blessed Trinity! Thrice Holy! Forever One!

It would seem to you, (that) you have been wandering through a dryness, and you have. But in that test you could not have known how close I was to you, for you were moving by your faith, praying with your faith, not with your feelings. How many of My children lose heart and fail to persevere through this test. It has been the fast that has brought you even closer to Me.

My word does not, cannot lie. If I lived, it was to show all how to follow in My footsteps.

Indeed in these days, there is nothing new that has not happened before. But yet, there is a very great difference that should be to all an absolute sign of these end times, that of the great apostasy in the Church. I do not have to explain teaching that I gave, instructions that I gave, the Body that I gave, the Blood that I gave. It was given and deposited in My Church, My vicar, My Word!

The rumblings within the Church are signs leading up to the revealing of this man of perdition, this man of destiny, this man: the Antichrist. That he would triumph, he has no delusions of his end, but desires to pull as many souls (as) possible into the fiery abyss of eternal torment. This battle has long been raging, but soon we will be in the final stages.

Again I ask you to pray for priests. Pray as you have, as you are for My brother priests. They embrace and fondle the evil one and lead many astray. Was not My pain in the agony in the garden the knowledge of many, many more who would give Me the kiss of Judas? The kiss of betrayal? Yes, even the Princes of the Church presume the God they serve will be forever mocked! But, not so, My child, not so!

I hear the cries of My children, the lamenting of their burdens, but still they do not give Me their hearts! They chose the way they would walk when they failed to defend the child in the womb.

This I tell you now, child, I have spoken once of a light that will brighten a night and will announce to you and to all, the greatest act of mercy since the beginning of creation! You are going to live through this tremendous evidence of My love. Tangible, physical evidence of God's infinite love for every creature alive on the face of this earth. You will be pierced with the sword of truth when all is revealed. You will be given all that is needed for you to continue in your walk with Me. Now you are praying for many who will not know of this event. My love and mercy desire all come to the font of My love.

My Brother Priests: You will see the serpent you now embrace and when you see the multitude of souls you will be held accountable for, you would not be able to survive but for the prayers and sacrifices afforded by the little remnant of My Mother and My Mother, the one whom I gave you, the one whom you abhor. She has wrought a tremendous triumph in the little army of heaven. Not one place has been left unprepared. (In the world.) You stamp Her out in one heart, She blooms in another. All this you have impeded and sought to destroy, but it was written long ago to be fulfilled in these days!

Very soon, as many events will follow one another quickly, you will be in the midst of the chaos, confusion and turmoil.

Look now, is that not what you see?

Do not let yourselves be deluded into thinking nothing will happen. It should have happened long ago, but I have desired

to show mercy and, through the great intercession of the Queen of Heaven, great acts of God's Justice have been averted.

But we are in the final hours and you have been prepared for this and raised with many others, that God's instructions should be heeded.

The economic ruin of this nation will come swiftly.

Again, prepare to receive priests who will flee.

Be as the brides with oil in their lamps, for you know not the hour in which the groom will arrive and you will have to flee. The graces for conversion are being showered upon humanity. They are bought by your prayers, fasts, sacrifices, and for some, by the shedding of their blood.

This Lent will be as no other. The sickle is put to the harvest.

I implore My priests: Return your hearts to Rome, the Chair of Peter, **My Vicar John Paul II** and all that he stands for. It is the truth, the life and the way.

Pray for the courage you need in days ahead.

If you have seen mighty things, mightier than these you will see, for I speak it, My will be done.

I bless you and all who follow in My footsteps!

(S.J., Amen.)

The Greatest Spiritual Battle of All Time

February 4, 1997 - 2:20 P.M.

(S.J., I heard a voice and I tested. The voice responded.)

Jesus: I am He Who directs you in My love, Jesus, the Son of God the Father in Whose presence I am. Praise, glory and thanksgiving be to the Holy Trinity!

367

I come to speak clearly to you in regard to many things spoken of that have remained veiled, as it were, until the proper time.

I tell you how this comet you have seen will announce to you, as the Star of Bethlehem to the shepherds and Kings, the coming of Light to the soul.

I was, and am, the Light announced and brought forth then, and I am the same Light which My Mother has announced and brought preparations that I might come forth again.

(Personal Message. Know that I am allowing your physical suffering, for to work through you, you must embrace this suffering. You will feel ill many more times until I speak through you. I am doing this work in you. I am well pleased with your efforts and cries to persevere. You see nothing but the holy will of God in your life. Heaven assists you at your prayers and protects you against the enemy. Oh yes, he hates you with vengeance as he does all who take up Heaven's call. Excuse me for this, (my experiences with the enemy in my home). I must allow this to remind My children of his reality.)

Within a very short period of time, you will be in the greatest spiritual battle of all time. I could not leave you or any untrained.

As the global situation is put in place more and more by My opposition, you and My Mother's army will raise your voices to heaven. The God of the faithful will hear, and Heaven, the angels and saints, will move and be given instructions as to your care.

It will seem that many events are happening simultaneously and that diabolical evil has total control, but it will be at the height of those moments that God's power and might will manifest itself to a height that can only be done by God.

Make no mistake about that, and of course you know that then no flesh can be glorified, only God in the Trinity! The crosses and signs . . .

368

(S.J., Immediately I had a vision in which I saw a globe with crosses raised upon certain locations around the world. I then asked "as signs", meaning more than one cross. Jesus responded.)

Jesus: Yes!

(S.J., I asked, "Luminous?")

Jesus: Yes!

(S.J. "Apart from the warning?")

Jesus: Yes! (The crosses and signs) . . . that will be raised, will draw multitudes upon multitudes and soon there will only be one Shepherd, one Church, after the purification.

The great era of evangelization is upon the whole of humanity and I will begin in My sanctuary! You will walk in My power and My boldness and My protection.

You will pass the height of the trial, bloody and terrible, but I am with you.

Pray with one heart, one voice and one accord.

(Personal. I call you to a nine-day fast, imploring Divine Mercy for the world.)

My peace and blessings upon you.

(S.J., Jesus I love you. Amen.)

Jesus, I Trust In You

February 24, 1997 - 6:00 A.M.

(S.J., I heard a voice and I tested. The voice responded.)

Mary: My little sorrowful rose, with you I have continually praised My God, God the Father, God My Son and God the Holy Ghost. My child how close I have been to you, though you could not feel My presence. Your life of interior solitude is greatly pleasing to the Father.

In the midst of this great physical suffering, it is as if you were being cloistered. Though you are seen outwardly, interiorly, you are with your Creator, sorrowing for what you see around you as I sorrow. Is it not My sorrow that I originally asked you to share? Why then do you not recognize my tears flowing from your eyes?

I weep for the many who have rejected My Motherly love and embrace. For I, the heavenly Mother of God, wish all My children to be healed of their spiritual and physical diseases, and this the Father will permit.

I weep for what even now hurls through space to bring this day of thunder to earth and all its inhabitants.

I weep for all the innocent babies of the womb, continuing to be offered to Satan, whose insatiable appetite for blood and sacrifice and souls, causes his infernal spirits to rage against humanity, a humanity that has itself opened the doors to them by allowing this abomination.

I weep for the cup of bitterness that all of humanity will drink of, and despite great love and mercy from the King of Mercy, as the Mother of Mercy, I weep, for not all will receive or accept this invitation.

No, God's enemies will plot and rage and begin the great apostasy. Even though they too have stood in the light of His love, they will deny the claim of kingship by Christ the Messiah, Jesus, Son of God.

Within the text of the many messages you have received, much has been hidden until now. For now it is time to trust. You were told the times of walking in complete faith would come. **Trust!** It is here.

Let "**Jesus, I trust in You**" be constantly on your lips and in your hearts. For the day of thunder is here! **Trust!** You will hear again the sound of many thunders and the godless, will be filled with fear. For you, **Trust Jesus!** There will be great upheaval in the natural elements. **Trust In Jesus!**

For this reason I have asked you to have a supply of provisions. (S.J. That is to say, water, food and blankets, etc.) The signs will bring the eclipse and great cosmic phenomena not able to be explained, though they will try. **Jesus I trust in You!**

Fear is not of God. Trust in My love and the ability to provide and protect, according to the permissive will surrendered to God. **I need your permission children to protect you!**

Do not stop imploring God the Father for mercy! What My Son Jesus has revealed to you is true. Your angels and the saints will make their presence **shown** in indisputable ways.

This day of love's illumination will set the countdown to Christian persecution. Remember you will see it, you will feel it! But, has it not all been foretold? *Jesus I Trust in You!*

All is in the hands of your Creator. Fear is useless. Trust in My Son Jesus. Nothing moves without His knowledge. The messages have been preparation, teaching, imploring and call to repentance and conversion.

Warning! I implore you, My children, surrender to your Creator and know this peace. Together (Our Lady and Jesus) we will bring the mass exodus of God's people through the bloody trial.

With great love in My Heart for all of My children I bless you in the name of the Blessed Trinity and seal it with My love.

(S.J. - I had been receiving promptings from Our Lord to review messages from the past four years. Key phrases or words were brought out to me by Jesus. He allowed me to understand that much of this material has remained hidden until the proper time. I now believe this it the proper time.)

September 30, 1993

Mary: Take heed of My words and warnings. The signs are all coming to the eclipse.

(Definition of eclipse used in this context: **cutting off of light**.)

March 10, 1994

Mary: These are indeed dire days and the day of thunder will catch many like a thief in the night.

March 24, 1994

Mary: This day of thunder is upon My children! To My own (the children of light), it is an awesome and wonderful thing! To the godless their hearts will be filled with terror!

May 12, 1994

Jesus: The time of tempestuous times is arrived! **Tumultuous and tempestuous time** for my people! The sun does not shed its light. The earth is in turmoil and there is no explanation. But to My own they see it as a sign, and indeed that is what it is.

June 13, 1994

Jesus: The threat of war looms on the horizon! The plagues are! The **cataclysmic** events begin and these My own, will know peace, protection and love; as the world, as it is known comes to a halt. My own, will walk through this valley of death, and I am with you.

August 16, 1994

Mary: The **upheaval** of the earth will bring such death and destruction as never been seen before!

372

September 1, 1994

Mary: I have made reference to this day before to you as the **day of thunder**. It will be a **day of reckoning**, everyone with their sins in clear view, just as they are seen by God. No longer will the darkness that has pervaded every inch of the world, be able to blind these souls.

September 10, 1994

Mary: I tell you this grave moment arrives for all humanity, all My children. The serenity of this day will be replaced by chaos and great reconciling of My children to there God, the Father. That, His just and holy justice will pass by them swiftly.

Jesus: Little daughter of My Heart, in a moment's flash, the reality of this world will pass away and great confusion come upon the world, though the world chooses ignorance to the warnings that have been given. The great illumination of men's souls will cause grief, anguish and repentance.

September 29, 1994

Jesus: The heavens will shake, the earth will tremble, all of creation will resound with this knowledge. In the light of Mercy, all will see the darkness of their soul. The moment is here.

October 10, 1994

Jesus: Only My own will know My protection, for in the coming days it will be. From the rising of the sun to its setting, there will rise the cries, lamentations and travail amidst the chaos and confusion that will exist.

October 21, 1994

Jesus: I am going to strike! I am going to strike all of humanity! I am going to strike this earth from the four corners!

November 13, 1994

Jesus: Write what was shown today to you at Holy Mass.

(S.J., After receiving Holy Communion, today at Mass, I was meditating during which time I saw the silhouette of a person standing on top of a globe of the earth. Then there are sudden explosions of bright light, great explosions, and this silhouette of blackness is intensified by the light. I see the person begin to move backwards and cower, as if in fear.)

Jesus: This illumination of men's souls is even now at the point of being. There will come mass confusion, chaos, darkness and despair.

November 30, 1994

Jesus: This is not to catch you unaware, but in peace and prayer. The days of darkness and distress, blood and trial, is not to catch the faithful unaware, but rather those who have not heeded My words.

December 13, 1994

Mary: But the moment draws near and, in the flash of one minute to the next, your prayers will be answered by means of the last great act of Divine Mercy.

December 30, 1994

Jesus: This warning, this light into your soul that will penetrate the impenetrable will be man's last chance and hope for salvation...

May 26, 1995

Mary: I want to tell you, that the **days of thunder**, and days of distress, are here.

August 1, 1996

Mary: I am the august Queen of Heaven, Mother of Jesus, the Christ. I dwell in the midst of the Blessed Trinity and I praise My Son Jesus for His coming in the flesh and I praise God the Father's great love of His gift to humanity. His only true beloved Son, and I praise the Holy Spirit, being poured out in abundance in these the latter days, by Whose power **He will change the hearts of mankind. Indeed He will change the very face of the earth.**

August 14, 1996

Jesus: As the darkness totally envelops this created world, your light will give light to others. When the light comes in darkness, it will bring the darkness that will reveal the Light.

While receiving these words, I had an interior vision: I saw first a dark night with stars in the sky, then a burst of light like a fireball with a tail, which I have been shown before. Then I see daylight suddenly growing darker until there is nothing but total blackness; then appears the Cross with Jesus Crucified.

November 9, 1996

Jesus: The stage is set for the fulfillment of great and wondrous things. The light that will break through the hardness of man's heart and conscience will suddenly break through, but their woes are yet to begin!

Chapter Ten

Final Dogma, Schism, Anti-Pope, Anti-Christ

**Messages From March 2, 1997
To March 1, 1998**

March 2, 1997 - 4:30 A.M.

(S.J., I was awakened and I heard Our Lord.)

Jesus: The hour is late. Will you keep watch with me?

(S.J., So I prayed a Chaplet of Divine Mercy.

Later I was again awakened by Our Lord.)

Jesus: It will be a full pardon.

(S.J., I took this to mean that a full pardon will be given to those who accept what they were shown in the warning and confess their sins in the sacrament of reconciliation.)

March 4, 1997 - 3:30 A.M.

(S.J., I began to feel pain in my head and also felt fear. I rebuked the voice if not of God. Jesus responded.)

Jesus: It was in the agony in the garden where the greatest temptations to fight the will of God My Father came. It was here where it was defeated. You feel the pain coming again (S.J. To my head.) and you fight it (S.J. Because of fear.) I ask your cooperation to participate fully in this work of My Mother and Myself to harvest the greatest number of souls.

(S.J., The Holy Spirit prompted me to say. "My Lord, then not only my head. Take my hands and feet as well." I wrote the following prayer through the inspiration of the Holy Spirit in response to what Jesus was saying to me.)

Sadie's Prayer To Our Lord

My God by virtue of this prayer of surrender,
which I first unite to the Passion of Your Son, united to:
His Holy Face,
His Sacred Wounds,
His Crown of Thorns,

378

His Holy Walk of the Via Dolorosa,
His Death and Victorious Resurrection,
and to all the Sacrifices of the Holy Mass being worthily offered,
and through the Holy Tears and Sorrows of the
Immaculate Heart of Mary and St. Joseph.
I place in Your Hands and Heart my will, to dispose of it forever,
that Your Holy Will be made clearly manifest in my life.
I humbly offer you who I am — nothing, sinful and wretched,
to dispose of me according to Your Design.

Ave Maria! Alleluia! Glory to the Trinity now and forever!

Jesus: And now, child, I your Jesus, Lord and King, Lover of
your soul, Joy of your spirit, receive and do take this prayer to
offer My Father and ask for pardon and mercy.

My Mercy will be full and complete. It will be for those who
accept a full unconditional pardon of their sins. They will emerge
cleansed as from the waters of Baptism, cleansed and immersed
in the source of Living Waters, Who I am. The world (to which
they emerge after the warning) will not be free much longer. Thus,
the purification of this created world and the height of the bloody
tribulation will be swiftly upon mankind.

**Thus, the importance of My promises for Mercy Sunday must
be propagated far and wide!**

**The time for souls to respond after the illumination will be
quick to end and it is during this time that My chosen instruments and persons will and must work tirelessly and
unceasingly, for the one who opposes Me will swiftly be
brought to the revealing and unveiling!**

(S.J., Our Lord refers to all persons from prayer groups, ministries, orders, etc. who recognize these events and have remained
prayerful and strong. Not just visionaries or prophets. He also
refers to the revealing and unveiling of the antichrist.)

Jesus: I will bring My priests to you and many others. For My priests, tell them to get ready to baptize, to feed My sheep, to bring this pardon of Mine to the multitudes that will inundate them. Tell them I say, "Fear nothing; I am at your side and within you. In the daily miracle, (Holy Mass) I, at the proper time, I AM speaks through you, (Consecration of the Eucharist) and you bring Me to My sheep."

"Worthily feed My sheep." To you I say; "Worthily feed My sheep." Much depends on you, My beloved brothers, My shepherds. Feed your sheep. Behold the Lamb of God slain for the ransom of many. He comes with pardon and mercy. AMEN

(S.J. I praise you, My Jesus!)

Jesus: And I love you, My Mother's little sorrowful rose.

From Me to all, I extend My blessings and peace.

(S.J., My understanding of this message is threefold:

1. *Many of our beloved priests do not know of the Devotion of Divine Mercy, and or the promises made for participating in, and observing the Feast of Divine Mercy Sunday. [First Sunday after Easter] Our Lord is imploring both priests and faithful to spread this information and observe this feast in their parishes.*

2. *For those who accept the invitation of Jesus' mercy after what is shown to them in the warning, and go to confession, they too will be completely pardoned for all the sins of their past life.*

3. *Our beloved Cardinals, Bishops and Priests must minister to the faithful who will want to return to the sacraments and receive instruction in the faith. For the time between the Warning and the revealing of the antichrist is very short. Just how short I do not know. But, we must unite, fast and storm heaven with prayers for mercy.)*

380

March 11, 1997 - 3:00 P.M.

(S.J., this was a day of extreme trial regarding the book containing the messages. I was inspired by the Holy Spirit to write the following:.)

Precious Face of the Child Jesus,
You became the wounded One of Calvary

Precious Face of the Child Jesus,
You died on the Cross for Me

Precious Face of the Child Jesus,
I have recourse to none but thee

Precious Face of the Child Jesus,
Became the Holy Face for me.

My Heart of Love

March 13, 1997 - Morning
(Message to Sadie Jaramillo. She tested.)

Jesus: Virtues - Humility, Chastity, Obedience, Charity, Poverty and Love.

Any one of these virtues or perhaps all of them may be at work in the Soul of one of My Creatures. But if it is not bound to My Heart of Love, it is nothing.

As I Am the Creator of the soul, I can see the intentions, be they pure or full of guile.

You have told many you were as My Magdalene. You have been forgiven much, but so has your capacity to Love been given, as it is offered to many.

381

Your desire then to love is My Love. In My name you renounce yourself to bring My Love, My Truth, to bear witness to many others. This is the love, (the charity) that binds you to Me.

If I had appeared to you as I Am, you would have acknowledged Me as your King, Lord and Messiah, but under the appearance of a ragged weather beaten immigrant, you still chose to love Me by showing compassion, not knowing it was truly Your King, Your Lord and Your Messiah.

If My children, My creation of Love, will love only under My Kingly appearance and not through the most despised, then they do not know Me!

Abandon Yourself Totally

March 17, 1997 - After Morning Prayer.

Jesus: You have been hearing Me correctly. I guard you jealously as My own! I Myself Am the One Who guards you and prompts you in what manner of action you are to take.

Jesus: It is true that the reward comes for the suffering. You are living out My Love, My plea for all to embrace their sufferings with love, My Love.

I will bring you yet deeper into My Love. But I will also assist you with all you need in these days.

Do neither rely on creatures or yourself. Abandon yourself totally as you have to My love, My care, My direction for your soul.

(S.J., Lord: I know only a small sliver, if that, of Your tender mercy and love. I am beginning to see when I hesitatingly began to pray for others rather than myself, even praying "if it means they receive their answer to prayer and not me," how very pleasing this is to you. Even that, however, came through grace given to me.)

March 19, 1997 - (S.J., after morning prayer I am inspired by the Holy Spirit to say.)

(S.J., Lord, thank You for the graces being poured out in abundance. Thank you for the great manifestation of Your Presence last night. I seek every minute to be diligent in squashing the demon of pride. For always and forever I acknowledge my sinfulness and unworthiness.

But, as I read My Sister of Mercy's words, it is clear to me when I stand before You with no guile in my heart, You are forced to respond, so great is Your love.)

March 20, 1927 - Early morning, after prayer.

(S.J., Our Lord indicates to me to write the vision given to me last night in the cenacle during the rosary.

I see an interior vision of Jesus, as in the Image of Divine Mercy, an illuminated cross above Him, a great chain, like the ones that anchor ships, and Our Lady standing on Satan's head.

I see myriads and myriads of angels. I also see a capital A with another capital A upside down resting on the first A. I later learn that this is the Masonic lodge symbol. Above this a Pope's Miter in black.)

March 20, 1997 - (S.J., later the same morning.)

Jesus asked me to look up the word trust and to add His Name in certain places.

TRUST. 1. Strong belief that some one (Jesus) can be depended on.

2. The one (Jesus) that is trusted.

3. Something that has been put in one's care (Jesus) or charge.

4. Rely, depend on (Jesus).

383

Choose Whom You Will Serve

March 29, 1997 - 3:30 P.M. Holy Saturday

(S.J., I heard a voice and I tested.)

Mary: Praise Be To Jesus. Glory To The Trinity!

My little sorrowful rose, I Am Your Virgin de Guadalupe! You have been in the crucible of God's Love, and oh how the enemy hates you and all those who have truly turned over their lives to Me to give their permission, their invitation to this Mother (given to all to Be their Mother) so I can come in and show them the Way, to encourage and console, to lead them deeper and deeper into the Heart, so Sacred, of Jesus, My Son.

You are amazed to see the fulfillment of words spoken to you. So it will be again as I brought My instruments, I brought My children. The graces being showered upon each one there will be made present in an ever stronger way in the days ahead.

For very quickly you will be called to take your places and stand for your God, your Faith and all you and countless others have been prepared for. For from the very smallest act done out of love for My Son and His Mother, who I am, to the greatest, all were received with great joy and love.

Understand, Body of Christ (believers), you are united in a powerful way spiritually to all My works. Pray for the strength of the priest sons of Mine, for they will be called upon in an overwhelming way. They are like the jewels which adorn My crown, the souls of these faithful priest sons of Mine and of the religions who, hidden and in contemplation, constantly implore the Father through this most sorrowful passion of Jesus and the power of the Holy Spirit for Mercy, pardon and graces, for more and more souls.

In this vision (March 20th) you see Me as described in Revelation 12, 1 who will see the ultimate defeat of Satan assured and final. The chain is broken, these chains of bondage by The King

384

of Mercy. But woe unto you, oh hardened of heart. To you quickly awaits enslavement, captivity and damnation!

Mary: You who have not chosen to follow in the footsteps of your Teacher, Woe, I cry Woe unto you. For all that could **possibly** be done, **has** been done. You must understand now and choose whom you will serve! I tell you, do not stand obstinate of heart, but humble yourselves unto the Lord. He cannot nor will He overrule your freedom to choose!

Pride is a very useful tool of the enemy, but be on guard lest any one think himself great. God will humble! You are drained (physically of strength) to rest for the coming days so quickly upon you. You have seen your sign!

(S.J., Our Lady refers to Father S. prayer at the Ninth Anniversary of the Cross of Peace, in Santa Maria. Ca. **that a sign would be Given to all in attendance.** Wednesday night I went to see a cross that has appeared on the bedroom window of a home in the Fillmore area. It appeared this night with no moonlight! It was bright white, an exact shape as the "Cross of Peace" in Santa Maria.)

Mary: On this day, Holy and Sacred, the only day in which I was separated from **My** Son, your imitation of Me is greatly appreciated and received. To all who keep Me company, I impart special graces from **My** Sorrowful, yet Immaculate, Heart.

Keep your eyes on your Risen Lord. Alleluia. With His Power and His Victory, you and many others will console the sorrowing.

Prepare to move quickly. Trust. Alleluia!!! Alleluia!!!! Alleluia!!!

From Heaven's Throne, I obtain special blessing and graces for you and for all who believe. Amen!

(S.J., I love you Mother. Who am I that have been given a Mother so tender and loving? **A** sinner, saved by grace which She obtained for me! Praise Jesus! Glory, Honor, Thanksgiving and Praise.)

385

My Mercy will Transcend All Boundaries

March 31, 1997 - 6:00 A.M.

Jesus: Sadie, come Forth!

(S.J., I tested, and commanded the voice to go if not of God!)

Jesus: I Am the same Jesus Who called Lazarus forth from the darkness yesterday and today, call you forth to live in **My** Light. You (and others), once dead in the darkness of your sins, who have said **yes"** to **My** invitation, have kept watch and in the remembrance of **My** Death and Sorrow thereof, anticipated with great joy the Vigil of **My** Resurrection!

Jesus: I AM the Resurrection! The Life! The Way and The Truth! He who believes in Me shall have life and live (eternally).

Father, I give you Glory, Praise and Thanksgiving for the wondrous works you have wrought!

1, Myself arrange all things for you. Have that total reliance upon Me. I love you and will never, never abandon you.

With what joy I see these faithful ministers in My service continue to lead their flock. A holy priest makes a people holy! Am I not the Holy One of Israel? Do I not make people holy? Not by force do I do this, but by My Great Love for souls! Love to send Me to creation, I love to accept the Holy Will of The Father, Love to suffer unto a death, Love to be placed in the tomb, Love to pass through the Shroud of linen and rise to the Glory of God! **For the love of one soul**.

As you, My Mother's little sorrowful rose, once came forth from the darkness and slavery of sin, so too do you live and illuminate with My Love. Those are the chains broken (vision March 20th.) by My Victory of The Cross. They were broken to free the captive!

So now keep your eyes on Me. Keep your eyes on Your King! Keep your eyes on your King of Kings and Lord of Lords! For My Mercy will transcend all boundaries, for today it is limitless!

But so very soon all this will change. The black Pope will soon ᵕ seated and reign with the one who opposes Me.

From the time of the illumination of your souls to the time of the revelation of this man of perdition will be short. (I hear the Number 6). And he will reign 6 and 6 and 6 more.

Of this be assured: The Queen of Mercy has obtained the shortening of his reign.

Scripture says **"if this time had not been shortened, not one would survive"**. (Douay Rheims Bible - Saint Matthew Chapter 24:22.) .

Through My Apostle of Mercy, Blessed Faustina, has the fulfillment of words come. As was told to her, **"You shall prepare the world for My Second Coming"**.

You are strengthened for the days ahead!

And know this mankind: The blows of justice from God are exact! They fall even now. **For My Justice will end your very sinful choices to serve other idols!**

Jesus: Prepare to hide the priests who will flee. My network will plug into each other, by My Power be protected and accomplish that which will reveal itself more and more as the darkness comes! The truth of My work will be brought together. The error of the deception of the enemy will be defeated, as My Mother stands on the head of the evil one.

If any man thinks himself to be wise, repent, for man's wisdom is foolishness to God! If you would be wise, humble yourself in My sight, and I will instruct you in the ways of God!

Tremendous graces and blessing do I pour out today on all who persevere and rejoice with joy at the Truth.

Peace, I say Peace unto you and all.

(S.J., Jesus, I love you, I love you, I love you. AMEN.)

Note: My understanding of the vision on March 20,1997: As I saw the image of Jesus, King of Mercy, the Luminous Cross and then Our Lady of Grace standing on the head of Satan, like we see Saint Michael doing. All of a sudden, this great chain is broken. Also I see many, many Angels.

*Right next to this vision I see the Masonic symbol with the Pope's Miter over it. **The broken chain represents the bondage of sin that will be broken by the Warning. This is what the Divine Mercy Image represents to me in this vision, the illumination of our soul.***

The defeat of Satan and the Triumph of Our Lady is represented by the vision of Our Lady of Grace, standing on the head of Satan. She is obtaining many, many miracles, as the time of darkness increases. The angels are in the vision because their role becomes stronger and more visible in these latter days.

*The Masonic symbol, with the black Pope's Miter above it, represents the anti-pope who will reign with the Antichrist. The fact that these two visions **are side by side represents the short length of time from the Warning to the revelation of the anti-pope and antichrist.***

Humanity Lives Out The Book of Revelation

April 25, 1997 - 2:20 P.M.

(S.J., I heard a voice and I tested. Our Lady responded this way.)

Mary: I identify Myself to you as Mary Ever Virgin, Co-Redemptrix and Mediatrix of all Graces! I forever magnify the Lord and Praise the Blessed and Holy Trinity forever. Amen.

Please child, write of your vision:

(S.J., This vision happened on April 24,1997, after receiving Holy Communion. I see interiorly steps leading to something like an undercover room that seems to have the doorway to it hidden within the house upstairs, as I continue to see this there is a group of believers and I see a priest lifting a monstrance giving Benediction. There is an absolute and total aura of our Lord's presence, holiness, reverence and silence. There is a glow that comes from our Lord that lights up that whole room, even though I only see a few candles lit. Then I see a map of the United States and I see lines that indicate some kind of path. These go in different directions.

I was then prompted to write of my vision of April 8,1997. During the rosary I see flashes of light and like balls of fire failing from the sky. I also see a man running like he is trying to avoid being hit. I hear "the time of conflagration is here." (Conflagration: a large disastrous fire.)

Mary: In the coming moments all this will be upon you. **My** Son, fulfilling the Prophet Joel, is already letting His Spirit fall in an extraordinary way amongst the believers.

Oh this year of blood, sorrow and tears! The cries of the just have been heard. So very much has been mitigated. But in this second outpouring of God's Spirit, He will burn and pu-

rify the consciences of men. And the purification of this world by fire will come.

You must hold steadfast to all that has been told and know that the moment of walking in faith has come. You have been shown the many paths **My** priest sons will take to continue the sacrifice in different gatherings of **My** remnant. (Vision 4-24-97)

You must continue to pray that the graces for them come. To spend endless hours reconciling **My** children to their God.

The Pope of My Heart, John Paul II, will proclaim this last dogma and My Triumph, and then he will be fiercely attacked and forced to flee. Many of My priest sons will be persecuted for to know this Truth will be the cause of the evil one's rage.

I am the Mother of all humanity, I have desired all to come and ask Me 'How to Love Jesus". Then I draw all near and deeper into the Sacred Heart of Jesus.

Mary: But the increase of evil and the coldness of men's hearts dictate now the Justice of God.

It has been previously said from creation to Noah, God used water to purify the world, from Noah to My Son Jesus, God gave the Blood of His Son that this world might be purified, from My Son's shedding of His Blood to this point, God will use fire.

For only Divine Intervention can save humanity from self destruction and from enslavement.

Woe to you who do not recognize the warnings and the signs, as humanity lives out the Book of Revelation!

Behold the heavens, they will be shaken and the signs continue.

Your time is short, prepare yourselves with prayer, for prayer moves the hand of God. If references have been made to specific chastisements, it is for you to pray. Continue to pray for My priest sons, it depends greatly on them.

Have faith in your prayers and know God will pour forth His protection and miracles.

He will confound the attacks of the enemies of God against the remnant, recall Scripture.

There will be signs that are permanent soon!

Peace and God's Blessing are upon you and all who persevere. (S.J. Amen!)

The Great Harvest

May 16, 1997 - 3:00 P.M.

(S.J., the following vision was shown to me at Mass on May 11, 1997.)

Vision: At the consecration of the host, just as Father C. elevates the host), I see interiorly an image of Jesus holding His Heart in the same way as Father is holding the host. His Heart is exactly like I see His Sacred Heart with, flames extending from around His Heart and I see a large gaping wound which shows where His Heart was pierced. I then heard Our Lord say: 'Behold, you are sons and daughters of the Fire of My Love!"

(S.J., On May 16,1997, 1 heard a voice and I test. Jesus responded.)

Jesus: I Am Jesus Who ascended to The Father that the Fire of Our Love may come to transform the hearts of mankind and to change and purify the face of the earth. I constantly praise My Father for the Love, which cannot be understood by the limited understanding of creatures!

First, let me address your concerns of frequency of My dictations to you. You in your silence and perseverance and even in your moments of weakness, are living in the Will, Divine, of My Father. It is the same as My acceptance of His Will for the salvation

391

of creatures. But as you have been taught to live every second of every day in Me, you are the delight of the Trinity.

Messages will cease, but I will not cease to be with all of you.

I have sought many more to co-operate in this plan, but many have fallen by the wayside. Many have their own desires instead of seeing Mine, and Mine is to say, that of My Mother's also.

No, the need for messages is not to change what has always been known, written and believed, but to **alert** humanity to it's most wretched state!

And oh My little daughter! The state of all creatures causes Me to suffer once again the Agony of Agonies!

Why have I sought and taken refuge in hearts such as yours? Why have I revealed mysteries of God to you and many others? Love, your love to respond 'yes'! Your 'yes' was not just for you, but that you might participate in this great era with many others.

Why have I chosen, from the time I was choosing My Apostles, the **least** likely to be what humanity would consider "of worth?" That I might be glorified and My Father Who is in Me and the Fire of Our Love, the Spirit of God!

Jesus: And I tell you do not doubt the purifying release of this Fire, and Love is **already** being poured on all those open at this time.

I say this time because it is the moment before the Great Prodigy for which you and other have been praying! (The Warning.)

The forces of darkness and evil, penetrated into My very sanctuary, prepare to lead many to the Great Apostasy.

I show you My Heart (in vision), for this is the essence of My Love, My Way, My Truth!

Am I not both Priest and Victim? Many do not know their Shepherd. For the voice they hear is not mine, but that of the wolves in sheep clothing. But I am about to bestow on My priests great graces for which you and many other have prayed, sacrificed and suffered. **You have been purified in the Fire of My Love and yet, this pales in comparison to the treasures I will allow to fall on My children preceding the Warning, and then after.**

For this is what the saints, who already behold Me, envy you, **The Great Harvest,** shining and ready souls I thirsted for on Calvary will be brought in if you continue to fall on your face and implore My Father for Mercy.

The signs which are beheld in the heavens continue, and soon the thunder will crack and you will know the second Pentecost comes!

Oh child, do not fear. Rejoice and know I already have a place prepared for you.

That all these things will come to pass, do not doubt! Be vigilant! Be prepared! This time must come. Do not fear!

All circumstances are being used to lead My children, and soon many will <u>know</u>, as you know, and take refuge. This Feast of Pentecost comes (remember) believe and receive!

You are My little voice, the sentinel I have placed in the watchtower! Give the sound of the trumpet. Alert My people, and continue to pray. Much <u>has</u> been changed for the Glory of God and Triumph of the Queen of Heaven!

Pray, Pray, Pray, child for many souls that have already perished and will continue (to perish). All that was shown to you has been fulfilled so that time of the tribulation has come! Many events will happen simultaneously. Do not fear, trust, and pray for My Brothers (priests). **That** is your purpose.

Love and Peace with blessings in the Name of the Trinity! Amen!

June 9, 1997 - 5:30 P.M.

(S.J., I heard a voice and I tested.)

Jesus: Tell Me daughter, what do you see?

(S.J., On June 8, a vision was shown to me after Holy Communion.)

Vision: I see a large bolt of lightening strike a church steeple. Then one-half of the church falls away, the other one-half is left standing.

Jesus: For 1, **Who Am**, Jesus The Christ, The Alpha and The Omega, The Beginning and The End, do solemnly tell you: The blows of God's Almighty Justice will strike as the lightening. It will be swift, mighty and exact.

The sanctuary of My Church lies in disrepair, turned over to the Pastors who are filled with self indulging design and who do not care for the sheep I have entrusted to them.

Is not the true shepherd, vigilant over his flock, leaving the many in search of the one? Suffering from the elements (of nature) to be with his flock? They know not the value of that one little soul that they foolishly overlook!

But I Who gave of My Very Soul and Body, My Divinity and My Blood, have continued to hold open My arms of Mercy, extended open on the Cross awaiting My pastors, My flock. My Mother weeps for this time to come to humanity.

We see the coldness of man's heart, the thickness of sin and evil so that the brilliance of God's Love has been cut off, so to speak, for man has freely chosen not to allow the Kingship of Christ to oversee all in the land and in My House.

Evil has devised a plan so insidious that woe to you who are hardened to not believe and/or receive Mercy! Woe again I say woe to you. I am Love and I Am Mercy. God is desirous of bestowing all upon those who come forward to ask.

But we wait and weep. For few are those who have forsaken all to follow Me. Those few give consolation and comfort to the Two Hearts that weep. Those few have already averted the Wrath of God many and many times over.

Can you not understand, My Children? The cries of Our Hearts are to convert. Become born of My Spirit, that My Law of Love will be engraved in your hearts, that Love (Mine) will enable you to forgive, to be gentle and meek and humble of heart, like Ours, that Love will bind up your open wounds and heal you of your spiritual blindness. You cannot say you love God and not change

Underground Network

June 9, 1997 - 5:30 P.M.

Jesus: The split comes, not without My knowing, for I do see all. Let it not catch you unaware but rather know the Triumph of The Immaculate Heart of Mary draws near and the Eucharistic Reign of Jesus draws near.

I have told you, My remnant will be in the eye of the storm. Fear not, I Am with you. I do give you physical signs of My Love and protection over you. These ones (the remnant) are placed to co-operate in My Will, My Will for them, My Will for you.

You will see greater than this, for you will fulfill My words given to you, (a time ago).

For one-half of the Church, left standing, indicates the Church that will be left standing for this short time will **not** be My Church. The one-half church, fallen away, is the body falling into the underground network already arranging and preparing.

You will have a house of prayer to teach and to give My Word which I give to you. It is the Body of Christ working together as one. Pray, unite, fast.

All events will strike quickly, many simultaneously.

Continue to pray, sacrifice for My Brothers, the Priests.

I bid you peace and blessing.

(S.J., AMEN!)

(Sadie - Note, this message was given with a very grave and firm sounding voice, a disciplining, father type, correcting his child.)

Catastrophes Will Suddenly Descend

June 26 1997 - 7:01 P.M.

(S.J., I heard a voice but did not respond. I had been going through a particularly difficult trial and was reluctant to receive a message. The voice continued.)

Mary: Come My little sorrowful rose, won't you respond to the call of Your Mother?

(S.J., Here I began to rebuke, and plead the Precious Blood of Jesus. I asked "My Mother, Protectress of my faith, hide me in the Wounds of Jesus." I said interiorly, "Oh Jesus this is just me making this up to console me." Our Lady responded.)

Mary: You know full and well the voice of Your Mother, whose voice speaks to and in the interior of your heart.

It is through My Virginal Womb the Incarnate Son of God came into the world, Body, Blood, Soul and Divinity to redeem mankind from the slavery of sin and death. All creation was created to **Praise, Love and Adore Him!**

With you, I praise God, Trinity Thrice Holy! With you I weep. I weep, for in the depth of your pain, I hold you up. I weep, for the cry in your heart is the cry in My heart. I weep, and with your offering, suffered in love, I present the tears, trial, pain and suffering of all, who like you, bring their offering to the Sorrowful and Immaculate Heart of Mary!

Through this time of the trial the sufferings increase, but to those who are anchored safety in My Heart, I say, DO NOT FEAR."

Even now God's Divine and Holy Will for you is being brought about. Have we ever failed you?

The mission and ministry of your work will heighten and increase, for a time. You are also the Herald of Truth for God. In this moment there is silence, but in the next a swarm of catastrophes will suddenly descend upon humanity. You must continue to proclaim the need to enter now into My Sorrowful Heart.

In that way only am I afforded the right to protect, lead and guide. I will arrange all that is necessary, I will provide -

What you suffer now will bring many souls to your Christ, what you suffer now is not comparable to that which it is gaining.

Yes, I come to confirm to you, that which My Son has spoken of to you. Not much longer now and those consecrated Son's of Mine will ultimately be given a choice: **Truth or Heresy?** It will be openly flaunted and will **be** the doorway of the schism. You must tell them, through your heart, to the pen you now hold.

Signs In The Heavens

June 26, 1997 - 7:01 P.M.

Mary: I ask them now to return to The Father's House, to the faith established on the Rock of Peter. To cease the Betrayal of all Betrayals! There is Mercy yet. Forgiveness and mercy yearn to fill their hearts.

I have been joyful in those who have lived the messages: Repent! Convert! Penance! Pray! That is the simplicity of the Gospel message. The reality of Christ in your heart will bring the joy, love and reverence of knowing His Presence in your midst.

It is now time for you to move, (to Santa Maria, Ca.), and all that will come, comes by Our preparation of many hearts and the circumstances you now face.

Humanity does not know what soon will come upon one and all. If I've come to you and others it, is to fulfill My promise to manifest My presence ever more fully as darkness descends. Does not Scripture say: 'Lift up your hearts! Your redemption draws nigh (near)"? What is required of each and all is complete Trust upon Our Two Hearts. Live with His Joy in your Heart. He gives you His Peace!

(S.J., Our Lady refers here to Jesus' 'Joy and Peace'.)

Mary, Prepare as the prompting of the Holy Spirit inspires. What is coming to all humanity, through the Mercy of God, is an event so prodigious (1), not since the beginning of creation has there been anything to compare! The signs in the heavens are there to point to the truth of these times.

As always I urge you to continue to be the instrument of God's message. As you pray and have risen to this degree, know that it consoles the Heart of God and your Mother. Count your sufferings as nothing and your joy complete.

To counter the seemingly (2) victory of Satan within the church, I will raise the signs of God and an army of believers, though small, and by your prayers will usher in The

Triumph of this Sorrowful Mother's Heart!

To the Glory of God! I am His Humble Servant! **My** Peace and Blessing of the Holy Trinity!

(S.J., Amen! Amen! Amen!)

(1) Prodigious: an extraordinary, wonderful, amazing, enormous, marvelous, an unusual accomplishment deed or event.

(2) Seemingly: that which seems real, true, etc. without necessarily being true.

Interior of The Church Grows Ever More Dark

July 20 1997 - 3:30 A.M.

(S.J., I was awakened at 3:00 A. M. and said a Chaplet of Mercy. At 3:30 1 heard a voice and tested. Mary answered.)

Mary: My little sorrowful rose, I am the Mother of God and of all humanity. I am the Mother of Jesus, Word Incarnate, Who came for the redemption of mankind. Praise Be to The Holy Trinity forever!

(Personal message. It is My desire you place yourself under the direction of Father J. He is the priest whose heart **is** like the Mother's, whose heart is like the Son's. Do not concern yourself with the futile thoughts that do nothing but rob you of your peace. Be assured all **is** coming to fruition and much is being accomplished through the efforts of your response. Not much longer and you shall find your home.)

Mary: And now I address you. The days of My children are numbered, to all that **has** been proclaimed.

My children exist without their God, without their Creator. They continue to offend Him very much by the indulgence of carnal pleasure and obstinate hard heartedness. They refuse to heed the plea of My Heart.

And in the House of **My** Son great errors are being and will be presented as Truth. The Interior of the Church grows ever more dark.

399

To those who are following the request of Heaven: Consecrate all whom you meet to My Immaculate Heart. Present to Me in the form of prayers all whose lives give you concern.

I plead with you to live in great hope and joy!

For all the saints in Heaven pointed to these days as the great harvest and by means of the great outpouring of God's love and power you are all called to respond and work united and in love to witness to the Truth.

Many of you, My children, will fall to your knees and implore God for mercy. Know that through the very events you will live (through), which may seem at first so terrible, will bring you to embrace the cross and accept the great act of man's salvation: the death of My Son and the shedding of His most Sacred Blood and Water for the ransom of many.

The more the Eucharistic presence of My Son is denied, the more I will show this to be **True!** The more denial of the Truths, on which the Church **was** founded, are promoted, the more **My** presence will **be** felt to counter these lies.

Suffering Has Wrought Great Fruit

July 20, 1997 - 3:30 A.M.

Mary: Rejoice for your suffering, and the suffering of many, has wrought great fruit that will be shown in days ahead. By means of an economic collapse many who now enjoy their comfort and consolation will know want!

I implore you, My children, for unity and love. Exclude none of My children. For your prejudices, you will be held greatly **accountable!**

Recognize the gifts and talents of all whose love in their hearts is to serve. That desire is to serve **God, not you.**

400

There is much dissension and division in the groups of prayer and this cannot be. For I tell you: if now you are blessed, but seek your own will, I will call forth another whose heart is pliable and yielding to the Mother's plea!

Whose life show compassion: God is with him.
Whose life show charity: God is with him.
Whose Heart is with God: God is with him.

Though many of the events will happen almost simultaneously, know that it is God's Hand. Be secure in the refuge of My Love, for neither God, nor I will abandon you.

I will lead you and the victory is **already** assured!

Remain steadfast in your prayers for My priest sons.

The time left, use wisely, My children. Recall the parable of the brides. Prepare to meet the groom!

The Blessings of the most Holy Trinity descend upon you and all who believe.

I will confirm through signs the mission and the message entrusted to you.

(S.J. Amen! Ave Maria!)

I Am The Alpha, I Am The Omega

August 13, 1997 - 1:00 P.M.

(S.J., today I am asked to write. I have seen several things in vision's but had not received understanding or any messages. I had been feeling very dry and abandoned by our Lord, but still persevering in prayer.

Sometime in July, during rosary, I saw a man, woman and child broken out all over their faces with sores. The looks on their faces were angry, even the child. These sores were oozing some sort of liquid.

Again, I have seen a ball of fire exploding and a brilliant light. The surface of its point of impact is very dark.

Today in Mass I heard three (3) sets of blows of a horn. Not an instrument, but like the horns I have seen make this sound are an animal's horn in biblical movies.

I heard: "The Glory of God will Reign. His Justice will prevail. I heard this three (3) times. I tested and the voice continued.)

Jesus: I Am the Alpha, I Am the Omega, I Am Who Am sent Me to dwell amongst mankind and bring Redemption through the price of **My** Blood! The Martyrs, Angels and Saints are constant in their Praise Ever lasting! Praise to God, **My** Father for His Great Love!

(S.J., the Lord had asked me to go to Jeremias chapter 25 verses 4 - 7 and 29 - 35 and write them here.)

Jeremias Chapter 25, Douay - Rheims Bible.

4. And the Lord hath sent to you all His servants the prophets, rising early, and sending, and you have not hearkened, nor inclined your ears to hear.

5. When He said: Return ye, every one from his evil way, and from your wicked devices, and you shall dwell in the land which the Lord hath given to you, and your fathers for ever and ever.

6. And go not after strange gods to serve them, and adore them: nor provoke Me to wrath by the work of your hands, and I will not afflict you.

7. And you have not heard Me, saith the Lord, that you might provoke Me to anger with the works of your hands, to your own hurt.

29. For behold I begin to bring evil on the city wherein My name is called upon: and shall you be as innocent and escape free? You shall not escape free: for I will call for the sword upon all the inhabitants of the earth, saith the Lord of hosts.

30. And thou shalt prophesy unto them all these words, and thou shalt say to them: The Lord shall roar from on high, and shall utter his voice from this holy habitation: roaring he shall roar upon the place of his beauty: the shout as it were of them that tread grapes shall be given out against all the inhabitants of the earth.

31. The noise is come even to the ends of the earth: for the Lord entereth into judgment with the nations: he entereth into judgement with all flesh; the wicked I have delivered up to the sword, saith the Lord.

32. Thus saith the Lord of hosts: Behold evil shall go forth from nation to nation: and a great whirlwind shall go forth from the ends of the earth.

33. And the slain of the Lord shall be at that day from one end of the earth even to the other end thereof: they shall not be lamented, and they shall not be gathered up, nor buried: they shall lie as dung upon the face of the earth.

34. Howl, ye shepherds, and cry and sprinkle yourselves with ashes, ye leaders of the flock: for the days of your slaughter and your dispersion are accomplished, and you shall fall like precious vessels.

35. And the shepherds shall have no way to flee, nor the leaders of the flock to save themselves.

Jesus: It is so! I have sent My prophets to proclaim the impending events and many refuse to hearken to My plea, to My requests: to return one and all to the Lord Your God that you would know salvation, peace and joy!

My Mother, assumed into the Glory of Paradise, has left countless signs among all God's children from one corner of this earth to the other. And they still have not believed! Amidst great confu-

403

sion, amidst great turmoil, amidst great signs shown forth in the heavens, many will come to believe.

And those who refuse will not believe those I have sent, but will believe he who comes to say he is Christ. His signs they will believe and accept. But woe to them who receive his mark. You shall seek death, but death will not come. And when you die, you will condemn yourself to the eternal fires of hell.

My Glory reigns in the hearts of the small remnant of My Mother's army. My Glory reigns in those who unreservedly serve Me.

My Glory reigns in the ministers of My Church, My Father's House of Great Love. For 1 Am Love. And in the sacraments of My Love, My people will know healing.

Jesus: The day draws ever nearer that the abolishment of My sacrifice will come, and those who know Me will know the True Church will exist as it did in the catacombs. Many will know persecution, some even death. For these souls you pray; for these souls of My ministers you pray.

Did I not tell you I would send My ministers to you? Pray as I asked, and I will reveal that which they are to know. They must remember: A Holy Priest makes a people holy!

(Personal... You are here now (Santa Maria, Ca.) according to My design and fulfillment of previous words. There is a home for you which shall contain prayer. For this too I will lead and fulfill. You have been as in the desert, that I might draw you ever deeper into My wounded heart. Do not concern yourself with J. He is and will be drawn by the prayers of many and his children.)

There is quickly coming this day of thunder, this cosmic disturbance. Pray for those souls who now revel in their sins. For disturbance will come, plagues will come, famine will come, the sword will come, yea. (Jeremias 25:31): "The noise is come even to the ends of the earth for the Lord entereth into judgement with the nations. He entereth into judgment with all flesh; the wicked I have delivered up to the sword." (The sword of My Truth.)

The signs of hope will come, the signs of peace will come, to draw many for the day of darkness to come.

Amen! I have said it is so!

(S.J., Regina Coeli, (Queen of Heaven). I heard a voice and I was prompted to greet Her this way.)

Mary: My little sorrowful rose! You were not abandoned, only being put through a test to draw you deeper and deeper into the Sacred and Holy Heart of My Son.

This announces to you a grave message given by My Son. For the Father is greatly offended and given to the anger of His Justice.

Pray this Justice, thrice holy, pass swiftly. For mockery by mankind of God cannot for the sake of all humanity, cannot be accepted any longer.

I have ceaselessly and tirelessly worked to this end: To prevent as long as possible this justice, and the reign of the Antichrist.

My prophets, those chosen long ago past and those who go forth now, will continue to lead and guide those whose hearts, minds, eyes and ears are open.

Mary: They can only be opened by grace, obtained by your prayers, sacrifices and fasts.

Tell them again and then again, consecrate themselves to My Sorrowful and

Immaculate Heart. Come to the river of life and everlasting peace and joy by means of Jesus **My** Son.

I am the Mother of all humanity, every pagan, Jew and Gentile, of all! Signs will increase to counter the signs of darkness.

Tell all to trust in Jesus because of His Marcy: Protection is afforded to **My** remnant. "For you have not seen, but believed."

Do not fear in the coming days for what you will **see**. The decree of God is against His enemies, not His children.

There is Triumph soon and in the midst of great difficulties, Triumph reigns!

Dominus Vobiscum. (The Lord be with you.)

See in the heavens a great sign!

Blessing upon you and all who believer (S.J. Amen!)

Economic Ruin Brought Forth On The Storms

September 8. 1997

(S.J., On the morning of the Feast of the Assumption, August 15,1997, 1 was awakened hearing these words by Our Lord: 'They will hate you on My account, they will throw you out of My House and all the while believe they are serving Me". I had kept these words in prayer for further discernment and/or message.

This morning, September 8,1997 at 10:45 A.M., I began to hear Our Lady. I tested and She gave the following message).

Mary: My little sorrowful rose, the time is come for the just retribution of God. Though this day commemorates My birth, My gift to My children of the remnant are My words of love, My words of encouragement and consolation, for the days of distress and extreme trial are just ahead.

I have asked you specifically to pray for the Princes of the Church, for soon they will stand one against another, openly. Whereas now, the division occurs where the heart of that shepherd is closed to the Vicar of Christ.

406

My priest-sons! Choose this day whom you shall serve! Remove the error you now embrace. It is up to you if you will hear the words of Your Mother.

You must foster true holiness by living it yourselves.

I will tell you where you will find this Holiness: In the Tabernacle of the house entrusted to your care. Do not deny any longer that Jesus My Son lies hidden for love of mankind in the appearance of the host, and by the words of consecration natural elements are changed to Divine. Then, next you will find the means of living this faith in the confessional of God's people.

You, through the power and manifestation of powers bestowed through your ordination, will bring healing and consolation to God's people. I ask you now to recognize this, for soon prophetic words will stand fulfilled.

If you (priests) now are preparing to face oceans of people clamoring to be reconciled, to have fears calmed, then you do well. If you are not, you too will be brought face to face with TRUTH, you too will seek consolation, you too will seek to reconcile first yourself, then many to God!

The signs of God's Omnipotent Power will continue to be made manifest. Many (priests) who have lived with compromise many who have falsely justified their errors, will not be able to stand in the light of Divine Mercy. In His Most Perfect Light of Judgement, all will see what lies hidden in the darkness.

For this reason persevere My children, you who know and embrace the Truth of which this Church, Holy and One was established.

Mary: For in the Triumph of this Mother's Heart is yet to be revealed the Power of God and His Protection that will be shown forth! With your transubstantial bread and with all the armor afforded you by God, lift your voices in unity. Pray My Most Holy Rosary and know these that seem so insignificant will bring Victory! I am Your Mother of Mercy and the Queen of Victory. Victory you will see over your persecutors.

The economic ruin of this nation will be brought forth on the storms, but you who have heeded and prepared, be at peace. I have received all prayers and sacrifices with a heart filled with Love and thanksgiving at your response. You will see the fruit of your labors.

To you I say, announce to My priest sons: Prepare sons of My Immaculate Heart, the Harvest is here. Pray for My Son's Vicar, for soon He will fall under the oppositions force, and so I say, "reconcile yourselves to your God and allow Me to guide and protect you."

The dawn of many storms Is upon you and in the midst of turmoil, again I tell you the cosmic disturbance brings forth your judgement in miniature.

My remnant, you are bound by the love of God and together you will assist one and another. Prepare to assist My priest sons, My children, for they will soon be at the cross-road of decision.

Pray! Pray much for this nation! This land cries out for God's Justice, for the sins of mankind are constantly beheld by God! The evil of this land is greed, abortion and sexual perversion. The critical time is here, My Children, but do not fear. Which one of you, as parents, would forsake your own children? Neither will I forsake you!

Let all who would participate in My work do so with no count of the cost. It will cost you (our sufferings and sacrifices etc.) in this world to enjoy consolation in the next.

The inspirations you receive are for you to pray and seek God for His answer. Allow yourself to be lost in My Love. And My Love is for God and Holiness and souls! Heaven's Blessings Upon You and All Who Believe!

(S.J., AMEN.)

(S.J., I immediately began to hear Our Lord and I tested. He gave me the following).

Jesus: And now My Mother's little sorrowful rose, I respond to your love, I ask nothing of you but your love. That all you do, you do in My Love. I AM consoled by your conversations of love, I delight in them! Yes! I am not an unapproachable God! 1 wait with Love for one, with Love for all.

Jesus: I tell you they (the enemies of God within the Church) will try to extinguish the Light of My Love in the Sacrament of My Love.

Multitudes upon multitudes, because of their luke-warmness, will fall prey to their discourse. Because of their pride to be first, they will fall prey to this discourse of deceit.

Now I call you who know the TRUTH to be at peace! For you will quietly exit this scene of scandal and gather as did the early church, yes, of the catacombs, in secret, but not in fear. For I have said; **"I Am With You Until The End Of Time."** (Matthew 28:20.)

The storms of God's justice bring to many the loss of your home, to many the loss of your means of employment and, at the height of tribulation once the man of iniquity is revealed, you will lose your means of providing food and external provisions, for the mark of this man will be required.

Therefore I ask you now to prepare as best as you are able. Heed well what I say, for then God will do the rest. Iniquity and his reign must abound for a short time more. But to you who hold fast and persevere, great is your reward.

The nations will soon be one. Your money will be one. Man's religion will be one, but in My Own, the Truth of the Gospel will be the light that will dispel the darkness. *My Light will keep you secure in the Refuge of My Heart!*

And soon, you will all know this by means of the two heavenly bodies which will cause such cosmic disturbance, and then you will see what I have called in the past the dread of your soul!

Remember My people: God **allows** all these things to bring His Justice! They are not just haphazardly happening! God is in control!

Be at peace!

Look expectantly towards the heaven! Prepare to harvest souls! And you I raise to teach!

Seek the counsel of those I place in your heart!

Special Blessings to God's Children on this day!

(S.J., I love you Lord. AMEN!!!)

The Father's House of Victory Through The Holy Family

September 20 & 23, 1997

(S.J., The following messages have come over a period of three (3) days, the first on September 20, 1997 and the second part on September 23, 1997. I was awakened by Our Lady around 5:00 A.M., September 20, hearing the following, I tested.)

Mary: I did not bring you here (Santa Maria) to start another prayer group. I brought you here to form the beginning of many prayer communities to receive and to teach the many who will come to take refuge under this "Cross of Peace." I am addressing you as Our Lady of Victory through the Holy Rosary to give Glory and Praise to God the Eternal Father and Victory for the Holy Family!

You shall call this apostolate: **"The Fathers House of Victory through the Holy Family"**!

You will embrace the Seven Virtues of the Holy Spirit and be the instrument to teach and do the Seven Corporal Works of Mercy, (and) you will console the Seven Sorrows of Mary! This shall be done by the Perpetual Adoration of Jesus in the Eucharist! True God and True Man! And by all the ways I have come to announce to all to pick up your weapon, the Holy Rosary, and wear your armor, the Scapular!

You will by lot (choosing lots), but first prayer and fasting, choose from those faithful to your group of prayer to be the governing body of this Apostolate. Your director will continue with the help of God to lead and guide through correct counsel. The house will come first and soon the people to come later (physically).

Let me explain the title: The Fathers House **Is** a house of prayer, for scripture says, "My house shall be a house of prayer.' (Matthew 21:13.) As the darkness pervades ever more in the sanctuaries of His Church, these small but powerful groups will continually keep the Light of Faith, the Light of Truth, the Light of Hope in the days of distress to come. Victory, for the victory comes from prayer, fasting and boldly proclaiming Truth in the face of lies. Victory comes with unity, and with unity comes unselfish acts of heroics that gives Glory to God!

I have proclaimed in all My valid apparitions victory would come through the small, the humble, the childlike who respond to the Mothers request of prayer, fasting, conversion, repentance and reparation, who unceasingly pray the powerful rosary!

The Holy Family is the Fathers Great Gift to mankind! I, who dwell in the midst, am called: **Daughter of the Father, Mother of the Son, Spouse of the Holy Spirit**. It is the Trinity that is blessed, worshipped and praised, each for their great manifestations of love on mankind.

How the Father's Love is great to allow Jesus so great to become so little, so that the sin of death to the soul could be erased in the living waters of baptism and the blood of the perfect and unspotted lamb, (and) Jesus in the arms of his earthly father, My chaste spouse and saint, Joseph.

Mary: Knowing the sanctity of family life, as intended by God, would be sorely attacked and families would lie wounded, scattered and bruised - the visible representation on earth of the Heavenly Jesus, Mary and Joseph!

But the victory of God will bring together that great Truth once again and the **Family of Nazareth will be the pattern for all in the coming era!** I, as the woman who stands on the head of the serpent, will bring about this victory in the hidden hearts and lives of My faithful.

We enter into the fullness of this battle.

In this house you will receive the broken, console and comfort the frightened and help prepare them (teach). The people who will come will come to assist in the works that consist of the corporal works of mercy. First and foremost, you will minister to My Sons Beloved Brother Priests. This can only come about if you believe with the faith of a child. I am arranging all through the hearts open to Me.

I bid you good night, we will continue later.

(S.J., on September 23, at 4:40 A.M., I heard a voice and tested. Mary answered.)

Mary: I reveal these things to you child, that you may be assured of My Victory, soon to be complete. Do not doubt that this is truly coming from your Mother, the Queen of Victory! Rise child and write!

I, My little sorrowful rose, am foundress of this apostolate, and as such will direct you, the visible representative to all, that will be required of you to organize this as such. The blessings upon all who participate and who in any way help bring this about will come through a special grace of protection for the coming days and let all who would participate do so for the greater Glory of God!

Though this seems overwhelming to you, it is precisely in your acknowledgment of your nothingness and weakness, God will show forth His strength and power. This is needed to be a pattern for the future gathering of the multitudes in this place (Santa Maria).

God is a God of order and peace, there is structure needed for the coming days. By the establishment of this apostolate, you will teach others.

There is great devastation and destruction on the horizon and as these things begin to happen, all of which has already been told, more and more will believe.

The great crisis in the church continues to be the catalyst for all prophecy coming to fulfillment.

Mary: As the True Light of Christ is extinguished in the coming days, the underground Church will prevail, will triumph, over this assault against God's children!

In this valley (Santa Maria) that bears My name, there **IS** special protection as in many other places. **Let the war in Medugorie be a sign of that same protection!**

I call all to help, to continue to persevere in prayer, in fasting, and sacrifices.

I call you to help renew the Truth! I fight with you, in prayer and supplication for souls, beloved souls of **My** Son.

Blessings and Peace descend upon you.

(S.J., Amen.)

Shepherds—Prepare Your Flocks

October 7, 1997 - 9:45 P.M.

Feast of The Holy Rosary

(S.J., I am lying down, resting, as the children and I prayed a nine hour novena today, in honor of this beautiful feast of Our Lady. I begin to hear Our Lord, as He gently reminds me that I have not written a series of visions I have received over the last three weeks. I had been shown similar visions about three and a half years ago, and feel that as Our Lord says in this message, the time of fulfillment is near.

Three weeks: At Tuesday night prayer, I see a massive wall of water, like a wave, first from a front view and then from behind. I see it at least two stories high. Maybe higher. I see the land, but I don't know where exactly this is.

Two weeks ago: At Tuesday and Thursday night prayer group, I am shown a vision of an immense earthquake. First, out in the hills. I see them (the land and the hills) going violently up and down. Second, I am shown a specific place in the Los Angeles area. **I see a huge opening in the ground and then buildings failing on people running. Great chaos and destruction. I am given an understanding to pray for the people who will die in these catastrophes. After I write the visions and test, Our Lord continues:)**

Jesus: It is I, Jesus, Your brother and lover of Your soul. Praise the Father for His Love is Great to bestow to mankind Love Incarnate!

The hour is late and the just retribution of God so very near. Thus your prayers today ascend, so that grace and blessings may descend! This is a great secret of My Mother's Most Holy Rosary!

414

With confidence you will face the oncoming battle, for your battle will become increased in strength, (for) the adversary knows his time grows short. **Thus, the sign of Assisi IS a sign for My body. If he (St.Francis) responded to My request to rebuild My Church, this (the destruction of the cathedral in Assisi) is a sign of how My Church, once again, lies in disrepair.** The pain of My heart is that now the destruction and disrepair of My sanctuaries is and comes from within!

But thus I say unto you: The blows of justice will fall upon the whole of mankind, prophecy is fulfilled and woe to you shepherds of My Church! For I will strike with My staff and the flock will be scattered!

Your complete trust and abandonment to the will of God is a joy to behold. I know the moment of your insecurities and of your human fear to be overwhelmed at the task given unto you. As you retreat in the prayer of silence, you are calmed by My very presence and thus you know, they that fight against you, fight the will of God. You have no fear of causing scandal by My words, better you know the great responsibility entrusted to you by these words. Thus you do not hide your lamp under the bad, but place it for all to see (By your silent signs of witness).

Jesus: This speaks louder than any great discourse, for I Myself have revealed these to you.

My True Presence is openly denied, so now I call My Princes of My Church and My Beloved Priest Brothers: **I call you to ascend the Calvary of the Church! Where you have fear, doubts, confusion, fill yourselves from the Living Waters that you may live! I call you to ascend the Calvary of the Church and lead your flocks! Teach your flocks! Prepare your flocks! This has been entrusted to YOU, no others!**

See My example: Did I not travel the length and width, and breadth, of the land so Holy to teach? Did I not preach uncompromising Truth to the point they cast Me out of the synagogue? For by the preaching and the Power of the Spirit, those in sin and error were brought under (the) conviction of their sin. Why do you betray Me? Why do you give Me the kiss of Judas? Yes, My House lies in a sad state of disrepair, that goes beyond reconstruction!

So I tell you, soon the True Church will separate, for they have been prepared, and the order, not so secret, will take up residence in that church that remains, but I AM is not there! You will be taken to task for your betrayal, sooner, rather than later.

(And) you, some not all, will lift your hearts in thanksgiving for the prayers that have gone up today, from this little instrument of mine and others who are compelled by My Love and Divine Will to spend much time in prayer on your behalf.

For the Victory of this battle will once again come through the Most Holy Rosary! The Victory of rebuilding and renewal will come through the Most Holy Rosary! For it (the rosary) is My Mothers and My Mother is Mine, and to deny Her is to deny Me. Many of My Vicars past, as the one present (John Paul 11), embrace this Truth. The Victory of the Rosary brings the Victory of the Cross!

I Myself fight for this House of Prayer, through your director and all who respond to the call to assist. The path becomes clearer in short days ahead.

These visions of storms are imminent upon happening. Thus I recall them to you again. But all will be in place at the proper time, for through the inspirations of the Holy Spirit, the exodus of the remnant to various places will be accomplished.

Continue to hold My Priest Brothers up in prayer. I love you with a Love you will never comprehend.

416

My Peace and Blessings to you and all who believe.

(S.J., Amen.)

November 5, 1997 - 11:30 P.M.

(S.J., I heard a voice and I tested. It was Our Lord and He asked me to write the text of these Scriptures as one message. They are according to Saint Matthew 7:21-23, 10:16-17, 10:19-20, 24:10-13, 24:24-25 and Saint Luke 21:11-16, 21:22, 21:25-27, 21:36. (Douay-Rheims edition of the "Holy Bible".) They are as follows:

Saint Matthew: Not every one that saith to Me, Lord, Lord, shall enter into the kingdom of heaven: but he that doth the will of My Father who is in heaven, he shall enter into the kingdom of heaven. Many will say to me in that day: Lord, Lord, have not we prophesied in thy name, and cast out devils in thy name, and done many miracles in thy name? And then will I profess unto them, I never knew you: depart from me, you that work iniquity.

Behold I send you as sheep in the midst of wolves. Be ye therefore wise as serpents and simple as doves. But beware of men. For they will deliver you up in councils and they will scourge you in their synagogues. But when they shall deliver you up, take no thought how or what to speak; for it shall be given you in that hour what to speak. For it is not you that speak, but the Spirit of your Father that speaketh in you. And then shall many be scandalized: and shall betray one another: and shall hate one another.

And many false prophets shall rise, and shall seduce many. And because iniquity hath abounded, the charity of many shall grow cold. But he that shall persevere to the end, he shall be saved. For there shall arise false Christs and false prophets, and shall show great signs and wonders, insomuch as to deceive (if possible) even the elect.

Behold I have told it to you, beforehand.

417

Saint Luke: And there shall be great earthquakes in divers (many) places, and pestilences, and famines, and terrors from the heaven and there shall be great signs. But before all these things, they will lay their hands on you and persecute you, delivering you up to the synagogues and into prisons, dragging you before kings and governors, for My name's sake.

And it shall happen unto you for a testimony. Lay it up therefore in your hearts not to meditate before how you shall answer: For I will give you a mouth and wisdom, which all your adversaries shall not be able to resist and gainsay (deny). And you shall be betrayed by your parents and brethren, and kinsmen and friends; and some of you they will put to death.

For these are the days of vengeance, that all things may be fulfilled, that are written. And there shall be signs in the sun, and in the moon, and in the stars; and upon the earth distress of nations, by reason of the confusion of the roaring of the sea and of the waves; Men withering away for fear, and expectation of what shall come upon the whole world.

For the powers of heaven shall be moved; And then they shall see the Son of Man coming in a cloud, with great power and majesty. Watch ye, therefore, praying at all times, that you may be accounted worthy to escape all these things that are to come, and to stand before the Son of man.

Jesus: I am Jesus come in the flesh, Praise God, My Eternal Father, I am the Alpha and the Omega! To you I come to announce grave tidings of events about to transpire.

I repeat: because you speak Truth, it will become increasingly more dangerous for you. Look neither to the left nor to the right. Keep your eyes transfixed on Me, for I am with you! Include your vision:

Note: (S.J., At the October 19th prayer meeting, I saw a block wall, and to this wall priests are being backed up. The expressions of these priests vary from extreme anger, confusion, and understanding. As these priests actually reach the wall, a door, like a trap door, swings open and some go through it. Then the door closes.

My own understanding of this vision is that the angry priests are the ones who knowingly are trying to destroy the church. The confused ones are good priests that perhaps were not trained correctly and know something is definitely wrong. The ones who actually go through the doors in the wall are the priests who right now know what is happening and know in their hearts they cannot stay, (in their particular parishes) and will go to places being prepared for them right now.

For it is my belief that the laity are right now preparing to receive many priests that will go underground. I also believe that many priests will have to make a decision one way or the other. Whereas right now they may go along with an abuse of the liturgy because they are afraid, if they take a stand, they will be let go and have no place to go.

It is my understanding that this will begin to happen very soon. I also have been shown at prayer, on Thursday October 30th and Friday October 31st, a place that has some kind of fencing with barbed wire up at the top, and I see military like vehicles. I see "soldiers" (?) dressed in black, with black ski masks, holding automatic weapons.

I also was shown a crown of thorns, and then I see a long stemmed red rose and that (by the stem) it begins to be entwined and woven into the crown of thorns. I hold the meaning of this vision in my heart. Our Lord continues:)

Jesus: I tell you now, My Mother's little sorrowful rose, the earth has been prepared to give vent to the fullness of the wrath of God and, in the cosmic flash coming, will confirm that which has already been announced.

Jesus: To the faithful remnant, pray for perseverance, for now is the time where many of the "elect will fall away, for those who come in My name, but I did **Not** send, will speak fables and show mighty signs worked through the powers of darkness.

Do not waver in your faith, and defend it when you are called, for in that moment I will give you the words and wisdom of God. The fullness of Gods wrath will seek out and destroy the kings and kingdoms of this earth for they have forgotten their God and Creator. Yes, even the princes of the Church have forgotten the Truth proclaimed, lived, and died for down through these ages of time.

But I am faithful and **True** to My promise. I AM with you always.

My vicar readies himself to **proclaim the dogma of My Mother's** that **Will** come, despite the opposition. Before and after that time will be tremendous testing for you, My Body. For those times will bring the persecution of the Truth of the faith to those who know and proclaim it. Be not afraid, for no power or force can come against you and prevail!

I have told you once of a night that would bring a great light and be a sign of the forthcoming prodigy. Therefore be yourself vigilant and prayerful. For what *comes* will bring the distress of the time of all times. All these things will bring great signs and prodigies given by Heaven for all God's people to confirm the impending events.

Grace abounds in this time, but more grace is rejected by the hardened hearts of humanity and by those consumed with the undertakings of their own endeavors, and not God's, rooted in self-pride.

Prepare to receive My brothers (priests) who will be backed up to this wall of decision, and those who, after the Light of Truth invades their souls, will see and reject the error they

420

now embrace, promote and teach. What I have given to you is that for which you have been prepared.

You must walk in the same footsteps of your Lord and Savior, who I Am.

Many have been prepared to help and will do so in the coming days, already fulfilling My Will.

Those, who have come to divide, are the weeds that grow in with the harvest, and they will be gathered and thrown into the fires of Gehenna if they do not repent.

There is no more time to waste. Let your time continue to be filled with My *Will*. Preparations will come for the many, and for you, to receive priests.

Jesus: My Beloved Brother Priests:

When I first gave the mission of preaching the Gospel, (hear what I say), I said take nothing with you! Be not concerned with the trivial cares of what you are to eat or where you will stay. This Gospel must and will be preached **Correctly!** That wall of decision will force many (of you) to take a clear, firm stand on what already is **Truth**. Do not be afraid of what they *say about you or what they* do to you, **Fear only your judgment before God!**

In all this you, My instrument, give voice to what I say, for the fullness of God's wrath is upon the whole of humanity. Very soon you will be in the height and peak of the tribulation period! WOE! For you, My creatures, who did not hearken to the voices crying in the wilderness, nor to the illumination of light and mercy!

In the hiddeness of your life, My Will is lived. Continue and pray much. Pray much, My Mother's little sorrowful rose, for I love souls, I thirst for souls!

Tell Father J. that now is the time to wear the full armor of God, that at all times he is known as Mine! There will be absolute signs for him to follow My Will in the very near future.

And for Father P., he will return to Rome, but only for a short while. Then he will be brought back to continue to work with His brother priests and God's people.

From where I AM with the Father and Holy Spirit, I bless you and all who believe. I am in your heart!

(S.J., Jesus I love you. Thank you. Give me strength and grace to persevere and die a holy death. AMEN. So may it be.)

November 22, 1997

(S.J., At prayer early in the morning I see this vision: I see the flames of hell and from these flames comes a roaring lion. He comes towards me and as he rears up on his hind legs, he is no longer a lion, but a man dressed in black. I have been shown this man before and told by our Lord that he is the antichrist.

This vision is taken away and then I see a balcony, and I can see a number of saints coming down a ladder, which is surprising to me. I see the Little Flower, Saint Theresa, and Padre Pio (not canonized yet.). I then see Our Lady as She comes to the edge of the balcony. She is in the position of Our Lady of Grace, but not dressed in blue and white, but rather in gold. She then extends her hands upwards and brilliant rays of gold seem to shoot out in every direction. The vision ends.)

The Day of The Lord Is Near

December 6, 1997 - 3:00 A.M.

(S.J., I am awakened by Our Lord, I test, and He gave me the beginning of Ezechiel, Chapter 30 verse 1-3 to read, which is as follows (Douay-Rheims version): "And the word of the Lord came to me saying: Son of man prophesy, and say: Thus says the Lord God: Howl ye, woe, woe to the day: For the day is near, yea the day of the Lord is near: a cloudy day, it shall be the time of the nations.")

Your Lives and This World Will Change Dramatically

December 8, 1997 - 2:30 P.M.
Feast of the Immaculate Conception

(S.J., I hear a voice and I tested. **Mary answered.**)

Mary: I am the Immaculate Conception. Today I come to speak to the children of Mary! Yes, My little sorrowful rose, Jesus Christ came once in the flesh and will come again! All creation praises God for His Wondrous Love!

(S.J., Our Lady instructs me to include my visions and the scripture given by Our Lord. She then continues.)

Mary: You see how many now have fallen by the wayside, following their own inclinations and seeking signs and wonders and not the essence of My messages. You see how the first love of many of My children has grown cold. You see the great complacency of most in this time that has been a time of mercy. To persevere in the face of many testings and trials, attacks and persecutions, few are they who are still trying, still standing.

But what is necessary now is that those still standing are the ones chosen by the Will of God to be strong in the face of all the adver-

423

sity up to now, for I tell you that soon you will be at the time of the man of perdition and all his offspring. You, My offspring and I, The Woman spoken of today (in the readings at Mass), will crush the head of the serpent, from where this man and all his forces come.

Mary: You the few, are the strong, and it had to be this way. For I have told you before, a chain is only as strong as its weakest link. But you and My other children are now the chain that cannot be broken!

In the period of the ten years from 1988 to 1998 has been the Age of Mary, Queen of Mercy, for Jesus in His Divine Mercy has awaited the return of His prodigal children. (And) if I could, I would keep from what is coming to happen to My children. (But) all those who have entered into the safety of My Immaculate Heart, I can protect and I will.

Strong prophecy has been given and as God's people, My children responded, **Much Has Been Mitigated**! But not only the sins of mankind that rise to call down the justice of God, **but the failure of His priests, bishops and cardinals to lead and prepare their flocks for what is coming, and their failure, for the most part, to propagate these messages!**

My little sorrowful rose, prepare well! And tell My children that I will protect them and lead them. They will know, for interiorly I will alert them to the coming dangers.

This next year will (because you have been in the tribulation) be the peak of suffering in the lives of all humanity!

The Holy Father will be forced into exile. More (people) will fall away from the Truth (of the Catholic faith). The underground church will be the only place the Holy Sacrifice of the Mass will be heard. The abomination spoken of in Daniel Chapter 12:10-11 will take his seat. Much of the hidden preparations of the antichrist will be revealed!

424

To counter these:

You will experience the **greatest miraculous prodigy of all time.** The whole of humanity will know there **is** a God, and how God sees them. **Your lives and this world will change dramatically.** Some who now fight against you, will fight **with** you!

The crosses as signs will rise and no force will be able to destroy them; the signs in the heavens will cause many to tremble with fear, (but) for the children of Mary you will marvel at the power of God!

You will be filled with the fearless love of Christ. The acts of charity and selfless love will abound. You will pray increasingly in this time. Many will be brought together in many places and you will have clergy, protected by the Holy angels, ministering to God's remnant.

Mary: Until the last moment when all events begin, you must tell all to give themselves to the **Love of the Two Hearts**! Cease their doubts and come in to the safety of the Ark of My Heart.

Have I not shown you the Will of God in this house that has been given? (House of prayer in Santa Maria). Then cease your fears and know that this will be completed through love, God's love, to serve Him, to Love Him, to reach His own! You will welcome some here and some will go (faithful and priests). But to all you will receive, for they are those I bring to you as I have since the beginning of your mission.

You will receive increased physical suffering in the days ahead, but be not afraid and your little ones will be cared for with you and help sent to you. I ask you and all to sacrifice from now until Christmas Day, the Day of Joy, for Love, Unconditional Love, came into the world! And it is this same Love that will save those destined to be saved in the days of trial ahead.

425

Rest assured, this dogma proclaimed long ago (Immaculate Conception), when love for Me still abounded, is not the last. The vision reveals that. And as the angel and My kinswoman greeted Me it was said, "Hail Mary, full of grace, . . ." and grace for Me is to be given to God's children. It was given unto Me to obtain from the Trinity all that is asked for in supplication and prayer that is in accordance with the Will of God, **for My Fiat to God**!

I have always been and always will be concerned for My children. So on this day of love and prayer I grace you with a special grace and your children. And so too, those who will read and believe My words. I encourage you with My Love to walk and persevere in your sacrifices, for they are applied to many priests, for your call and mission is for My beloved priests sons.

(S.J., Message ended at 4:00 P.M., but She did not dismiss me as usual so I am waiting, I believe for Our Lord.)

December 9, 1997 - 9:00 A.M.

(S.J., Our Lord begins to summon me to take up my pen and write. I am reminded of many things that I fought to do because of the severity of the message, and Our Lord had reminded me that I would be given this message over the course of three summons (calls to write). I tested and Jesus responded).

Jesus: I am the Alpha and the Omega, I am the Bridegroom who prepares to come for My Body! I am Jesus who came once in the flesh and will come again!

My Mother's little sorrowful rose, My discourse to you today will be short, I remind you of words you fought to receive, that this message would be given over the course of three times called, and that it would be important for Gods people.

(S.J.: I'm sorry Lord, please forgive me. Our Lord continues.)

Jesus: Yes, I look with favor upon you and in the weakness of your humanity I still find a willing heart, a heart where I dwell to be consoled, as in many others (hearts).

But I ask you now to write. Behold the fulfillment of all things is at hand! I say, "Be sober and awake, vigilant and prayerful," for these things must come to pass for the Triumph of My Mother's Heart! (and) it is the Will of the Trinity to bring now to completion events prophesied for so long.

So that soon there may be One Shepherd, then, One Flock, and holiness and devotion to My Mother may flourish and surpass the days of old. (And) the glory of My church will shine more brilliantly than ever before.

Now there are some who think they will enter into this Kingdom of Mine, but for their errors and prideful ways will wind up punished forever in eternity. (These will be sent to hell). All that My Mother has revealed to you in these words will come to pass. Some will be hard pressed to find the words they ignored become a reality.

I desire to assure My faithful priests, "**Do not be afraid**," My bishops, "**Do not be afraid**," My cardinals, "**Do not be afraid**." This moment in this time will stand for all eternity and you will be held accountable. My Mother's words in days long ago foretold the errors of freemasonry, the errors of modernism and the infiltration of them into My church.

(S.J., here I was interrupted, and Our Lord dismissed me to tend to my children. At 12:05 P.M., I was called back to continue).

Jesus: Child, we continue. For this reason We have together, (Our Lord and Our Lady), arranged many things (projects, apparitions, ministries, apostolates, etc.) and called many to respond to the pleas of My Mother. Some have responded to such a degree that because of this response, though there are few, We can do much!

My Father is a Father of Love, for He gave Me, Love incarnate, to the world!

Jesus: This time of Advent spend in your spiritual preparations and last minute preparations to receive My faithful, My brother priests.

Look to the New Year as the time of liberation, though the suffering for many will be great. You will do all you have been called to do and many have been placed to assist you.

Pray, for if you do not pray, grace cannot be given!

It will not be much longer and My Mother will cease Her messages, for you will be living them!

(S.J., at this point I knew Our lady was going to give me Her blessing along with Our Lord, and I heard Hers say:)

Mary: I love you, My little sorrowful rose, and great things will be accomplished for you and God's people!

(S.J., then Our Lord spoke:)

Jesus: We both are with you and now bid you peace and blessings, and for all who believe!

(S.J., Jesus I love you. Lady, what can I say? But not for you, I would still be lost and for that alone I love you and would serve you forever. The messages can cease, but I know your love and efforts will never cease. AMEN. **So It Is. So May It Be.**)

A Note to this Message: (S.J., It is impossible for me to convey all the things that will happen even though, Our Lady did mention some. The understanding I received in this message, while words did not say it, **the trials people will begin to suffer through these storms (weather related), will be the beginning of the tremendous sufferings we will go through.**

Even though we will see the **Real** financial crash, civil strife, extreme conditions that we can only pray we have prepared ad-

428

equately for, but especially what we will see in our churches, we cannot be afraid, we must rejoice and look expectantly for the hand of God to intervene in our trials ahead.

The vision written at the beginning of the message clearly show that the antichrist, with all his forces from hell cannot prevail, for we have at our disposal (if you will), the Saints, Angels and Our Lady, **for whom this last Marian Dogma will be proclaimed.** She is mighty, powerful, and loving. To know this should keep us expectant. Be at peace. Be hope filled people, people filled with joy, especially at this time of year when the true meaning of **CHRIST**mas is forgotten.)

The Great Sign And God's Final Warning

December 30th - 1:45 A.M.

(S.J., I am awakened by hearing my name, "Sadie!" And then I hear, "Sacrifice and oblation I desired not, but a contrite heart I will not turn away." I test at this point.) I am asked by Our Lord to write of my recent visions. They are as follows:

Approximately three weeks ago, at a prayer group here (at the House of Prayer in Santa Maria, CA), I am first shown a rain swollen river that seems to be raging furiously. I can see homes been taken in this river. Then I am shown a volcano. I don't know where it is, and it seems that I am given the understanding that there is very intense pressure building up and when this volcano erupts, it will be very severe.

I have had these two visions constantly in these last four weeks. I have been praying for those who might die.

On Sunday, December 28th, the feast of The Holy Innocents, I'm making my thanksgiving after receiving Holy Communion, when I see a brilliantly illuminated cross against a very dark sky. It seems as if this cross is beaming rays of light down

towards the Earth. There is some light, and I see people prostrate in adoration, like the kneeling Maji in my nativity scene. This is very intense and seems to be occurring for each person individually. It seems that this cross is close enough that I could reach out and embrace the foot of it.

Even where there is no light, I can see silhouettes of people, cowering back in intense fear, almost to the point of despair, hands up to their faces, crying, and then some falling to their knees. I have been shown this before.

At this point, I begin to see scenes of my own life from early childhood, beginning around 7 years of age. It seems as if I am seeing a series of still photos of many scenes that lead to the time of my conversion. I feel intense shame and I begin to cry uncontrollably (yet silently, for I am still in Mass). Through all of these scenes I did not see Our Lord, but I felt His Presence of Love. Though I did not hear these words, this understanding was given: "I beheld all these things of your life and I still love you. For I do not remember them ever. I reveal them to you, for I place you in the crucible of My Love."

(S.J., I heard a voice and I tested.)

Jesus: Yes child, it is I, Jesus. Born as a child to walk among men, to be crucified and die, so that many could live and experience the Glory of My Resurrection!

The hour is late and I had told you, "I am going to place you in the crucible of My Love," to experience, if you will, a mini-judgement.

Jesus: The illuminated cross all will see, and if it seems you could embrace the foot, (it) is because (on) Calvary I saw each and all and it is a personal experience for those who finally surrender unto Me their heart.

430

How can I give life to a person if not in the place that gives life to your human body? How can a person know the walk with Me, spiritually, if I do not have 100% of that heart? The heart of your body gives you life. My Heart in your heart gives life to your soul and your spirit lives with Me to give action to your physical body. Thus your lips and voice I use to speak to My Children. Your arms to console My Children; your feet to go where I send you; and your heart to **Know** the Love of My Heart. That is your zeal: to tell one and (to) tell many.

My Love will sustain you when you are tired and feel that you cannot go any further. **I Only Ask For Total Surrender!**

Again I show you those in the darkness are the ones you pray and sacrifice for; they now, who enjoy the sins of the world, who conspire to destroy **what they cannot destroy!** Yes, for these too, pray.

For My brother priests, who again cause me to experience the scourging, pray. For My brother priests, who again cause Me to experience the crowning of thorns, pray. For My brother priests who again cause Me to experience agony, pray. For My brother priests who will cause My body to be crucified, pray.

You **ARE** in the final moments.

And because you pray, and because My Mother asks for these, many will be given the grace to embrace the foot of My Cross, and carry theirs!

Though there is stillness now, in a short moment the storms of justice will be. Do not consider how can these things come to be, or how many things must occur, for I Who Am tell you they **Will** be. The divinity of the Trinity **Is!** Though there are those who deny it! The reality of My Presence in the Bread of Angels Is, though there are those who deny it! **In That Know The Power Of God Who Proclaims It!**

You tire, for now I give you rest. Be thou open for My words to you.

This House of Prayer (in Santa Maria) is Mine. You have been entrusted for a time to care for it. I know the attacks of the enemy against you, but stand firm. I **Will** prevail against **All** your enemies.

Jesus: You will see the violent eruption of this volcano, and know then the decisive events are in progress.

Do not worry for the money will come, though this pilgrimage will be for My children a sacrifice. You will by prayer and sacrifice join many who will offer this for My Vicar, and My Mother will shower abundantly graces to be given for the time immediately following.

I will not fail you My Mothers little sorrowful rose, and you will not fail Me, for I know your heart.

I bid you now blessing and grace. For you and all who believe. PAX!

(S.J., AMEN, MY SWEET JESUS, AMEN!)

(Note: Our Lord refers to a pilgrimage I have been asked to make which will take us to Fatima, Lourdes, Garabandal, Turin, Padua, Assisi, and to be in Rome on May 31, 1998.)

I have been wondering how I could go and take my children with me. Thus Our Lord assures me not to worry. The purpose is to join with many others who will make this pilgrimage, and other pilgrimages at this same time to be a force of prayer for the Holy Father, John Paul II. Although his burden is quite heavy, with many praying for him he will be able to do what is required of him.)

War Is On The Horizon

January 30, 1998 - 7:00 A.M.

(S.J., after morning prayer, I hear Our Lady, I test, and She asks me to take up my pen and paper to write. During the rosary at the Thursday night cenacle, I was shown the following visions:)

I was shown a procession of cardinals. At the head was one dressed in pontifical garb, but he was all in black. I could see a very ornate red chair that was empty. This man dressed as a pope, but in black, was walking towards the empty chair.

I was then shown the graph that indicates the activity of the stock market. I saw it at a certain point, then the line began to go down until it was no longer visible. I then saw the Stock Exchange, and their were bodies lying on the floor.

Then I was shown an image of Our Lady embracing the Holy Father, John Paul II, as he seemed to be resting his head on Her shoulder. Our Lady was dressed in a white gown and she wore a very ornate crown on her head.)

Mary: Now My little sorrowful rose, I address My children through you: "Behold, people of God, the signs that will soon be in your midst. Blessed are they who have believed without seeing, so that they who are blind may see!"

Jesus Christ, Son of God, My Son, walked here in the flesh to leave His Church on Rock! To gift the whole of humanity with salvation! The price He paid was His Passion and tortuous Death, the shedding of His Precious Blood! By the power of His Blood, He has won the victory!

To you My fallen My weak, My lukewarm, to you who have believed and fallen away, you will find yourselves living that which you denied! You along with those who walk in total darkness, Mercy yet awaits you!

433

You were shown he, who opposes My True Vicar, will take the seat left empty when the Pope of My Heart is forced to flee. I wear a crown, for he (John Paul II) will crown Me with the title Co-Redemptrix, Mediatrix, Advocate of all graces!

The warning of God's Love will be upon you and the whole world! In the crucible of Truth and His Love the lost will be found; the lukewarm will be fanned into flame; the fervent will rise to the degree of heroics needed for the Truth of the Church to flourish once again!

This sign of My beloved daughter's healing is a sign for My remnant! You will see greater than this in days ahead!

(S.J., I had been praising God, Jesus and Our Lady for Mother Angelica's physical healing!)

Mary: There is no turning back the events even now in progress. This nation will be brought to its knees. See the leader of your country and how his moral behavior is condoned and accepted! His unwillingness to end the scourge of the slaughter of the innocents brings now the wrath of God to him and to this nation!

War is on the horizon! Chaos will be the norm! Control will be enforced, but My remnant will be led and guided by their Queen! God will open doors no one else can open and shut what no one else can close.

Be not fearful, My remnant. You are led by the Woman who has stepped on the head of the serpent! Continue to pray for My priest sons, you and those praying with you. Many priests will come back to the harbor of Truth, who would be totally lost otherwise.

My little sorrowful rose, I ask you to fast from the Feast of the Presentation to the Feast of The Lady of Lourdes who I am (February 2nd to 11th, 1998). Those who wish to accompany you may do so. Great mercy and graces will be obtained for My children; My priest sons.

All that will be needed to complete My House of Prayer will come. All that is needed for the pilgrimage will come. Cast yourself in the Will of the Father and the Mercy of My Son. Listen to the promptings of My Spouse the Holy Spirit, and I who called you to share My sorrow, will obtain all you stand in need of.

I call the servants of My valley to unite under My banner of Love and be encouraged in knowing this, My project (Cross of Peace) will be completed for the greater glory of God and for great consolation to many of My children. I am gathering your prayers, your tears, your sufferings, and pain and take them to the father of Love to bring salvation and grace to many souls.

I have sent you the priest (Father Jim) whose heart is like the Mother's, whose heart is like the Son's. Listen to him, for he will speak the Will of God for you, for the project.

(S.J., Here I did something I don't normally do, I asked about Carol, who has been ill.)

Mary: Tell Charlie, "Charlie the cross you have been given has been measured and weighed and entrusted to your care, for the good of your soul, for the good of the project. Love your cross and allow those God is drawing once again to help in the final stages of the project! You Are Not Alone! My Son and I walk with you! In all things know you are loved and blessed to complete the mission entrusted to your care. I obtain blessings of the Trinity for you and all who believe."

(S.J., Lady, My Mother, I Love You! Amen. So May It Be.)

(S.J., **Note:** In this message, I am given the understanding the Pope's proclamation of the Dogma will come, and sometime after this, the anti-pope will come on the scene. The stock market crash will indicate the closeness of the revelation of the Antichrist, and the bodies I saw symbolize the many who will despair when the crash comes. I had been wondering if I would receive any more messages and I know everything that could possibly be said Has been said. Your prayers and mine are accomplishing much, if not now, in the next moment when all will change after the Warning. Please be expectant and joyful and at peace. **Go To Confession Now! Do Not Wait! Continue To Pray For Our Lady's Beloved Priests! They Hold The Key To What Happens To God's People!! Pray, Pray, Pray.**)

Priests Hold The Key For My People

February 10, 1998 - 2:00 P.M.

(S.J., I heard a voice and I tested. Jesus responsed.)

Jesus: My Mothers little sorrowful rose and children of My Heart: **I AM the Alpha and the Omega**, the Beginning and the End, the First and the Last. I was given to the world by My Father of Love, who sent Love to the world. In the flesh I came to all who would receive Me, who would open their hearts so that I could live in them and them in Me.

(S.J., during Holy Mass, February 9, 1998, I had been looking at the beautiful crucifix and meditating before Mass. As the priest pronounced the words of consecration, I had my eyes closed and interiorly, I was show the corpus of Jesus on the altar. I was awe struck by what I saw. But this IS the Truth of the Real Presence! Our Lord continues):

Jesus: Many words have been given to you and to others to mark the time when the fulfillment of prophecy was to come. What is there left but that you now follow with your eyes of faith the path that has been shown to you and all? This is the path humanity must now follow.

The wrath of My Father is for the silence of the pastors who neither believe nor prepare their flocks! Oh yes, there ARE some and these I know, for they hear the voice of the Shepherd and speak Truth! Yes, these I know and love with a boundless love, a limitless Love. The Great Queen of Heaven, who is Advocate of All Graces, she has carefully formed and prepared these her beloved priest sons. **For You, My Brothers, Hold The Key For My People.**

In this instrument of mine (S.J.), I have revealed Truth. Am I not made present on the Altar of sacrifice? Do I not speak through you to make this so?

(S.J., our Lord refers to the above vision.)

Jesus: The days immediately before you bring all that has been revealed! Do not cease your prayers! Though your efforts are imperfect, **I Am Perfect**, and your will fused to mine makes all that you do for Your Love great! Yes **I Am Your Love: that you give, that you speak; that you desire all to know!**

You to whom much has been forgiven, have the capacity for a great love. This you will bear witness to, you and others will testify on My behalf. You will be given all that is needed in that moment.

I ask you not to fear. Be expectant, for the Light of My Love is upon you. You have been told it is upon you, this night of bright light announcing to you the Coming of My Mercy! (The Warning.)

Jesus: As you, the True Church go underground, as you become more and more persecuted, keep your eyes and your heart looking towards the East! As the way you will worship during this time (persecution) is not the same as you have had up to now. (To worship openly).

You and others have prepared as well as possible to keep the flame of Truth burning in the darkness that now comes to my people. What has been placed in your heart is by direct inspiration of My Spirit. Thus those who are bringing it about follow My Will. For My Spirit has spoken to you and to others the same (words).

437

Again, keep your eyes and your hearts eagerly anticipating My coming! From the East I will come! Yes! As sure as the flash of lightening!

Much will come ever so swiftly, but you are following Her (The Virgin Mary), who has come to lead the remnant into the battle! **It has already been won! Do not fear!**

The elements of nature mirror the fury of God's wrath! My priests and My people will be shaken from their complacency! My priests will look for rest, but it will not come! For now the harvest, ripe and full, is ready! And you who were blind will see! The false and the evil and the chaff will be thrown into the fire! **I will lead you and continue to guide you, but My words to My people have ended!**

This fast (February 2nd to 11th. 1998) has borne much fruit yet to be seen! I encourage you and My Mother's remnant. The weapon has been given! Do not lay it aside!

From the Blessed and Holy Trinity, blessings descend on you and all who believe!

(S.J., AMEN. SO IT IS, SO MAY IT BE! I love You My Love, Lover of my soul, light of my spirit, I love You.)

(S.J., NOTE TO THIS MESSAGE: It is my understanding that the messages from Our Lord to be given publicly have ended. The crisis immediately before us will be what Our Lady and Jesus have been preparing us for. Walk by faith, keep peace in your hearts and be joyful, for if you read this and believe, you already are walking in faith. Pray for those who yet remain for awhile in darkness. As future events unfold by the power of God's Holy Spirit, you and I will testify for what we believe, and for what is TRUTH!

I am given the understanding that They will continue to lead me and for this (you who have prayed and read the messages and are on the mailing list). I will keep you informed. I am praying for all

438

of you. Please pray for me. This is how we will get through. **May We Who Are United In Prayer Soon See The Triumph Of The Two Hearts!**

Note:

Our Lord promised Blessed Faustina that anyone who confessed their sins to a priest in the Sacrament of Reconciliation on the Feast of Divine Mercy will be granted a full pardon by Him and the remission of the punishment due to all the sins of their past life.

> **I want to grant a complete pardon to the souls that will go to Confession and receive Holy Communion on the Feast of My Mercy. [1109]**
>
> **Whoever approaches the Fountain of Life on this day will be granted complete forgiveness of sins and punishments. [300]**
>
> **The soul that will go to Confession and receive Holy Communion will obtain complete forgiveness of sins and punishment. [699]**

In 1937 our Lord asked Blessed Faustina to make a special novena before the Feast of Mercy, beginning on Good Friday, and completing on the Feast of Divine Mercy Sunday. Jesus Himself, dictated the intentions for each day.

This is now called the Novena to The Divine Mercy [Diary 1209-1229] and has become very popular with people praying for a wide range of intentions. This chaplet can be found in The Divine Mercy Message & Devotion. Most Catholic bookstores will carry copies of this booklet from the Marian Helpers in Stockbridge, Massachusetts 01263.

See Appendix A for Divine Mercy Devotion and Prayers

Are You Prepared for the Harvest?

March 1, 1998 - 5:30 P.M. (Message to Sadie Jaramillo.)

(S.J., I heard a voice and then tested. Our Lady responded.)

Mary: My child, It is I, Your Mother and the Mother of all humanity. My little sorrowful rose, I who dwell in the midst of the Trinity, I who gave the world through My Virgin womb Jesus, the Son of God and flesh of My flesh, I too, praise the Omnipotent God Who gifted the world with Love Incarnate!

This is the month of the Annunciation. Now, I announce to you, as the Herald of Truth, and Sentinel set in the watchtower: weep and pray with Me! Bind your heart to Mine, Whose heart is bound to My Son's. Share My Sorrow for what now comes to humanity!

My Son has announced to you the end of public messages, and I, but a few more will proclaim what the world will know, because it will begin to live out the fulfillment of them. Bind your heart to Mine and do not stray, for in that moment you will be caught unprepared!

Many times I have interceded and stayed the hand of God's Justice! For you, dear and faithful remnant, so few, but so strong, you have continued to persevere, a virtue that comes with great difficulty!

But look and see what We (Our Lord and Our Lady) have done to prepare humanity for this, "the time of all times!" Where the voices of the shepherds have been silent, I have made present in strong ways the words God would speak through so many! Be not fearful, for you, My children, are assured of My faithful promises! I will protect you! I will shield you from the foe! I will guide you!

But the world continues on its path of self destruction, for obstinate hearts persist. And faith? Oh My little sorrowful rose, will My Son find true faith when He returns?

Division abounds everywhere; confusion, and the blind lead the blind! (In matters of the Church). The leaders of nations proclaim

440

peace, but I tell you the contrary is true and war is imminent! Stay on bended knee! In the midst of great confusion will the illumination of your souls come! (And) yet a short time and the man of iniquity appears!

The Divine and Miraculous signs of God will come to confound the Godless! You, My children, will stand in awe of God's might and power, for what you have seen in these storms is but the beginning!

Are you prepared for the harvest? Are you prepared for the harvest? Are you prepared for the harvest? For amidst trials will come triumph and ultimately the Victory of the Two Hearts!

Pray the exorcism prayer of St. Michael, for the enemy knows no rest!

I tell you there is a breakthrough for the Cross of Peace Project and there will be at the Anniversary great outpouring of graces!

My priest sons, prepare to reconcile My children to their God! My priest sons, prepare to receive your brothers now embracing error, soon accepting TRUTH!

My child, prepare to receive many who will come for counsel and teaching, instruction and Love! My children, prepare to take in My priest sons. Darkness falls upon the Church!

Walk in My Love. Let there be no discord, but unity. There is POWER in unity of prayer! Walk in My humility! Walk in the assurance of My promises, for the storm of all storms arrives!

My Blessings to you and all who believe! AMEN.

APPENDIX A

Blessed Faustina

Blessed Faustina Kowalska, a Polish nun who died in 1938 at the age of 33 was beatified on April 18, 1993 by Pope John Paul II, who as Archbishop of Crakow had re-introduced her cause of beatification in 1978. Six months later he was elected Pope.

With the words **"Oh what great graces I will grant to souls who recite this Chaplet,"** Jesus gave Blessed Faustina **The CHAPLET OF MERCY** with instructions to make a Novena, in particular for nine days from Good Friday to the following Saturday.

Jesus also asked that at three o'clock, the hour at which He died, we should say the Three O'clock prayer saying **"At Three O'Clock implore My mercy, especially for sinners. . . I will refuse nothing to the soul that makes a request of Me in virtue of My Passion."** (1320).... **"Run through the whole world and tell of My mercy."**

He requested that she paint His image with the signature **JESUS I TRUST IN YOU** which should be venerated, first in her Chapel and then throughout the world. In her Diary, she records promises connected with the Devotion to the Divine Mercy.

- **"The Souls that will say this Chaplet will be embraced by My mercy during their life time and especially at the hour of their death."**

- **"To Priests who proclaim My mercy, I will give wondrous power and touch the hearts of those to whom they will speak."** (1521)

- **"I promise that the soul that will venerate My image will not perish."** (48) **"The two rays denote blood and** water....These two rays issued from the very depths of My tender mercy when My agonized Heart was opened by a lance on the Cross." (299)

- "Souls who spread the honor of My mercy....at the hour of death I will not be a Judge for them but a Merciful Saviour." (1057)

- "The prayer most pleasing to Me is prayer for the conversion of sinners. Know my daughter that this prayer is always heard and answered." (1397)

- "I desire that the Feast of Mercy be solemnly celebrated on the first Sunday after Easter. The soul that will go to Confession within 8 days and receive Holy Communion and spend some time in adoration before the Blessed Sacrament on this day shall obtain complete forgiveness of sins and punishment." (699)

- "When they say this Chaplet in the presence of the dying, I will stand between My Father and the dying person, not as the just Judge but as the Merciful Saviour," (154)

"By this Novena I will grant every grace to souls" (796)

The Novena

Jesus asked that this feast of the Divine Mercy be preceded by a Novena to the Divine Mercy which would begin on Good Friday. He gave her an intention to pray for on each day of the Novena.

Day 1. "Today bring to Me all mankind, especially all sinners and immerse them in the ocean of My mercy. In this way you will console Me in the bitter grief in which the loss of souls plunges Me"

Day 2. "Today bring to Me the souls of priests and religious. They gave Me the strength to endure My bitter Passion. Through them, My mercy flows out upon mankind"

Day 3. "Today bring to Me all devout and faithful souls. These souls brought Me consolation on the Way of the Cross. They were that drop of Consolation in the midst of an ocean of bitterness."

Day 4. "Today bring to Me the unbelievers and those who do not yet know Me. I was thinking of them during my bitter passion and their future zeal comforted My Heart."

Day 5. "Today bring to Me the separated brethren. During My Passion they tore at My Body and Heart; that is My Church. As they return to unity with the Church, My wounds heal and in this way they alleviate My Passion."

Day 6. "Today bring to Me the meek and humble souls and the souls of little children. They strengthened Me during My bitter agony. Only the humble soul is able to receive My grace."

Day 7. "Today bring to Me the souls who especially venerate and glorify My mercy. These souls will shine with a special brightness in the next life. Not one of them will go into the fire of hell."

Day 8. "Today bring to Me the souls who are in the prison of Purgatory. They are greatly loved by Me. They are making retribution to My Justice. It is in your power to bring them relief."

Day 9. "Today bring to Me souls who have become lukewarm. My Soul suffered the most dreadful loathing in the Garden of Olives because of lukewarm souls. For them, the last hope of salvation is to flee to My mercy." (1210-1228)

(Anyone making a Novena to the Divine Mercy should include a Novena of Chaplets as part of it.)

444

APPENDIX B

Poems & Prayers of
The Little Sorrowful Rose

Sadie has received and written some poems and prayers in the past several years. Here are a few for your reference and your own prayer time.

The Cross of Peace

I've been to the Hill again,
many times, I know I will return,
and when I do,
there will be someone return to you.
Hail, Most Holy Queen,
Our lives you came to redeem,
back to Our Lord and Savior.
In whom you have so much favor.

The Cross of Peace will appear to draw all,
far and near for Jesus' return is close at hand
so you've come to dwell in our land
until the appointed time
when Mercy flows no more
and all who have shut the door
will be left behind
and know in their heart
It was God's plan fulfilled,
right from the start.

[August, 25, 1991]

Dialog With Jesus Before a Message

Jesus how profoundly I adore you. When will I understand the immensity of Your love for me? I praise and love my Eternal Father for calling me to You. Someday I'll know whose prayers broke the bondage of the evil.

The agony in my heart! I want to cry out and scream at seeing the woman who cared for me when I was a little girl, lying in such a state. But, I suffer in silence as You, My Beloved Mother, have asked to use my suffering to bring more glory to your Beloved Son! By converting more souls, precious souls who will live eternally with Him! What have I to give? Only my heart. That is all.

[October 3, 1992]

Prayer to Mary for Help With Our Children

Beloved Mother: I sit in silence to see if there are any words you would have me know. I call upon the whole celestial court to help me - strengthen me by the graces you pour upon those who ask.

How can I serve you better? How can I know you better? My time is so limited when I have my - your two angels J. and C.

[January 2, 1993]

The Call of God the Father

I call your name, I God Omnipotent Who gave My only begotten Son, Jesus as ransom to be praised!

I, the great I am call you to greatness in My Kingdom. None of My chosen can glory in themselves, only I am glorified and when I am glorified, My Son Jesus Is glorified. This glory is preceded by My Spirit, for it is My Spirit, the Spirit of the Living God that calls My Children...

First to repentance and sorrow....
then to purification and expiation.....
then on to the glory brought by
the redemptive suffering
for more of My souls......
created by Me.....
to be loved by Me.....
to be filled with Me.....
to be moved by Me.........

but, I cannot withhold My justice that will fall in recompense for
all these who offend Me greatly!

[August 11, 1993]

Prayer For Our Lord's Mercy

My God by virtue of this prayer of surrender,
which I first unite to the Passion of Your Son, united to:
His Holy Face,
His Sacred Wounds,
His Crown of Thorns,
His Holy Walk of the Via Dolorosa,
His Death and Victorious Resurrection,
and to all the Sacrifices of the Holy Mass being worthily offered,
and through the Holy Tears and Sorrows of the
Immaculate Heart of Mary and St. Joseph.
I place in Your Hands and Heart my will, to dispose of it forever,
that Your Holy Will be made clearly manifest in my life.
I humbly offer you who I am - nothing, sinful and wretched,
to dispose of me according to Your Design.

Ave Maria! Alleluia! Glory to the Trinity now and forever!

[March 4, 1997]

THE GREAT SIGN

Messages and Visions of Final Warnings

A Powerful book on God's warnings and great mercy to prepare us, His children for a new Era of Peace. His greatest act of mercy will be a universal warning or illumination of souls, accompanied by a miraculous luminous cross in a dark sky.

This is a book you must read if you want to learn how:

- ✞ The Mother of All Humanity warns her children.
- ✞ Priests must inform and prepare God's people, with faith, hope, love, prayer and sacrifice.
- ✞ The thunder of God's justice will resound and nature will mirror the fury of God's anger, bringing mankind to its knees.
- ✞ Worldwide economic and financial collapse will far surpass anything that has ever happened.
- ✞ The Church and the Pope will be attacked.
- ✞ **The GREAT SIGN, a miraculous, luminous cross in the sky,** will accompany **the warning or illumination of souls**
- ✞ Forces of Antichrist will impose worldwide order and the sign of the beast.
- ✞ The Holy Rosary is a most powerful weapon to strengthen and protect.
- ✞ Christ will end the rebellion and bring a glorious, new Era of Peace for His Father's remnant which remains true.

Order Form

☐ **Yes**, I would like to receive **THE GREAT SIGN!** Please send me ___ copies for **$14.95**, plus **$3.95** shipping and handling within the U.S.
Please call for exact foreign shipping rates.

Check or Money Order enclosed. U.S. funds only.

☐ MasterCard   ☐ VISA   ☐ Discover   Expiration Date _____

Card# ☐☐☐☐☐☐☐☐☐☐☐☐☐☐☐☐ (Include all 13 or 16 digits)

Signature (required for credit card orders) _____

Name/Recipient _____

Address _____

City _____ State _____ Zip _____

Work (_____) _____ Home (_____) _____

Please make checks to **SIGNS AND WONDERS** for Our Times
PO Box 345, Herndon, VA   20172-0345.
For immediate attention, call our Order Department at (703) 327-2277 or
FAX (703) 327-2888
Thank you for your love and support.

Read Tomorrow's News TODAY!

Subscribe to Catholic Prophecy Update!

Bimonthly reports on:

- **The Warning / The Miracle**
- **The Mark of the Beast**
- **The Smart Card and the Microchip**
- **The Fate of Pope John Paul II**
- **The Great Tribulation**
- **The Persecution of the true Church**
- **The Antichrist and One World Government**
- **Natural Disasters and the Comets**
- **The New Era of Peace, And MORE!**